Financial Policies in Emerging Markets

Financial Policies in Emerging Markets

Mario I. Blejer and
Marko Škreb

The MIT Press
Cambridge, Massachusetts
London, England

The MIT Press is pleased to keep this title available in print by manufacturing single copies, on demand, via digital printing technology.

This book was set in Palatino on 3B2 by Asco Typesetters, Hong Kong, and was printed and bound in the United States of America.

Library of Congress Cataloging-in-Publication Data

Financial policies in emerging markets / edited by Mario I. Blejer and Marko Škreb.
p. cm.
Includes bibliographical references and index.
ISBN 978-0-262-02525-6 (hc. : alk. paper)—978-0-262-52622-7 (pb.)
1. Finance—Developing countries. 2. Finance. 3. Monetary policy—Developing countries. 4. Developing countries—Economic policy. I. Blejer, Mario I. II. Škreb, Marko, 1957–
HG195 .F5355 2002
332′09172′4—dc21 2002022760

Contents

1 Financial Vulnerability and Exchange Rate in Emerging Markets: An Overview 1
Mario I. Blejer and Marko Škreb

I New Evidence on Financial Policies and the Impact on Emerging Markets 17

2 Original Sin, Passthrough, and Fear of Floating 19
Ricardo Hausmann, Ugo Panizza, and Ernesto Stein

3 Banking Crises in Emerging Markets: Presumptions and Evidence 47
Barry Eichengreen and Carlos Arteta

4 International Financial Crises: The Role of Reserves and SDR Allocations 95
J. Onno de Beaufort Wijnholds and Arend Kapteyn

II The Euro and Financial Policies in Central and Eastern Europe 163

5 The Eastern Enlargement of the EU and the Case for Unilateral Euroization 165
Jacek Rostowski

6 The Costs and Benefits of Euroization in Central and Eastern Europe before or instead of EMU Membership 193
D. Mario Nuti

7 Currency Substitution, Unofficial Dollarization, and Estimates of Foreign Currency Held Abroad: The Case of Croatia 217
Edgar L. Feige, Michael Faulend, Velimir Šonje, and Vedran Šošić

Index 251

1 Financial Vulnerability and Exchange Rate in Emerging Markets: An Overview

Mario I. Blejer and Marko Škreb

1.1 Introduction

When one is approaching the analysis of recent trends and current economic conditions prevailing in the set of countries characterized as "emerging market economies," there are at least two clear conceptually separated but analytically connected questions. The first question relates to the degree of financial vulnerability of emerging markets (EMs), and the second addresses the issue of the possible connection between the exchange rate regime and financial vulnerability. Although it does not attempt to provide full answers to these questions, the aim of this overview is to discuss some of these matters as they have evolved and attracted attention in the last decade of the twentieth century.

The overview is divided into three main sections. Section 1.2 explores the question of whether the EMs are indeed financially vulnerable. Section 1.3 deals with the question of the "optimal" exchange rate regime for EMs. Some concluding remarks are provided in section 1.4. The overview also incorporates and discusses some of the main results of the volume's chapters.

Before discussing the issues embodied in the previous questions, let us point out that to the best of our knowledge there is as yet no clear and broadly accepted definition of an EM. The IMF, for example, usually classifies countries into three categories: advanced economies, developing countries, and countries in transition. So EM economies are not explicitly defined, although the term is widely used anyway.[1] Wijnholds and Kapteyn (chapter 4) define EMs as developing countries that have access to private capital flows (i.e., excluding eligible countries that receive loans from the IMF at subsidized interest rates). Others assume under the definition of EM "more important financial markets outside the longer-standing OECD members" (Hawkins and Klau 2000, 1). Finally, some simply use the term without defining it in more details.

1.2 Are Emerging Markets Financially Vulnerable?

The second part of the last decade of the twentieth century was marked by EM financial crises. It started with the Mexican crisis in 1994–1995. After Mexico, the crisis traveled a long way, slowly, as it moved to the other side of the globe to Southeast Asia in 1997.[2] Starting with the fall of the Thai baht in July 1997, the crisis rapidly spread from Thailand to Indonesia, Malaysia, South Korea, and (to a lesser degree) the Philippines. What was interesting about this crisis was that it was to a large degree not anticipated in the affected countries and that contagion seemed to be strong. Other Asian economies (Hong Kong, China, Taiwan, etc.) came under pressure as well but managed to avoid a crisis.

From Southeast Asia the crisis spread, with a time lag of one year, to Russia and later on to Latin America. The famous Russian default on domestic debt on August 17, 1998, was a big shock for emerging markets and especially for transition economies, although interestingly, and contrary to expectations, the crisis caused difficulties and pressures in the transition economies (like the Czech Republic, Hungary, and Poland), but it did not end in a full-blown crisis.

The crisis scenario moved next to Brazil, which started facing liquidity problems in late 1998. As a consequence Brazil floated its currency, the real, in January 1999 and decided to adopt an inflation targeting regime by mid-1999. Brazilian troubles immediately augmented pressures on the already troubled Argentinean economy. Brazilian depreciation, combined with the strengthening of the U.S. dollar and high debt servicing for Argentina, opened discussions on the sustainability of its decade-long currency board peg to the U.S. dollar. Argentina's high external debt, in spite of its being swapped for new bonds in the amount of US$29.5 billion in June 2001, seems to continue to put pressure on the currency board regime ("Cavallo pawns" 2001). The most recent emerging markets crisis has affected Turkey. Pressures started in the second half of 2000, but a currency crisis erupted in spring of 2001 and resulted in the abandoning of the peg of the Turkish lira and a subsequent significant depreciation.

Sure enough, neither the character nor the causes of all these events is the same. The Asian crisis was to a large extent due to the region's fragile financial sector and a highly indebted corporate sector (combined with the foreign exchange mismatch). A peg to the U.S. dollar that has become unsustainable with the strengthening of the U.S. currency has affected Asia's competitiveness. The Russian crisis was caused by the lack of efficient domestic financial intermediation and problems in controlling public finances (especially in the light of falling commodity prices) linked with political problems. In Turkey the combination of excessive government spending and lag in structural reforms (particularly in the banking area) led to political troubles that ended in a rapid depreciation.

But in almost all of the crises in EMs, banking problems were severe. In Mexico, Asia, Russia, and Turkey, the banking "component" of the crisis was a central part of the broader financial problems.

Chapter 3, "Banking Crises in Emerging Markets: Presumptions and Evidence," deals specifically with banking crises in EMs, stressing the importance of banking problems in detonating and magnifying the crises. Its authors, Barry Eichengreen and Carlos Arteta, identify the instability of the banking system as the main difference between an ordinary recession and a full-scale economic crisis. Banking crises have indeed disrupted EMs very seriously in the last two decades. The goal of chapter 3 is therefore rather ambitious, as the authors attempt to identify what is known and what is not known about the causes of the banking crises in emerging markets.

Eichengreen and Arteta start the chapter by presenting a comprehensive review of the literature on banking crises. They proceed to present a vast number of empirical results, and they summarize their main results as follows. Three causes of banking crises in emerging markets are econometrically identified as robust: (1) the rapid growth of domestic credit (domestic credit booms are directly linked with banking crises), (2) the large size of bank liabilities, measured by M2, relative to international reserves, and (3) financial liberalization in the form of deregulation of interest paid on deposits. On the other hand, they find no stable relationship between the exchange rate regime and banking crises. This is an important result, as it is often assumed that "inappropriate" exchange rate regimes are important causes of banking crises. In fact, the finding of chapter 3 points to just the opposite: banking crises cause currency crises.

Another factor often mentioned as a possible cause of banking crises is deposit insurance. Eichengreen and Arteta's estimates find no major impact of these types of arrangements on the prevalence of banking crises. Furthermore, their evidence does not support the intuitive and seemingly straightforward assessment that quality of institutions (banking supervision, contract enforcement, etc.) is an important factor in causing banking crises. But, we have to conclude by quoting the authors that "on the causes of banking crises in emerging markets, it is fair to say that the jury remains out" (p. 55). Even if the causes of banking crises may be disputed, everyone agrees that the consequences of the crises for emerging markets are, in general, very severe. As the international financial environment has rapidly changed in the last decades (liberalization and deregulation of financial flows, deepening of financial markets, and innovations in financial transactions)[3] the consequences of crisis are usually seen first in the external sector. A good illustration of such developments is the change in net capital flows to emerging markets when a crises occurs.

In the early 1990s, private net flows to emerging markets were increasing rapidly. On a yearly level in the early 1990s they averaged about US$100 billion and more than doubled up to 1996. But as a consequence of the Asian and later the Russian crises, the perception of the risks of EMs among major investors has rapidly changed. So those countries faced an abrupt reversal of capital flows. From the second half of 1997 to 1999, total flows (private and official) steeply decreased from their peak in 1996. According to IMF data (IMF 1999, 2001) the flows decreased from about US$225 billion to only US$37 billion, or only about one sixth of their maximum level.

From figure 1.1 it is obvious that this rapid decrease was mainly due to the decrease in net private capital flows. It is certainly worth nothing that the official net flows that alleviated the problem in 1997–1998 seem to be almost nonexistent after 1998, which tends to reconfirm the long-term trend that private flows are bigger than official ones, though the later play a crucial role in a crisis situation.

But all private capital flows do not have the same characteristics. Indeed, as shown in figure 1.2, foreign direct investment (FDI) remained the only stable and constantly growing component of private capital flows through the decade, whereas portfolio investment and other private flows contributed to the overall rapid decline. The constant increase in FDI can be interpreted as a sign that investors

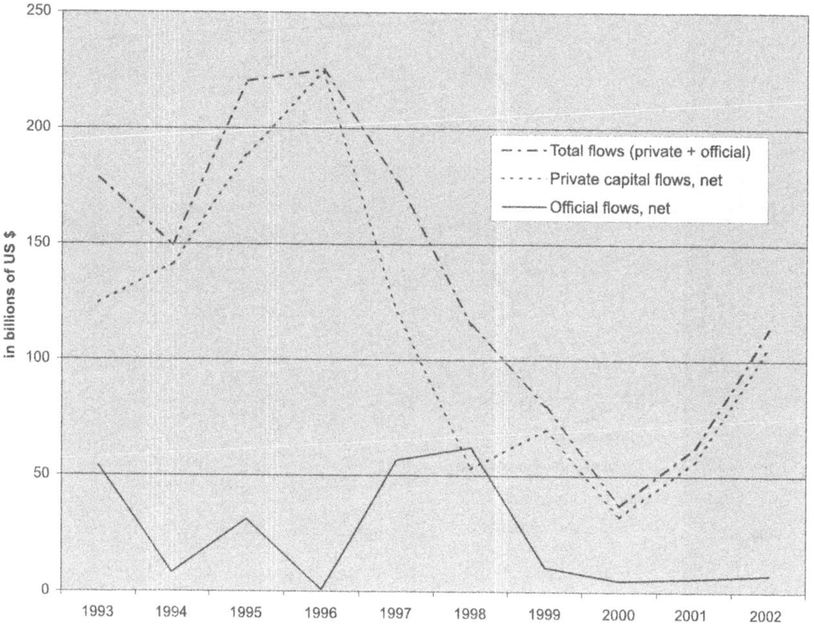

Figure 1.1
Net capital flows to emerging-market economies. *Source:* IMF 2001. *Note:* Figures for 2001 and 2002 are estimates.

remained optimistic about the long-term prospects of EMs. Interestingly, this development has confirmed the conventional wisdom that FDI is more sustainable, whereas other flows are more volatile. Other forms of inflows to EM economies (such as bond issues, bank loans, and equity issues) reveal a similar reversal of trend after 1997.

As a consequence of the crisis and reversed external flows, short-term interest rates in EMs increased significantly—sovereign bond spreads in some cases increased by more than 1,000 bps (Indonesia and Brazil, for example)—but later came down. In addition, the greater uncertainty about the EMs was reflected in the increased volatility of other major financial indicators. The negative shock of falling commodity prices in 1997–1998 certainly did contribute to the overall situation. It should be noted, however, that commodities prices did rebound in 1999 and 2000. So did the equity prices of emerging-market economies.[4]

Financial crises (whether linked with the exchange rate problems, external debt crises, banking problems, or a combination of them)

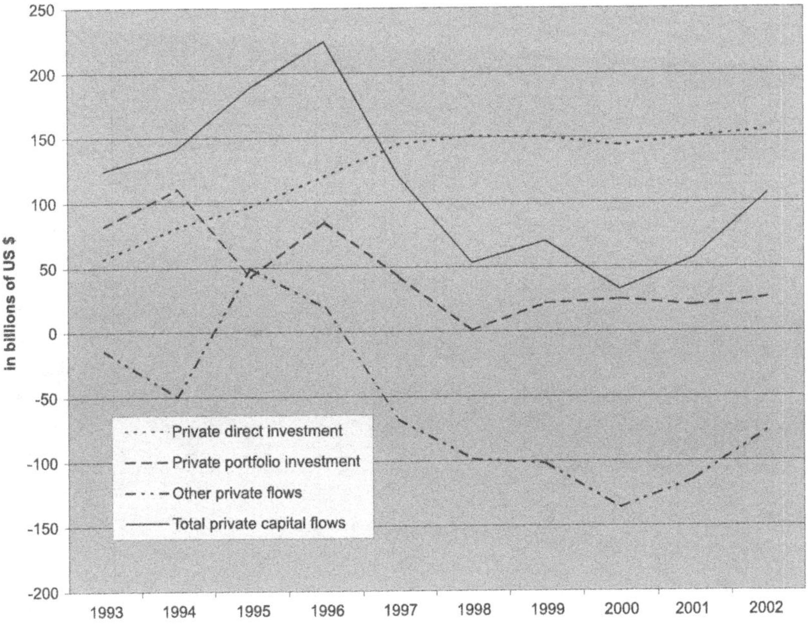

Figure 1.2
Private net capital flows to emerging markets. *Source:* IMF 2001. *Note:* Figures for 2001 and 2002 are estimates.

are also typically very costly in terms of both direct budgetary expenditures (or lost output) and the overall costs on the economy. Rising spreads and devaluations can be a significant strain on a country's budget as debt servicing becomes more expensive (especially in domestic currency). Severe policy adjustments are usually needed, and the short-run output "response" to the crisis is usually negative and very severe. Only in Asia, however, did the output fall by more than 8 percent.

Having examined these facts, the answer to the question on financial vulnerability seems clear. Yes, emerging markets are financially vulnerable. So the natural question might then be whether crises can be predicted and possibly averted. But measuring and predicting vulnerability in EMs is not an easy task by any means. The recent EM crises have led to extensive research that has tried to identify those variables that can measure the strengthening of pressures on EMs and has tried to develop "early warning indicators."[5] Despite all these efforts, the econometric results are uneven, and therefore the incidence of unexpected and unpredicted crises will remain with us, at least for some time. So what can EMs do to avoid a crisis? It is clear that, first and foremost, they should follow sound macroeconomic policy. There is no substitute for stable macroeconomic environment and sound financial system.

But in addition, some argue, EMs would be well advised to hold an adequate level of international reserves. This is a central suggestion in chapter 4, "International Financial Crisis: The Role of Reserves and SDR Allocations," by J. Onno de Beaufort Wijnholds and Arend Kapteyn. But in a globalized world, with open capital accounts and an increase in cross-border flows, the traditional definition of the adequate level of international reserves is obviously obsolete. The rule of thumb that reserves should be at the level of three months' worth of imports of good and services was valid when major external shocks could arise mainly from terms of trade, that is, from the current account. But the recent major crises in EMs have shown that a major feature of these events is the reversal of capital flows. Thus it is the capital account, and not the current account, that is the major source of variability or vulnerability for EMs today.

Wijnholds and Kapteyn attempt to update the rule of adequate level of reserves. They start their approach with the so-called Guidotti rule. The criterion that the former Argentinean deputy finance minister Pablo Guidotti used to determine the adequate level of reserves was that countries should manage their external liabilities in such a way as to "live without foreign borrowing for up to one year." U.S. Federal Reserve Chairman Alan Greenspan proposed adding the so-called liquidity-at-risk standard, which requires that country's external position be calculated over a range of possible outcomes (similar to the *value-at-risk* technique for the commercial banking sector). Wijnholds and Kapteyn build on this proposal. They start with the short-term external debt on a residual maturity basis. In their view, this amount needs to be fully covered with reserves. To this they add the estimated amount of the so-called confidence crisis cost, that is, internal drain. If there is a confidence crisis, people will vote with their money, and one will observe a capital flight among residents (not just among nonresidents).

Holding adequate reserves is important, but it has its costs too. As EMs with relatively large reserves withstood the recent financial crises much better than those with modest levels, however, the costs of increasing reserves to adequate level can be viewed, according to the authors of chapter 4, as the insurance premium for protection against financial crisis.

1.3 Emerging Markets and the Exchange Rate

The choice of the exchange rate regime to be used in a particular economy is probably one of the most contested in modern international economics, and controversies about the "appropriate" regime for EMs naturally abound. There is a vast choice of regimes, indeed, from freely floating and managed floating, over a variety of pegs, today divided into soft pegs (such as conventional fixed pegs, horizontal bands, diagonal bands, and crawling pegs) and hard pegs (such as currency boards), to the other extreme of a country's completely abandoning its own currency and adopting another country's, that is, dollarizing.[6] So, which regime is more appropriate for an EM?

Some currently hold (e.g., Fischer 2001) that the world is moving toward bipolarism. In short, this view is that, to be sustainable, a country should adopt either a free-floating exchange regime or a hard peg, that is, a currency board or a dollarized economy. Soft pegs are out of fashion, at least for the time being, and there is a general (although certainly not universal) view that for countries that are open to international capital flows, adjustable pegs have not proven to be viable. And EM experience has more or less confirmed this view. But can EMs really float their currencies? In chapter 2, "Original Sin, Passthrough, and Fear of Floating," Ricardo Hausmann, Ugo Panizza, and Ernesto Stein claim that, de facto, EMs do not float their currencies, even if they have a de jure floating regime. To advance their hypothesis, Hausmann and his colleagues focus their analysis on countries that have a de jure floating exchange rate regime. One of the main benefits of such a flexible system is believed to offer a country is the ability to conduct independent monetary policy. But in the view of Hausmann, Panizza, and Stein, this may not be the case in emerging markets. Hausmann and his coauthors start their analysis by studying the degree of passthrough (from the exchange rate to prices) and considering the ability of a country to borrow (both domestically and abroad) in its own currency. In this context they develop the concept of "original sin," which indicates that a country cannot borrow long term, either domestically or abroad, in its own currency.

The main conclusions of chapter 2 can be summarized as follows. First, countries that are officially classified as having flexible exchange rate regimes actually have a very low degree of flexibility. Second, empirically, countries that cannot borrow in their own currency have low exchange rate flexibility. These results are very important, as they indicate that EMs actually do not have the "luxury" of exchange rate flexibility and independent monetary policy, even if they want to adopt a flexible regime.

If EMs cannot float, what then are their options regarding the choice of an exchange rate regime? Should they adopt a currency board or even dollarize? This issue is dealt with in detail in chapter 5, "The Eastern Enlargement of the EU and the Case for Unilateral Euroization," by Jacek Rostowski, which focuses on the so-called applicant countries (countries that are recognized as candidates for EU membership) and their choice of exchange rate regime.

It is well known that Economic and Monetary Union (EMU) is part of the *acquis communautaire* (the common legal framework of the EU member countries), meaning that new (since 1998) members of the EU will not have available to them the so-called opt-out clause. Therefore, future members of the EU will not have the choice to be a member of the EU and not be part of EMU (as is the case today for the United Kingdom, Denmark, and Sweden). In other words, countries that aspire to EU membership and become EU members will have to adopt the euro as their currency immediately upon becoming members. But adopting the common currency is subject to strict criteria (the Maastricht criteria) and involves a country's demonstrating its exchange rate stability by being within the EU's exchange rate mechanism (ERM-II) for at least two years.

Within this context, it is clear that the main challenge in the choice of the exchange rate regime for applicant countries is not whether they will eventually adopt the euro as their currency, but rather when will this happen. Or, in other words, what exchange rate regime optimizes the path to EU membership and ultimately to the euro? Rostowski's views are very clear. He stresses that the traditional route to EMU membership seems to be fraught with difficulties. Applicant countries will be faced with rapid economic growth, real appreciation as a result of the Harrod-Balassa-Samuelson effect, free capital movements, and the need to satisfy the Maastricht criteria. Those developments will result in high current account deficits and subsequent problems in joining the EMU. Therefore, Rostowski proposes unilateral euroization (adoption of the euro as a country's currency without its being a member of EU and EMU), stressing that this should be the best way to achieve the necessary convergence.

On the same subject, chapter 6, "The Costs and Benefits of Euroization in Central and Eastern Europe before or instead of EMU Membership," by D. Mario Nuti, takes a broad view on the question of whether a country should euroize or adopt a currency board. He weights the costs and benefits of euroization in Central and Eastern Europe before EMU membership. As the main advantages of a unilateral and early euroization, he stresses lower transaction costs; greater economic integration, both through trade (especially if linked with trade liberalization) and foreign direct investments; lower interest rates, avoidance of volatility in the exchange rate, and less vulnerability to changes in capital flows due to speculative crises; and the avoidance of Hausmann, Panizza, and Stein's original sin. But Nuti claims that adopting another currency has costs and disadvantages for a country as well. First, large international reserves are needed, and they may not be available to some of the EMs pursuing EMU membership. Borrowing is an option, but it might undermine the credibility of the whole exercise. Additional costs arise from the fact that a country may not be at the same business cycle as the country whose currency it has adopted, so it may be subjected to asymmetric shocks that may not be compensated for by the use of the exchange rate as a shock absorber. Moreover, the expected rapid increase in productivity after euroization will result in the adjustment of the real effective exchange rate only through inflation, as the nominal rate is fixed. Also, the loss of seigniorage may be a problem for some countries, and so can be the loss of the lender-of-last-resort function (both of which can be resolved in different ways).

In Nuti's view the net balance of costs and benefits of euroization is an empirical question the answer to which depends on the degree of convergence (nominal, real and institutional) of each country, its level of reserves, invoice and payment practices in its foreign trade, and the size and denomination foreign debt, among other factors. His conclusion is that early euroization certainly has its advantages, but they should not be taken for granted, and the costs of such a step should not be neglected.

But even without intending, as a policy matter, to dollarize an economy, there are countries where the process of dollarization has already taken place spontaneously. To measure, how dollarized a country is, however, is not an easy task at all. The common way to measure dollarization is by calculating the share of foreign currency deposits in broad money (Balino, Bennet, and Borensztein 1999). But with this indicator a large part, that is, foreign currency in circulation, may be missing from the picture. It is common knowledge that foreign-currency banknotes are widely used in a number of emerging markets. Edgar L. Feige, Michael Faulend, Velimir Šonje, and Vedran Šošić, in chapter 7, "Currency Substitution, Unofficial Dollarization, and Estimates of Foreign Currency Held Abroad: The Case of Croatia," try to measure what has indeed proven very difficult to quantify: the amount of foreign currency in circulation in a country.

Unofficial dollarization (a situation in which individuals and firms use foreign currency as a substitute for some of the monetary services that the domestic currency should provide) is without any doubt a wide phenomenon. Feige and his coauthors estimate that out of the total number of U.S. dollar bills in circulation, 40–60 percent are held abroad. In 1999 the total value of U.S. dollar banknotes was US$480 billion. Similar estimates (30–69 percent) exist for German mark banknotes. But of course, the problem is how to measure the circulation of those banknotes in individual countries. This information is indeed very important for monetary authorities, since without it, it would be difficult to conduct monetary policy with a reasonable degree of certainty, since the effective money supply may be larger than perceived by the authorities. In addition, unofficial dollarization has consequences not only for monetary policy but for fiscal and social policy as well. As foreign-cash transactions are usually part of the underground economy, they stimulate rent seeking and corruption.

Feige and his collegues distinguish first between currency and asset substitution. Currency substitution takes place when foreign currency is used as a medium of exchange. Asset substitution takes place when foreign-denominated monetary assets substitute for domestic ones. As an illustration, the proxy used in the IMF study (Balino, Bennet, and Borzenstein 1999)—foreign-currency deposits in broad money—measures only asset substitution, and not currency substitution. Unofficial dollarization is a summary measure of the use of foreign currency as a substitute for all money services of the domestic currency.

In their attempt to measure dollarization, Feige et al. use first the so-called denomination displacement method, which is based on the assumption that when currency substitution occurs, it often results in high-denomination domestic banknotes' being "displaced" by high-denomination foreign notes. Therefore, if a country is highly dollarized, then the distribution of domestic banknotes should be skewed; that is, large-denomination domestic notes should be less used than normally. The second method used in the study is the estimation of a demand function for money in a well-known, highly dollarized country for which the actual amounts of U.S. dollars in circulation is known. The parameters obtained from that estimation are then used to estimate the demand for U.S. dollars in the country being studied, where there is an unknown volume of currency substitution.

Both methods were applied to the case of Croatia, a highly dollarized (or euroized) country by any standard. Through the first method, Feige and his coauthors conclude that the average dollar value (of German marks) in circulation in Croatia in 1994–1998 was about US$400 per capita. For the second method, the country used as a model for estimating money demand was Argentina. By this method the estimated foreign currency in circulation in Croatia on a per capita basis in the same period was twice as high, between US$800 and US$1,000 per capita. These numbers are unusually high and indicate that the degree of dollarization in Croatia is extremely high.

And these estimates are of crucial importance for policymakers in their choice of exchange rate regime. If unofficial dollarization is very high and irreversible, the benefits of the flexible exchange rate regime are called into question. One conclusion might be that highly dollarized economies cannot count on the floating exchange rate regime as a shock absorber.

1.4 Concluding Observations

Emerging markets are rapidly being integrated into the world economy, especially into the international capital markets, due to at least two factors. On the one hand, there has been a broad movement toward market-oriented reforms in developing economies (liberalization and deregulation) that has speeded up economic growth in some EMs, separating them from other developing economies whose reforms were slower. On the other hand, capital investors from advanced economies have been trying to diversify their portfolios, directing much of the available fund toward the new set of emerging markets. And no doubts these reforms and trends have been very positive. But as we have mentioned, a very high level of capital flows can also be the root of problems. And indeed if there is a lesson to be learned from the last ten years, it is that EMs are financially vulnerable and therefore extra caution is warranted. One should be especially concerned about the financial system in general and the banking system in particular, as banking crises are costly and unfortunately frequent in EMs.

A great deal has been written about the choice of the exchange rate system for EMs. Lately, and as a consequence of various crises in EMs, soft pegs are out of fashion, and the bipolar view (at least for countries with open capital account) is gaining more ground. But as Hausmann et al. demonstrate in chapter 2, EMs cannot afford the luxury of floating. Even more so, as Feige et al. show in chapter 7, unofficially dollarized countries cannot count on the benefits of flexible exchange rate regimes. Proponents of unilateral official dollarization are obviously against floating as well. So is the trend toward hard pegs clear?

This is an interesting question, as some countries that have abandoned their unsustainable pegs and in need of a monetary anchor have adopted an inflation-targeting framework in monetary policy.[7] This is the case in Brazil, Mexico, Israel, the Czech Republic, and Poland, but it implies a flexible exchange rate regime. In this context, one should remember the words of Thomas Alva Edison: "There is no substitute for hard work." By the same token there is no substitute for "getting the fundamentals right" and pursuing sound macroeconomic and structural policies. No exchange rate regime will do the trick. Or in other words, if countries do not have internal discipline in the conduct of their economic policy, external discipline (by a hard peg) will not suffice in the medium term.

Therefore, the question remains: what is the best choice for EMs in the area of exchange rate policy? According to Sebastien Roch Nicolas dit Chamfort, an eighteenth-century French philosopher: "Le bonheur, disait M... n'est pas chose aisée. Il est très difficile de le trouver en nous, et impossible de le trouver ailleurs."[8] Applied to EMs, Chamfort's words mean that EMs must realize that their solutions lie within themselves. They must look within their own respective countries and find specific answers to specific problems for a better future. There is no alternative to a home-grown development strategy.

Naturally, they should not neglect looking outside as well. There is not a single doubt that for EMs to be successful, they need to open up, promote foreign direct investment as much as possible, embrace transfers of knowledge, and participate in and benefit from globalization. All those elements are indeed necessary. But the ultimate factor for successful and sustainable economic development lies within them, within their available human and social capital.

Notes

1. See, for example, IMF 1999, IMF 2000, and IMF 2001.

2. For a more detailed chronology of the emerging market crisis see BIS 1999, chap. 3, "The Spreading Crisis in Emerging Markets," and BIS 2000, chap. 3, "Recovery from the Crisis in the Emerging Markets."

3. More details about these trends can be found in Blejer and Skreb 1999.

4. For more details on these trends, see, for example, BIS 2000.

5. For a review of the literature on early warning indicators, see Hawkins and Klau 2000.

6. The term "dollarization" is used as a generic one, without specific reference to the U.S. dollar, but is applied to any use of foreign currency in a country as the only legal tender (be it euro, yen, U.S. dollar, or any other currency).

7. For more on inflation targeting, see Blejer et al. 2000 and Bernanke and Mishkin 1997. On Inflation in EMs see IMF 2001, chap. 4.

8. "Happiness ... is not an easy thing. It is very difficult to find it in our souls; it is impossible to find it elsewhere."

References

Balino, Tomas J. T., Adam Bennet, and Eduardo Borensztein. (1999). Monetary Policy in Dollarized Economies. Occasional Paper no. 171, International Monetary Fund, Washington, D.C.

Bank for International Settlements (BIS). (1999, 2000). Annual Report Nos. 68, 69, 70. Basel, Switzerland.

Bernanke, Ben S., and Frederic S. Mishkin. (1997). Inflation Targeting: A New Framework for Monetary Policy? *Journal of Economic Perspectives* 11, no. 2: 97–116.

Blejer, Mario I., Alain Ize, Alfredo M. Leone, and Sergio Werlang (eds.). (2000). *Inflation Targeting in Practice.* Washington, D.C.: International Monetary Fund.

Blejer, Mario I., and Marko Skreb. (1999). Transition and the Open Economy: An Overview. In Mario I. Blejer and Marko Skreb (eds.), *Balance of Payments, Exchange Rate and Competitiveness in Transition Economies*, 1–16. Boston: Kluwer Academic.

Cavallo pawns an uncertain future. (2001). *Economist*, June 8.

Fischer, Stanley. (2001). Exchange Rate Regimes: Is the Bipolar View Correct? Distinguished Lecture on Economics in Government American Economic Association and the Society of Government Economists. Presented at the meetings of the American Economic Association, New Orleans, January 6, 2001. Available online at ⟨http://www.imf.org/external/np/speeches/2001/010601a.htm⟩.

Hawkins, John, and Marc Klau. (2000). Measuring Potential Vulnerabilities in Emerging Market Economies. Working paper no. 91, Bank for International Settlements, Basel, Switzerland. Available online at ⟨www.bis.org/publ⟩.

International Monetary Fund (IMF). (1999–2001). *World Economic Outlook*. Washington, D.C.

I

New Evidence on Financial Policies and the Impact on Emerging Markets

2 Original Sin, Passthrough, and Fear of Floating

Ricardo Hausmann, Ugo Panizza, and Ernesto Stein

2.1 Introduction

The currency and financial crises of the last decade gave new strength to the debate on monetary policy and exchange rate options for small open economies in general and for emerging-market countries in particular. On the one hand, some economists highlight the risks of floating and noncredible fixed exchange rate regimes and point out that since emerging markets have a very limited ability to conduct an independent monetary policy, they should move to super–fixed exchange rate systems, such as a currency board or dollarization (Calvo 2000a; Dornbusch 2000; Hausmann 1999). On the other hand, some economists point out that dollarization and currency boards cannot solve the fundamental problems of emerging markets and may end up being more of a straitjacket than an anchor of salvation (Chang and Velasco 2000; Mishkin 1998; Sachs and Larrain 1999).

Yet other economists suggest that there are no one-size-fits-all monetary policy regimes and that "no single exchange rate regime is right for all countries or at all times" (Frankel 1999; Mussa et al. 2000). Although there is disagreement on the best exchange rate regime for emerging countries, there is now some agreement on the fact that the standard textbook model—suggesting that the main benefit of a flexible exchange system consists of the ability it provides for a country to conduct an independent monetary policy—may not be applicable to emerging-market countries. In particular, some authors emphasize that emerging-market countries with an open current account may have a limited ability to conduct an independent monetary policy, both because they have a high degree of passthrough from exchange rate to prices (and therefore nominal devaluations will not affect the real exchange rate) and a limited ability to borrow long term (either domestically or abroad) in their own currency (what Hausmann [1999] calls the "original sin" of emerging markets).

This new awareness of this particular peculiarity of emerging-market countries has generated a new class of model that explicitly includes the role of liability dollarization and high passthrough. Some models in this class (Céspedes, Chang, and Velasco 2000a, 2000b) show that the standard analysis applies even when one considers liability dollarization and find that even for emerging market countries, a flexible exchange rate system is superior to a super-fixed exchange rate system. Other research, however, finds that there are conditions under which the option of conducting an independent monetary policy has very limited value, and therefore a strong fix could be superior to a floating exchange rate (Mendoza 2000; Ghironi and Rebucci 2000). Lahiri and Végh (2001b) show that in countries that face small monetary shocks, policymakers may find it optimal to let the exchange rate adjust to partly offset the shocks. In countries that face large shocks, however, policymakers may find it optimal to stabilize the exchange rate completely. Lahiri and Végh conclude that this nonmonotonic relationship between exchange rate and the size of the shock may explain the fact that developed countries (which are likely to face smaller shocks) tend to let their exchange rates float freely and developing countries (which are likely to face larger shocks) tend to manage their exchange rates heavily.

Together with this new theoretical literature, a series of empirical studies has documented that countries with a formally floating exchange rate show remarkable differences regarding the way in which they intervene in the exchange rate market (Hausmann, Panizza, and Stein 2001; Calvo and Reinhart, 2000a, 2000b). In particular, these studies document that whereas most OECD countries hold limited international reserves and tend not to intervene in the foreign exchange rate market, most emerging-market countries tend to hold large amounts of international reserves and use these reserves to intervene in that market. Furthermore, Levy-Yeyati and Sturzenegger (1999) show that there are important differences between the de facto and de jure exchange rate policies for countries with both fixed and flexible exchange rates.

This chapter focuses on countries with a formally flexible exchange rate and tries to provide an explanation for their different de facto exchange rate policies. In particular, the chapter considers the degree of passthrough from exchange rate to prices in a country and on the country's ability to borrow in its own currency. After building an extremely stylized model that relates the degree of exchange rate flexibility to passthrough and ability to borrow in own currency, we test the model and find a strong and extremely robust positive correlation between ability to borrow in own currency and degree of exchange rate flexibility. We also find a negative but not statistically significant correlation between passthrough and exchange rate flexibility and conjecture that the weak correlation between passthrough and exchange rate flexibility could be due to the presence of noise in our passthrough index.

The chapter is organized as follows: section 2.2 presents evidence of large differences in exchange rate management among countries that have a de jure floating exchange rate regime; section 2.3 sets the stage for the empirical analysis by discussing a very stylized model that highlights the relationship among passthrough, ability to borrow in own currency, and exchange rate flexibility; section 2.4 builds an aggregate index of (in)ability to borrow in own currency and uses this index to test the model of section 2.3; and section 2.5 concludes.

2.2 Do Emerging Markets Really Float?

The aim of this section is to document differences regarding the way in which countries with a formally flexible exchange rate manage their exchange rate policy. To this purpose, we follow Hausmann, Panizza, and Stein (2001) and classify as having a de jure flexible exchange rate all countries that, according to the November 1999 IMF classification of exchange rate regimes (International Monetary Fund, 1999), adopted one of the following exchange rate arrangements: (1) independently floating (forty-nine countries); (2) managed floating with no preannounced path for exchange rate (twenty-five countries); and (3) countries with a crawling exchange rate or a horizontal band with a width of at least 18 percent (five countries).

Even though the above classification should yield a sample of seventy-nine countries, we lack data for many of the countries included in the first two categories. As a result, our sample includes only thirty countries: the G3 (the United States, Germany, and Japan),[1] nine other industrial countries (Australia, Canada, Greece, Israel, New Zealand, Norway, Sweden, Switzerland, and the United

Kingdom), and eighteen developing and emerging-market countries (Brazil, Chile, Colombia, the Czech Republic, the Dominican Republic, Guatemala, India, Indonesia, Jamaica, Mexico, Paraguay, Peru, the Philippines, Poland, Singapore, South Africa, South Korea, and Thailand).[2]

As in Hausmann, Panizza, and Stein (2001) we focus on three aspects of exchange rate management policy: (1) the stock of international reserves, (2) the relative volatility of exchange rate and international reserves, and (3) the relative volatility of exchange rate and interest rate. For the first indicator, we focus on the ratio between the average stock of international reserves and broad money supply (M2) over the April 1998–April 1999 period. We think that this is a good indicator of exchange rate management policy because whereas a country with a freely floating exchange rate does not need a lot of reserves to defend its exchange rate, the opposite is true for countries that intervene (or plan to intervene) in the exchange rate market. Therefore, countries with an active exchange rate management policy should be characterized by high reserves/M2 ratios, and countries with freely floating exchange rates should have much lower reserves/M2 ratios.[3]

Appendix table 2.1 documents that there are large cross-country differences in the stock of international reserves. Whereas most industrial countries hold levels of reserves that are well below 10 percent of M2 (the average for the group is 12 percent), emerging-market countries have an average reserves/M2 ratio of 33 percent. Interestingly, this value is higher than the reserves/M2 ratio of Argentina (28 percent), a country with a very strong commitment to a fixed exchange rate. If we divide the group of developing countries into two subgroups, emerging-market countries (we follow Bordo and Eichengreen 2000 and classify countries as emerging markets on the basis of whether they are net recipients of substantial capital inflows) and other less-developed countries (LDCs), we find that the level of reserves in emerging-market countries is higher than in countries in the LDC group (37 versus 21 percent; see figure 2.1), suggesting that emerging countries that do not rely (or rely less) on the international capital market need lower levels of international reserves.[4] Figure 2.1 provides strong support for Calvo's statement that emerging-market countries, instead of floating freely, tend to float with a life jacket (i.e., with a large amount of international reserves).

Table 2.1
Measures of exchange rate flexibility

	RES/M2		RVER		RVEI		FLEX	
	Level	Rank	Level	Rank	Level	Rank	Level	Rank
Australia	0.06	25	6.91	5	90.21	3	0.30	26
Brazil	0.25	14	2.92	8	12.13	24	0.12	17
Canada	0.06	26	3.37	7	23.46	12	0.17	23
Chile	0.49	3	0.42	25	7.96	27	0.04	3
Colombia	0.41	5	0.93	19	8.48	26	0.06	5
Czech Republic	0.31	8	1.26	16	13.97	20	0.09	12
Dominican Republic	0.09	23	1.58	14	11.57	25	0.12	18
Germany	0.11	21	2.84	9	157.91	2	0.29	25
Greece	0.36	6	0.39	28	25.02	9	0.08	9
Guatemala	0.30	9	0.42	26	24.94	10	0.09	11
India	0.13	20	1.21	17	3.70	29	0.10	15
Indonesia	0.34	7	2.15	13	23.38	13	0.11	16
Israel	0.26	12	0.76	21	21.38	15	0.09	13
Jamaica	0.25	15	0.27	30	2.75	30	0.07	6
Japan	0.05	28	30.45	1	377.26	1	1.00	30
Korea	0.24	16	1.35	15	14.14	19	0.10	14
Mexico	0.30	10	0.84	20	6.99	28	0.07	8
New Zealand	0.06	27	12.68	4	23.78	11	0.33	27
Norway	0.29	11	0.36	29	12.34	23	0.07	7
Paraguay	0.26	13	0.62	23	12.38	22	0.08	10
Peru	0.64	2	0.51	24	13.13	21	0.03	2
Philippines	0.24	17	2.32	11	38.5	8	0.14	19
Poland	0.45	4	0.42	27	14.58	18	0.05	4
Singapore	0.88	1	0.69	22	20.0	16	0.00	1
South Africa	0.06	24	2.47	10	22.8	14	0.15	20
Sweden	0.14	19	0.98	18	62.59	5	0.16	21
Switzerland	0.09	22	2.27	12	40.43	7	0.16	22
Thailand	0.23	18	6.62	6	15.16	17	0.19	24
United Kingdom	0.02	29	17.95	3	46.54	6	0.45	28
United States	0.01	30	19.38	2	69.63	4	0.50	29
Average	0.25		4.18		40.57		0.17	
St. Dev.	0.19		6.99		70.99		0.20	
Min.	0.01		0.27		2.75		0.00	
Max.	0.88		30.45		377.26		1.00	

Note: RES/M2, RVER, and RVEI are from Hausmann, Panizza, and Stein 2001. FLEX is obtained by applying factor analysis to RES/M2, RVER, and RVEI.

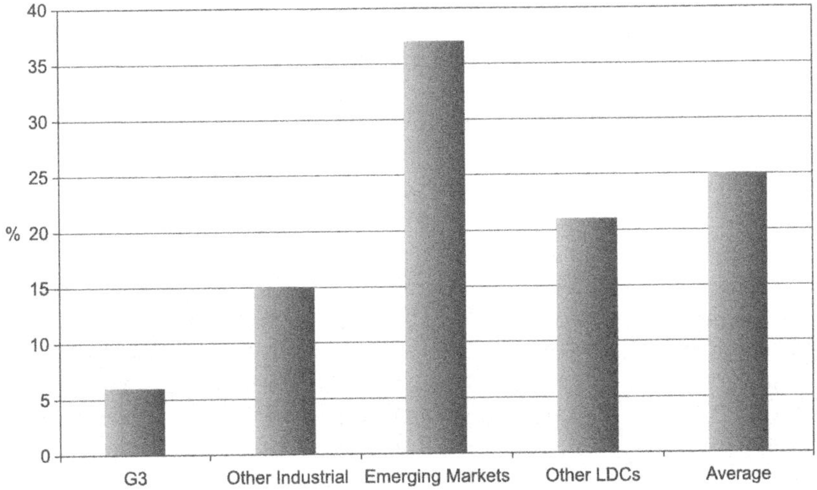

Figure 2.1
International reserves over M2

After having established that emerging-market countries tend to hold a large amount of international reserves, we move on to explore whether these countries use their international reserves to defend their exchange rate. In order to do so, we look at the relative volatility of exchange rate over reserves (Hausmann, Panizza, and Stein (2001) discuss why comparing relative volatilities is better than comparing the absolute volatility of reserves or exchange rate). We measure the volatility of the exchange rate by using the standard deviation of the rate of depreciation. This is a better indicator of exchange rate volatility than the standard deviation of the exchange rate, because the latter would not be able to capture the fact that one possible objective of monetary policy is the achievement of a stable crawling peg. To prevent changes in the exchange rate from affecting the dollar value of the denominator of the reserves/M2 ratio, we average M2 over the period under consideration. Formally, we measure the degree to which countries intervene with reserves with the following ratio:

$$RVER = \frac{\sigma(DEP)}{\sigma(RES/\overline{M2})} \tag{2.1}$$

where

RVER is the relative volatility of exchange rate and reserves,

σ(DEP) is the standard deviation of exchange rate depreciation, and

$\sigma(\text{RES}/\overline{\text{M2}})$ is the standard deviation of international reserves divided by a measure of money supply.

Clearly, under a perfectly flexible exchange rate system, the volatility of international reserves would be low (approaching zero), and therefore the relative volatility of exchange rate and international reserves (RVER) would be high. In the opposite case of a fixed exchange rate or a constant crawl, the numerator of equation (2.1) would be zero (or close to zero), yielding a low RVER. Hence, RVER gives us a good indication of a country's willingness to use international reserves to defend its exchange rate. In particular, the higher the RVER, the lower the degree of exchange rate interventions. To compute the RVER index, we need to decide which exchange rate should be used for each country. We follow Hausmann, Panizza, and Stein (2001) and use the deutsche mark for European countries, the Australian dollar for New Zealand (the results are also robust to the use of the U.S. dollar), and the U.S. dollar for all the other countries in the sample.

The second column of table 2.1 shows the values of the RVER index for all the countries in our sample.[5] As in the case of the stock of reserves, we find strinking differences in our sample (figure 2.2). The G3 and other industrial countries have very high average values of the RVER index (17.5 and 5, respectively), whereas emerging markets and other developing countries tend to have extremely low values of the RVER index (1.7 and 0.8, respectively). Although this leads us to conclude that emerging-market and developing countries seem to be characterized by higher degrees of intervention in the foreign exchange market, it should be pointed out that there are large within-group differences. In fact, table 2.1 shows that there are some developed countries with low values of the RVER index (Norway, Israel, and Sweden) and also some developing countries with high values of the RVER index (Thailand and, to some extent, Brazil, South Africa, the Philippines, and Indonesia).

We now move on to a different kind of intervention. Besides buying and selling international reserves, the monetary authority can affect the behavior of the exchange rate by tightening or relaxing monetary policy. In practice, when a country wants to defend its

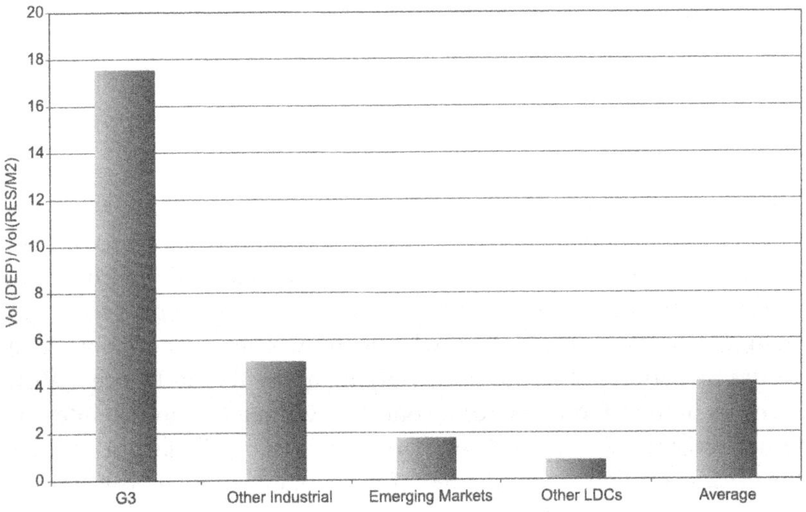

Figure 2.2
Relative volatility of exchange rate and international reserves

exchange rate, it will often both sell international reserves and adopt a tight monetary policy (Lahiri and Végh 2001a). To capture this kind of intervention, we build a measure of the relative volatility of depreciation and interest rate (RVEI).[6] Formally, we measure interest rate interventions with the following index:

$$\text{RVEI} = \frac{\sigma(\text{DEP})}{\sigma(i)} \tag{2.2}$$

where

RVEI is the relative volatility of exchange rate and interest rate,

$\sigma(\text{DEP})$ is the standard deviation of exchange depreciation, and

$\sigma(i)$ is the standard deviation of interest rate.

Countries with limited interest rate interventions will have a relatively low volatility of the domestic interest rate and a higher volatility of their exchange rate; the opposite is true for countries that actively try to manage their exchange rate.[7] Therefore, as in the case of the RVER index, the RVEI index will tend to assume large values for those countries that allow their exchange rate to freely float and low values for countries that heavily manage their exchange rate.

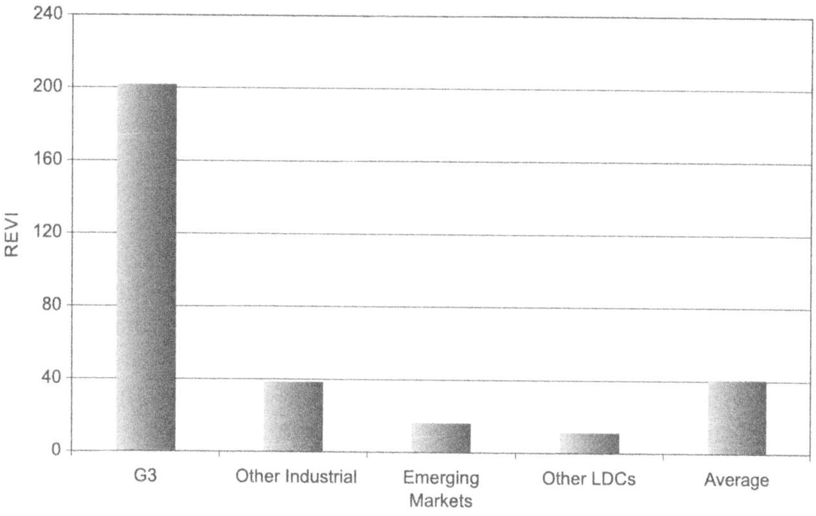

Figure 2.3
Relative volatility of exchange rate and interest rate

Table 2.1 presents individual country values for the RVEI index. As in the case of the first two indices, there are large cross-country differences in the relative volatility of depreciation and interest rate. The G3 countries are characterized by very high values of the RVEI index (Japan has the highest value), and developing countries are characterized by extremely low values of the index (figure 2.3). Even if we exclude the G3 countries, the average value of the industrialized-countries group is more than twice the average value of the emerging-market and other LDC groups (thirty-eight versus sixteen and eleven, respectively).

One possible critique of the RVEI index is that although large movements in interest rate may originate from an attempt to manage the exchange rate, they are also consistent with a floating exchange regime cum inflation-targeting framework (Levy-Yeyati and Sturzenegger 1999), and this is especially true in countries with a large passthrough from exchange rate to prices. However, as pointed out in Hausmann, Panizza, and Stein (2001) this observational equivalence is not an issue here. In fact, we are not interested in knowing if the actions of the monetary authority are dictated by a concern about the exchange rate per se; what matters to us is whether the authorities act "as if" that concern existed. Furthermore, it is easy to find many real-world examples in which, during periods of crisis, the monetary authority completely subordinated its interest rate policy to the defense of a given exchange rate parity. An interest rate defense of the exchange rate, aimed at preventing a vicious cycle of devaluation and inflation, often coincides with the policy advice of the IMF (Ghosh and Phillips 1998).

Whereas in Hausmann, Panizza, and Stein (2001) we consider the above three indices of exchange rate flexibility separately, this chapter uses factor analysis to build an overall index of exchange rate flexibility (FLEX). The aggregate index of exchange rate flexibility is reported in the last column of table 2.1 (we normalize the index so that all its values are included between 0 and 1). As one would expect, FLEX is highly correlated with the reserves/M2 ratio and the RVER and RVEI indices. However, as factor analysis gives more weight to RVER and RVEI, the correlation between FLEX and each of our two measures of relative depreciation (0.96 for RVER and 0.87 for RVEI) is higher than the correlation (0.57) between FLEX and the reserves/M2 ratio. FLEX has an average value of 0.17 and ranges between 0 (Singapore) and 1 (Japan). As in the case of the individual indicators, there are large differences among groups of countries, with the group of industrial countries (especially the G3) characterized by high degrees of exchange rate flexibility and the group of developing countries characterized by low degrees of flexibility (figure 2.4).

We conclude that there is ample evidence that countries with a formally floating exchange rate do follow very different policies regarding the way in which they manage their exchange rates and that industrial countries (especially the G3 countries) seem to follow a policy of "benign neglect" characterized by limited interventions in the exchange rate market, most emerging-market and developing countries heavily intervene in the exchange rate market. Hence, a good answer to the question in the title of this section is: "Not too much." The remaining part of this chapter will try to provide an explanation for this behavior.

2.3 A Simple Model

Even though this chapter is mainly empirical, we set the stage for the empirical work with a simple and stylized model of the behavior of a country's central bank. The building blocks of the model are the following three equations:

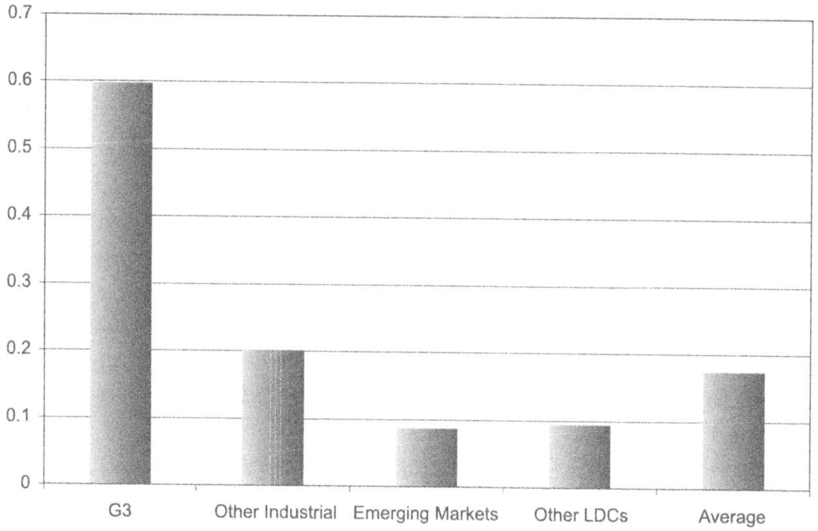

Figure 2.4
Aggregate index of exchange rate flexibility

$$Y = Y(i, \kappa(\dot{e} - \pi), (\dot{e} - \pi)). \tag{2.3}$$

$$\pi = \gamma \dot{e}. \tag{2.4}$$

$$i - i^* = E(\dot{e}_{+1}) + \varepsilon. \tag{2.5}$$

Equation (2.3) states that income (Y) is a function of the nominal interest rate (i) and the real exchange rate ($\dot{e} - \pi$).[8] We also assume that $Y_1 < 0$, $Y_2 < 0$, and $Y_3 > 0$. Equation (2.3) is derived under the assumptions that firms are credit constrained and that their ability to borrow (and produce) depends, through a credit multiplier, on profits (Aghion, Bacchetta, and Banerjee 2000). Furthermore, we assume (but Aghion et al. derive it formally) that both profits and the credit multiplier are inversely related to the interest rate, hence $Y_1 < 0$. The assumption that $Y_3 > 0$ comes from a standard competitiveness effect (i.e., a real depreciation increase competitiveness and hence the profits of firms). $Y_2 < 0$ comes from assuming that a fraction $\kappa \in [0, 1]$ of firms' total liabilities is denominated in foreign currency. Therefore, a depreciation of the real exchange rate will increase the real burden of debt repayment and decrease profits, production, and income. Hence, whereas equation (2.3) postulates a negative relationship between income and the nominal interest rate, the relationship between income and the real exchange rate is uncertain and will depend on the sign of $\kappa Y_2 + Y_3$. Clearly, if the fraction of liabilities denominated in foreign currency is low, devaluations will always be expansionary.

There two possible interpretations for κ. The first is that firms find it convenient to have some of their liabilities in foreign currency, and therefore the parameter κ is endogenous and derived within the firms' maximization process (Aghion, Bacchetta, and Banerjee 2000). The second interpretation is that firms are unable (at least at a reasonable rate) to contract all their debt in domestic currency and therefore κ is exogenous to the firm. This second interpretation is closer to Hausmann's (1999) "original sin" idea and is formally modeled by Chamon (2001).

Equation (2.4) describes the short-run links between inflation and devaluations. The key determinant of this relationship is the coefficient of passthrough γ. When $\gamma = 1$, real devaluations are impossible, and purchasing power parity (PPP) will hold in both the short and long run. However, when $\gamma < 1$, PPP will not hold in the short run, and nominal devaluations are translated into short-run real devaluations.

Equation (2.5) is the standard uncovered interest parity condition and states that the difference between domestic (i) and foreign (i^*) interest rate is equal to expected devaluation ($E(\dot{e}_{+1})$) plus country risk (ε).

Before moving to the central bank's (CB's) objective function, let us assume that there is a sudden jump in country risk (possibly due to international contagion) or in the foreign interest rate and discuss the CB's policy options in such a situation.[9] On the one hand, it is clear that the CB can just let the domestic interest rate increase and compensate the increase in country risk (i.e., set $\Delta i = \Delta\varepsilon$). On the other hand, the CB could try to balance the sudden jump in country risk by generating expectations for a currency appreciation. As the exchange rate is a jump variable, the only way to generate expectations for a future appreciation is to let the exchange rate jump above its equilibrium value. As long as $\gamma < 1$, this will generate a real depreciation and hence expectations for a nominal appreciation. Hence, the only way to set $E(\dot{e}_{+1}) < 0$, is to let the exchange rate to jump to a value above its long-run equilibrium and therefore to suddenly depreciate ($\dot{e} > 0$). It should be clear that this is an option only if $\gamma < 1$, in the case of perfect passthrough it is not possible to engineer real depreciations and therefore the only response to a sudden increase in country risk is an increase in the domestic interest rate. We assume that it takes one period for the real exchange rate to go back to its equilibrium level, therefore expected nominal appreciation needs to be equal to the real depreciation: $E(\dot{e}_{+1}) = -(\dot{e} - \pi)$.[10] We also assume (without loss of generality) that $i^* = 0$, and rewrite equation (2.5) as

$$i = -(\dot{e} - \pi) + \varepsilon. \tag{2.6}$$

Having discussed the central bank's policy options, we are now ready to describe its objective function. We assume that the CB sets the interest rate (and through equation (2.5) the exchange rate) in order to minimize a standard Barro-Gordon quadratic loss function of the kind

$$L = \frac{\lambda}{2}\pi^2 + \frac{1}{2}(Y - \bar{Y})^2. \tag{2.7}$$

For sake of simplicity, and without loss of generality, we assume that target inflation is zero and that target income $(\bar{Y})$ is equal to the natural rate and therefore that there is no inflation bias. We also assume that we start at a point in which $\varepsilon = 0$ and $\bar{Y} = Y$ (therefore, equation (2.6) is minimized by setting $i = i^*$ and $\dot{e} = E(\dot{e}_{+1}) = 0$) and analyze the CB's optimal response to a sudden jump in country risk to $\varepsilon = \varepsilon > 0$.

To study the CB's optimal response, we substitute equations (2.3), (2.4), and (2.6) into equation (2.7) and express the CB's problem as[11]

$$\min_{e} L = \frac{\lambda}{2}(\dot{e}\gamma)^2 + \frac{1}{2}[(\varepsilon - (\dot{e} - \pi), \kappa(\dot{e} - \pi), (\dot{e} - \pi)) - \bar{Y}]^2. \tag{2.8}$$

Equation (2.8) yields the following first-order condition:

$$\frac{\partial L}{\partial \dot{e}} = (\lambda \dot{e}\gamma^2 + (Y - \bar{Y})Y_{\dot{e}} = 0, \tag{2.9}$$

with

$$Y_{\dot{e}} = (1 - \gamma)(-Y_1 + \kappa Y_2 + Y_3). \tag{2.10}$$

We are now ready to analyze how passthrough and liability dollarization affects the optimal response of the exchange rate and therefore the degree of exchange rate flexibility. Let us first look at the role of passthrough. If $\gamma = 1$, real devaluations are not possible, and the nominal exchange rate will have no effect on output. Hence, if the CB had no concern for inflation ($\lambda = 0$), any exchange rate policy would be consistent with the CB's optimal policy, but none could isolate the domestic interest rate from external shocks (Calvo 2000b makes the same point). However, if $\lambda > 0$, devaluations will have a cost in terms of inflation, and therefore the optimal policy will be $i = \varepsilon$ and $\dot{e} = 0$. Next, let us consider the case in which $0 < \gamma < 1$ and $Y_{\dot{e}} > 0$.[12] In this case, the first term of equation (2.9) measures the marginal costs (in terms of inflation) of a devaluation, and the second term of equation (2.9) represents the marginal benefits (in terms of output stabilization) of a devaluation. Equations (2.9) and (2.10) clearly show that the higher is γ, the higher are the marginal costs and the lower the marginal benefits of a devaluation. Finally, if $\gamma = 0$, there are no inflation costs of a devaluation, and therefore the CB will let the currency depreciate up to the point where the output is fully stabilized (i.e., $Y = \bar{Y}$). The above discussion clearly shows that, other things equal, the higher is γ, the smaller is the exchange rate (and the higher the interest rate) response to a given ε shock.

Let us now move to the relationship between κ and e. Unlike γ, κ does not enter into the first term of equation (2.9) and therefore does not affect the marginal costs of devaluation. However, κ does enter into the second term of equation (2.9) and therefore it does affect the marginal benefits of a devaluation. In particular, equation (2.10) shows that the higher is κ, the lower are the marginal benefits of a devaluation. Hence, as in the case of γ, the higher is κ, the smaller is the exchange rate (and the higher the interest rate) response to a given ε shock.

It is also important to analyze the joint effect of κ and γ. In particular, equation (2.10) shows that the higher is γ, the smaller is the impact of κ on the marginal benefits of a devaluation, and hence the smaller is the impact of κ on the CB's monetary policy decision. The intuition for this result is the following: κ affects the marginal cost of a devaluation by increasing the real value of foreign currency liabilities; however, the higher is the degree of passthrough, the lower is the impact of a nominal devaluation on the real value of foreign currency liabilities. At the limit, when $\gamma = 1$, a nominal devaluation will have no impact on the real exchange rate and therefore on the real value of foreign currency liabilities.

We conclude that the very stylized model of this section has three testable implications for the relationship among a country's willingness (or ability) to let the exchange rate float freely, the degree of passthrough from exchange rate to prices, and the ability to borrow in own currency:

1. Other things equal, the higher the passthrough, the lower the degree of exchange rate flexibility.
2. Other things equal, the lower the ability to borrow in own currency, the lower the degree of exchange rate flexibility.
3. Other things equal, the higher the passthrough, the lower the impact of ability to borrow in own currency on the exchange rate policy.

The next section tests these three implications of the model.

2.4 Taking the Model to the Data

The model of section 2.3 illustrated that the degree of exchange rate flexibility is a function of passthrough (γ) and inability to borrow in own currency (κ). We can therefore test the implication of the model by estimating a linearized version of the following equation: $\text{FLEX} = f(\gamma, \kappa, z)$. In particular, we focus on the following specification:

$$\text{FLEX}_i = \alpha_0 + \alpha_1 \text{PT}_i + \alpha_2 \text{SIN}_i + \alpha_3 (\text{PT}_i * \text{SIN}_i) + \alpha_4 \mathbf{Z}_i + u_i, \qquad (2.11)$$

where FLEX, as noted above, is a measure of exchange rate flexibility, PT is a measure of passthrough from exchange rate to prices, SIN is a measure of the inability to borrow in own currency, **Z** is a vector of controls, and u is a random error. Following the discussion of the previous section, we expect α_1 and α_2 to be negative and α_3 to be positive. Although we can use the indices discussed in section 2.2 to measure the degree of exchange rate flexibility, we still need to develop measures of passthrough and inability to borrow in own currency. This is the object of the next section.

2.4.1 *Measures of Passthrough and Ability to Borrow in Own Currency*

To estimate equation (2.11), we need to have a measure of passthrough from exchange rate to prices and an indicator of the ability (or inability) to borrow in own currency. The most difficult task consists of finding a good index of passthrough. In this chapter, we will make use of the coefficients of passthrough estimated in Hausmann, Panizza, and Stein 2001. The full set of coefficients is reported in column 1 of table 2.2.[13] We need to point out, however, that estimating passthrough for a large cross-section of countries is an extremely difficult exercise, and the data set of Hausmann, Panizza, and Stein 2001 is far from being problem free. In that article, we do our best by estimating error correction models for a sample of twenty-seven countries, and we show that although for some countries we do find reasonable results, for other countries we obtain very puzzling results. For instance, we find that Singapore (one of the most open economies in the world) has an extremely low passthrough (approximately 2 percent) and that the correlation between PT and openness is negative. Therefore, PT has a large measurement error that is likely to cause an attenuation bias in the estimation of the relationship between passthrough and flexibility.

To measure a country's inability to borrow in own currency, we rely on the three indices developed in Hausmann, Panizza, and Stein 2001. In that article, we make the point that the inability of countries to borrow abroad in their own currency is a fundamental determinant of the existence of currency mismatches in the country's balance sheets, since this inability makes it more difficult for agents to hedge their currency risks. The three indices were built using two different databases from the Bank of International Settlements (BIS). The first records international transactions involving the banking sector, and the second reports international debt securities transactions (including bonds and money market instruments). The first indicator derived in Hausmann, Panizza, and Stein (ABILITY1, column 2 of table 2.2) measures the ratio between the stock of international debt securities issued by a country in its own currency and the total stock of securities issued by the country in all currencies. This ratio is zero in almost half of the countries, and it is very small (lower than 3 percent) in more than two thirds of the cases. There is also a high correlation between this indicator and the level of development (figure 2.5). In fact, South Africa is the only developing country with a significant amount of debt securities denominated in its own currency. A drawback of ABILITY1 is that it captures only one third of the total claims registered by the BIS.

To address the limited coverage of ABILITY1, we (Hausmann, Panizza, and Stein 2001) compute a second indicator (ABILITY2,

Table 2.2
Explanatory variables

	PT	ABILITY1	ABILITY2	ABILITY3	SIN	MONTHS
Australia	0.21	0.21	0.25	0.44	0.73	189
Brazil[a]	0.81	0.00	0.05	0.00	0.97	5
Canada	0.07	0.15	0.17	0.27	0.81	359
Chile[a]	0.18	0.00	0.03	0.00	0.98	6
Colombia	0.38	0.00	0.00	0.00	1.00	1
Czech Republic	0.02	0.00	0.24	0.00	0.86	26
Dominican Republic	0.25	0.00	0.02	0.00	0.99	32
Germany	0.07	0.28	0.46	0.87	0.54	323
Greece	0.15	0.03	0.15	0.25	0.88	298
Guatemala	0.28	0.00	0.00	0.00	1.00	118
India	0.07	0.00	0.04	0.00	0.98	250
Indonesia	0.49	0.01	0.05	0.00	0.97	23
Israel	0.16	0.00	0.02	0.00	0.99	25
Jamaica	0.31	0.00	0.01	0.00	0.99	122
Japan	0.04	0.51	0.49	1.52	0.36	250
Korea	0.18	0.00	0.01	0.00	0.99	237
Mexico	0.58	0.00	0.01	0.00	0.99	56
New Zealand[b]	0.07	0.04	0.14	1.05	0.81	175
Norway	0.09	0.01	0.13	0.05	0.92	80
Paraguay	0.59	0.00	0.00	0.00	1.00	127
Peru	0.22	0.00	0.05	0.00	0.97	109
Philippines	0.30	0.01	0.04	0.02	0.98	180
Poland	0.62	0.02	0.15	0.32	0.88	17
Singapore	0.02	0.01	0.03	0.00	0.98	318
South Africa	0.11	0.11	0.23	1.17	0.72	250
Sweden	0.14	0.02	0.21	0.08	0.87	81
Switzerland	0.02	0.16	0.27	2.06	0.60	237
Thailand	0.03	0.02	0.02	0.00	0.98	24
United Kingdom	0.03	0.47	0.19	0.94	0.60	330
United States	0.04	0.78	0.80	2.33	0.00	359
Average	0.22	0.09	0.14	0.38	0.84	153.6
St. Dev.	0.21	0.19	0.18	0.65	0.23	121.6
Min.	0.02	0.00	0.00	0.00	0.00	1
Max.	0.81	0.78	0.80	2.33	1.00	359

Note: Except as noted below, PT coefficients are from the ECM estimations of Hausmann, Panizza, and Stein 2001. The ABILITY indices and the MONTH variables are also from Hausmann, Panizza, and Stein 2001. The SIN variable is obtained by applying factor analysis to the ABILITY variables.
[a] PT coefficients estimated by regressing changes in prices over changes in lagged exchange rate. [b] PT coefficient from Calvo and Reinhart 2000b.

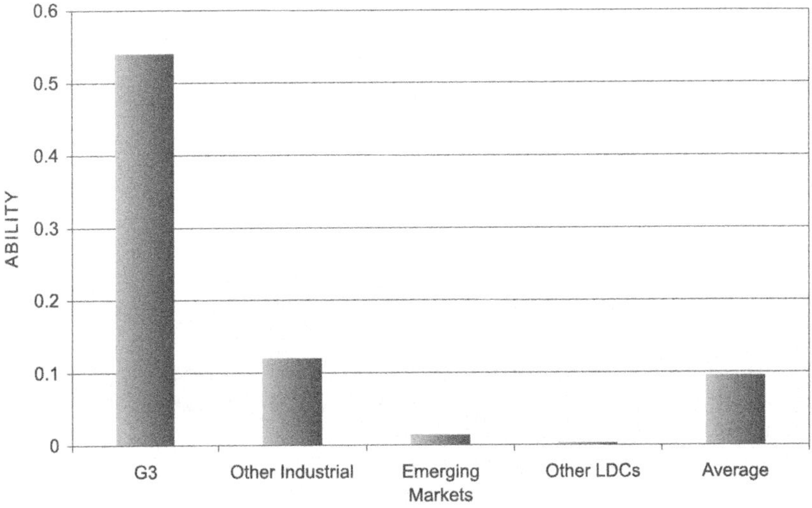

Figure 2.5
ABILITY1 index

column 3 of table 2.2) using, together with the data on debt securities included in ABILITY1, BIS data on total claims of the banking sector. As BIS provides the currency breakdown of the claims of the banking sector for only six of the thirty countries in the sample, for the remaining twenty-four countries all bank debt in "other currencies" was assumed to be denominated in a country's own currency. Hence, ABILITY2 overestimates a country's ability to borrow abroad in own currency. The main advantage of ABILITY2 is that it covers more than 60 percent of the total foreign debt of the countries in the sample. As in the case of ABILITY1, industrial countries (especially G3) tend to have much larger values of ABILITY2 (figure 2.6).

The third indicator of Hausmann, Panizza, and Stein 2001 was built using the debt securities database. ABILITY3 is the ratio between the stock of foreign securities issued in a given currency (regardless of the nationality of the issuer) and the amount of foreign securities issued by the corresponding country. As expected, several developed countries have values greater than one, indicating that other countries issue securities in the currencies of those countries (the average value for the G3 countries is 1.57; see figure 2.7). Not surprisingly, the value corresponding to the United States is the largest (the data are reported in column 4 of table 2.2). In fact, by

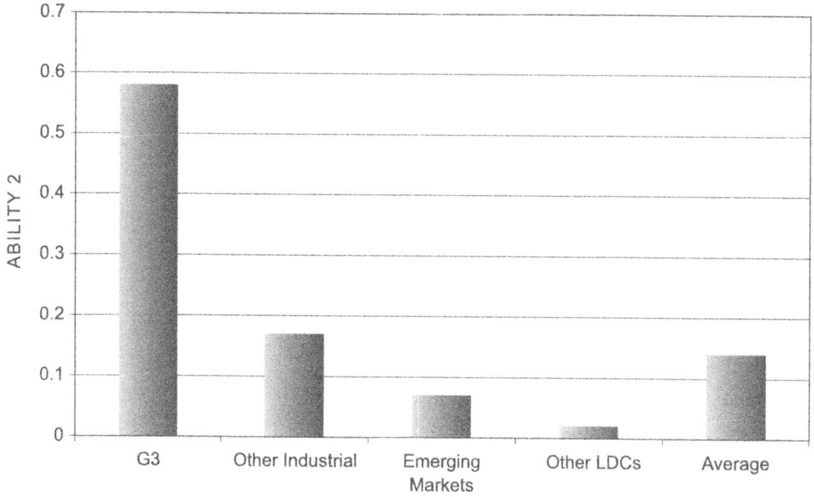

Figure 2.6
ABILITY2 index

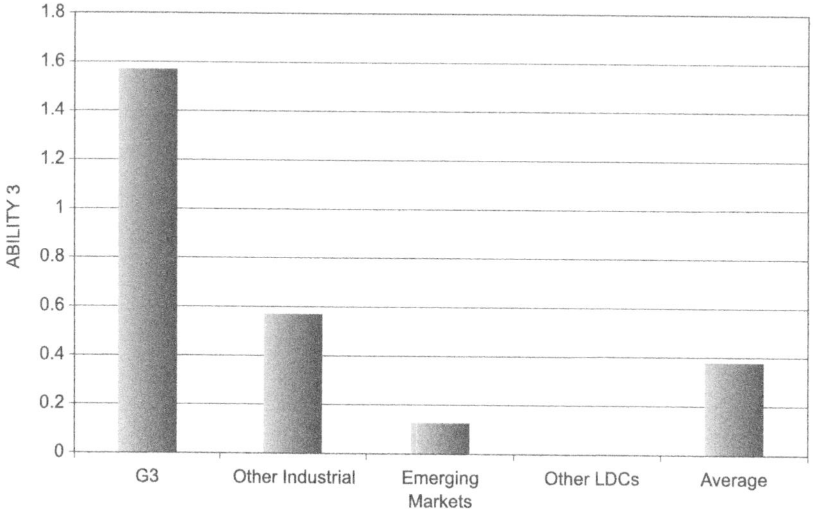

Figure 2.7
ABILITY3 index

comparing ABILITY1 with ABILITY3, we find that about two thirds of the total stock of dollar debt instruments has been issued by countries other than the United States. More surprising is the fact that South Africa has a value greater than unity, suggesting that its currency is widely used by nationals of other countries. Hausmann, Panizza, and Stein (2001) make the point that although ABILITY3 may seem less precise than the other two indices, it is a good measure of the potential for foreign currency mismatches and of a country's ability to hedge its foreign currency risk.

Rather than working with each index separately, we here use the same strategy as in section 2.2 and use factor analysis to build an aggregate index of the inability to borrow in own currency.[14] Following Hausmann's (1999) definition of "original sin," we label this index SIN. The values of SIN are reported in the fifth column of table 2.2. Interestingly, large values of SIN do not seem to be characteristic of developing countries only, and even our group of industrial countries has a high average value of SIN (figure 2.8).

2.4.2 *Estimations*

Equipped with our measures of passthrough and original sin, we are now ready to estimate the relationship between these two variables

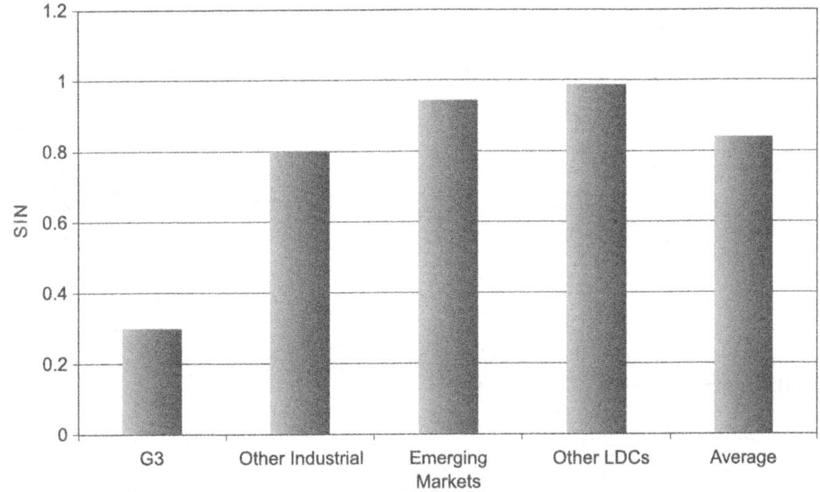

Figure 2.8
Index of original sin

and the degree of exchange rate flexibility (all the regression results are reported in table 2.3). We start with a very basic specification in which we regress FLEX on PT and SIN only, and then we check whether the results of this basic regression are robust to the inclusion of a series of controls that are likely to be correlated with both our explanatory and our dependent variables.

The results of columns 1 and 2 of table 2.3 are consistent with the prediction of the model of section 2.3. In fact, they show that although both PT and SIN are negatively correlated with FLEX, their interaction (PT*SIN) is positively correlated with FLEX. Whereas the coefficient attached to SIN is highly significant, however, the coefficients attached to PT and PT*SIN are not statistically significant. Next, we control for the strong correlation between the level of development (measured with per capita income) and both FLEX and SIN (0.55 and −0.64, respectively) by augmenting the regression with the log of per capita GDP (GDPPC). Column 3 of the table shows that controlling for the level of development does not change the results discussed above. In particular, we still find a negative and highly significant relationship between SIN and FLEX, a negative (nonsignificant) relationship between PT and FLEX and a positive (nonsignificant) relationship between PT*SIN and FLEX. Furthermore, column 3 shows that once we control for SIN and PT, the correlation between FLEX and level of development completely disappears.

Three other variables that are likely to be correlated with PT, SIN, and FLEX are the degree of openness (OPEN), total GDP (GDPT), and the number of months since the country started floating (MONTHS).[15] The degree of openness is likely to be important, because countries that trade a great deal with the rest of the world are likely to be more concerned with the behavior of their exchange rate. Furthermore, even though this is not the case in our sample, the degree of openness should also be correlated with the degree of passthrough (Goldfajn and Werlang 2000). The rationale for including total GDP comes from the observation that if the willingness to hold assets in a given currency is positively correlated with the amount of transactions executed in that currency, then currencies of large countries will have deeper markets, and residents of these countries will find it easier to borrow in their own currency. There is in fact a strong negative correlation between SIN and GDPT (−0.88). Furthermore, there is a strong positive correlation (0.67) between

Table 2.3
Determinants of exchange rate flexibility

	(1)	(2)	(3)	(4)	(5)	(6)	(7)	(8)	(9)	(10)	(11)
PT	−0.017	−0.99	−1.01	−1.17	−1.13	−1.01	−0.09	−0.04	−1.24	−0.79	−0.6
	(−0.136)	(−0.136)	(−0.58)	(−0.68)	(−0.65)	(−0.57)	(−0.66)	(−0.28)	(−0.69)	(−0.44)	(−0.58)
SIN	−0.65***	−0.65***	−0.7***	−0.63***	−0.61***	−0.71***		−0.41**	−0.57**	−0.31	−0.54**
	(−5.69)	(−4.73)	(−4.39)	(−3.66)	(−3.12)	(−4.28)		(−2.01)	(−2.72)	(−1.17)	(−2.58)
PT*SIN		1.016	1.04	1.16	1.14	1.02			1.23	0.74	0.59
		(0.58)	(0.58)	(0.65)	(0.63)	(0.56)			(0.66)	(−0.4)	(0.52)
GDPPC			2.E−03	1.E−02	−3.E−03	2.E−03	2.E−02	4.E−03	8.E−03	2.E−02	−0.01
			(0.07)	(0.46)	(−0.11)	(0.08)	(0.94)	(0.16)	(0.26)	(0.53)	(−0.08)
OPEN				−5.E−04					−5.E−04	−6.E−04	−3.E−04
				(−1.11)					(−0.90)	(−1.15)	(−0.96)
GDPT					0.02				0.014	0.006	0.006
					(0.84)				(0.57)	(0.24)	(0.44)
MONTHS						0.001			0.005	0.008	0.005
						(0.001)			(0.24)	(0.36)	(0.40)
G3							0.42***	0.21		0.22	
							(4.65)	(1.58)		(1.47)	
Constant	0.73***	0.78***	0.76**	0.65**	0.63*	0.76**	−0.04	0.47	0.53	0.26	0.59*
	(7.91)	(6.04)	(2.52)	(2.05)	(1.83)	(2.27)	(−0.20)	(1.42)	(1.36)	(0.61)	(1.95)
Adj. R^2	0.57	0.56	0.54	0.54	0.53	0.52	0.53	0.58	0.51	0.53	0.38
Number of observations	30	30	30	30	30	30	30	30	30	30	27

* Significant at 10 percent; ** Significant at 5 percent; *** Significant at 1 percent.

FLEX and GDPT. Finally, the rationale for including the number of months since the country started floating is based on the idea that countries need time to "learn how to float" and therefore their "fear of floating" could be negatively correlated with the duration of their floating experience. Our estimations show that once we control for SIN and PT, none of these variables is significantly correlated with FLEX and that including them in the regression, either one at a time (columns 4, 5, and 6 of table 2.3) or all together (column 9), does not affect the result of a strong negative and significant correlation between SIN and FLEX.

One last problem with the estimations of table 2.3 is that both FLEX and SIN take extreme values for the G3 countries (see figures 2.4 and 2.8). Therefore, SIN could simply be capturing some G3-specific factor that does not have anything to do with the ability to borrow in own currency. In fact, if we drop the SIN variable and substitute for it a G3 dummy (taking a value of one for the United States, Japan, and Germany, zero otherwise), we find that G3 countries have an average degree of flexibility that is forty-two percentage points higher than the average degree of flexibility of the other twenty-seven countries in the sample (column 7 of table 2.3). This is a very high number, corresponding to more than two standard deviations of the FLEX index. If we include both the G3 dummy and the SIN index in a horse race regression, however, we find that whereas SIN remains statistically significant at the five-percent confidence level, the coefficient attached to the G3 dummy drops substantially and becomes insignificant (column 8 of the table). This last result indicates that the ability to borrow in own currency is an important determinant of exchange rate flexibility, independent of the extreme behavior of the G3 countries.

Admittedly, if we include the G3 dummy in the model with all controls, both the SIN and G3 variables become insignificant (column 10 of table 2.3). However, the high R^2 and low t statistics of this regression signal that there is a clear multicollinearity problem, as shown when we regress SIN over the other explanatory variables and note that these variables explain 87 percent of the variance of SIN and that therefore their inclusion in the regression leads to very unstable estimates of the SIN coefficient.[16] In any case, to ensure that the strong negative correlation we found between SIN and FLEX is not driven by the inclusion of the G3 countries, we drop United States, Japan, and Germany from our sample and then reestimate the model with the full set of controls. The results of this experiment (column 11 of the table) clearly show that our findings are not driven by the G3 countries. In fact, even after dropping these three countries, we still find a negative and significant correlation between SIN and FLEX.[17]

We conclude that there is a strong and robust correlation between the ability to borrow in own currency and the degree of exchange rate flexibility. In particular, our results suggest that a one standard deviation decrease in SIN would be associated with a fourteen-percentage-point increase in FLEX. This is equivalent to bringing the Philippines or South Africa to the same level of exchange rate flexibility as Australia or Germany. In the case of PT, our results always have the expected sign (in the case both of PT alone and of its interaction with SIN) and suggest that PT has an *economically* significant impact on exchange rate flexibility (they imply that a one-standard-deviation decrease in PT is associated with a twenty-percentage-point increase in FLEX). However, the PT coefficient is never *statistically* significant.[18] Although we like to think that this finding is due to the attenuation bias caused by large measurement errors in PT, we must conclude that we have no proof that passthrough significantly affects the degree of exchange rate flexibility.

We conclude by mentioning that although we work with aggregate indices of flexibility and original sin, in Hausmann, Panizza, and Stein 2001 we work with disaggregated indicators of both exchange rate flexibility (the three indicators discussed in this chapter as well as one from Levy-Yeyati and Sturzenegger 2000) and ability to borrow in own currency (the three ABILITY indicators discussed in this chapter plus a dummy variable aimed at capturing nonlinearities in the relationship between ability to borrow in own currency and exchange rate flexibility) and show that the negative relationship between original sin and exchange rate flexibility is extremely robust across specifications and definitions of the variables.

2.5 Conclusions

In this chapter, we documented that there are large differences in the exchange rate management policies of countries with a formally flexible exchange rate. In particular, we showed that countries hold different levels of international reserves and are characterized by different degrees of intervention in the exchange rate market. After building an aggregate index of exchange rate flexibility, we showed that emerging markets are characterized by an extremely low degree of flexibility.

After documenting striking cross-country differences in the degree of exchange rate management, we discussed a model that relates the degree of exchange rate flexibility to the passthrough from exchange rate to prices and to the ability to borrow in own currency. Our model found that the higher is the degree of passthrough in a country and the lower is its ability to borrow in own currency, the lower is its degree of exchange rate flexibility. The model also suggests that the higher is a country's degree of passthrough, the weaker is the connection between its ability to borrow in own currency and its exchange rate flexibility.

We tested the model by using the passthrough coefficient estimated in Hausmann, Panizza, and Stein 2001 and an aggregate index of (in)ability to borrow in own currency and found a strong and extremely robust negative correlation between inability to borrow in own currency and exchange rate flexibility. We also found the expected negative correlation between passthrough and exchange rate flexibility and positive correlation between flexibility and the interaction of passthrough and inability to borrow in own currency. The coefficients attached to these variables, however, were never statistically significant. We conjectured that these weak results are due to the attenuation bias caused by measurement errors in the passthrough variable; however, we have no proof for this conjecture.

Notes

We would like to thank Patricia Cortés for excellent research assistance and Eduardo Fernández Arias, Michael Gavin, and participants in the Dubrovnik Conference, the Inter-American Seminar in Economics held at the Universidad del CEMA, and seminars at the Inter-American Development Bank (IDB) and Latin American and Caribbean Economic Association (LACEA) Winter Camp for very helpful comments. We are also grateful to Melissa Fiorelli, Denis Petre, and Rainer Widera for making unpublished Bank for International Settlements data available. All remaining errors are our own. The views expressed here are those of the authors and do not necessarily reflect those of the Inter-American Development Bank.

1. Even though Germany is formally classified as a part of a monetary union, we assume that during the period considered in this chapter, the Bundesbank was actually dictating the European monetary policy and therefore the deutsche mark was floating against the U.S. dollar.

2. Hausmann, Panizza, and Stein (2001) study a sample of thirty-eight countries and find similar results.

3. One caveat is that countries may also accumulate reserves to be able to cope with the shutdown of the international capital markets that characterizes periods of financial turmoil.

4. We classify as emerging markets the following countries: Brazil, Chile, Colombia, Czech Republic, Indonesia, Mexico, Peru, the Philippines, Poland, Singapore, South Africa, South Korea, and Thailand.

5. For most countries, the values of the index are computed for the January 1997–April 1999 period. However, for countries that started floating after January 1997, we start the period of measurement three months (five months in the case on Indonesia) after the shift in the regime.

6. As in Hausmann, Panizza, and Stein 2001, we compute the RVEI index by using money market interest rates from International Financial Statistics (IFS) and, when these are not available, using data on money market interest rates from Bloomberg and lending or deposit rates from IFS (see Hausmann, Panizza, and Stein 2001 for a detailed definition of the variables).

7. As in the case of the RVER index we focus on the January 1997–April 1999 period. For those countries that adopted a floating exchange rate after January 1997, we started three months after the regime shift. As we use nominal interest rate, countries with a downward trend in inflation could end up showing excessive volatility of the interest rate. To attenuate this problem, we transform annual interest rate into monthly rates. The rationale for this transformation is the following: If a country has a downward trend in inflation during the period under study, this will translate into a downward trend in interest rates, as well as in monthly devaluation. By using the same unit of time for the devaluation and the interest rates, we ensure that the effect of these trends because of changes in inflation on both volatilities will be fairly symmetric and will cancel out when the relative volatilities are calculated.

8. All the results carry on to using the real interest rate $(i - \pi)$ instead of the nominal interest rate.

9. We will focus on a jump in country risk, the discussion for an increase in foreign interest rate would be identical. A real shock that pushes income below potential and, in order to stabilize income, requires either cut in the real interest rate or a real devaluation would also lead to an analogous discussion.

10. If we assume the real exchange rate takes more than one period to go back to its equilibrium level, we need to write expected nominal appreciation as $E(\dot{e}_{+1}) = -\theta(\dot{e} - \pi)$, with $\theta < 1$. All the results carry on to this case.

11. Note that as devaluation and nominal interest rate are linked by equation (2.6), the two instruments are equivalent, and we can express equation (2.8) as a function of either variable. We choose e because it simplifies the algebra.

12. $Y_{\dot{e}} > 0$ implies that devaluations are expansionary; the discussion carries on (substituting devaluation with appreciation) to the case of contractionary devaluations $(Y_{\dot{e}} < 0)$.

13. Hausmann, Panizza, and Stein (2001) estimated passthrough for twenty-seven countries; we fill in the three missing observations in the following way: for New

Zealand we use the estimations of Calvo and Reinhart (2000b), and for Brazil and Chile we obtain an estimate of passthrough by regressing the changes in prices over lagged changes in the exchange rate.

14. Clearly, as we are interested in an index of the inability to borrow in own currency, we need to multiply ABILITY1, ABILITY2, and ABILITY3 by −1. As in the case of the FLEX index, we apply a linear transformation to SIN, so that the index lays in the 0–1 range.

15. We actually use the log of GDPT and the log of MONTHS.

16. Formally, assume that we are interested in estimating the model $FLEX_i = \alpha_0 + \alpha_1 SIN_i + \alpha_2 X_i + u_i$ and define RS as the R^2 in the regression of SIN over X. Then, it is easy to show that $Var(\alpha_1) = \frac{\sigma^2}{(1 - RS \sum(SIN_i - \overline{SIN})}$. Therefore, $\lim_{RS \to 1} Var(\alpha_1) = \infty$.

17. We report that SIN is statistically significant at the five-percent confidence level. However, with a p value of 0.018, the coefficient of SIN is close to being significant at the one-percent confidence level.

18. Attempts to treat PT as a discrete variable by dividing our sample into two groups (countries with low and high passthrough) or three groups (low, medium, and high passthrough) did not yield any interesting results.

References

Aghion, Philippe, Philippe Bacchetta, and Abhijit Banerjee. (2000). Currency Crises and Monetary Policy in an Economy with Credit Constraints. Unpublished manuscript, University College London. Mimeographed.

Bordo, Michael, and Barry Eichengreen. (2000). Is the Crisis Problem Becoming More Severe? Unpublished manuscript, University of California at Berkeley. Mimeographed.

Calvo, Guillermo. (2000a). The Case for Hard Pegs. Unpublished manuscript, University of Maryland. Mimeographed.

Calvo, Guillermo. (2000b). Capital Markets and the Exchange Rate. Unpublished manuscript, University of Maryland. Mimeographed.

Calvo, Guillermo, and Carmen Reinhart. (2000a). Fear of Floating. Unpublished manuscript, University of Maryland. Mimeographed.

Calvo, Guillermo, and Carmen Reinhart. (2000b). Fixing for Your Life. Unpublished manuscript, University of Maryland. Mimeographed.

Céspedes, Luis Felipe, Roberto Chang, and Andrés Velasco. (2000a). Balance Sheets and Exchange Rate Policy. Working paper no. 7840, National Bureau of Economic Research, Cambridge, Mass.

Céspedes, Luis Felipe, Roberto Chang, and Andrés Velasco. (2000b). Balance Sheets, Exchange Rate Regime and Credible Monetary Policy. Unpublished manuscript, New York University. Mimeographed.

Chamon, Marcos. (2001). Why Developing Countries Cannot Borrow in Their Own Currency Even When Indexing to Inflation. Unpublished manuscript, Harvard University. Mimeographed.

Chang, Roberto, and Andrés Velasco. (2000). Exchange Rate Policies for Developing Countries. *American Economic Association Papers and Proceedings* 90 (May): 71–75.

Dornbusch, Rudiger. (2000). Millennium Resolution: No More Funny Money." *Financial Times*, January 3.

Frankel, Jeffrey. (1999). No Single Currency Regime is Right for All Countries or at All Times. Working paper no. 7338, National Bureau of Economic Research, Cambridge, Mass.

Ghironi, Fabio, and Alessandro Rebucci. (2000). Monetary Policy Rules for Emerging Market Economies. Unpublished manuscript, Federal Reserve Bank of New York, and New York, N.Y., International Monetary Fund, Washington, D.C. Mimeographed.

Ghosh, Atish, and Steven Phillips. (1998). Inflation, Disinflation, and Growth. Unpublished manuscript, International Monetary Fund, Washington, D.C. Mimeographed.

Goldfajn, Ilan, and Sergio Werlang. (2000). The Passthrough from Depreciation to Inflation: A Panel Study. Unpublished manuscript, Pontifica Universidade Católica, Rio de Janeiro. Mimeographed.

Hausmann, Ricardo. (1999). Should There Be Five Currencies or One Hundred and Five? *Foreign Policy* 116: 65–79.

Hausmann, Ricardo, Ugo Panizza, and Ernesto Stein. (2001). Why Do Countries Float the Way They Float? *Journal of Development Economics* 66: 387–414.

International Monetary Fund. (1999). *Annual Report on Exchange Rate Arrangements and Exchange Rate Restrictions*. International Monetary Fund, Washington, D.C.: Author.

Lahiri, Amartya, and Carlos Végh. (2001a). Fighting Currency Depreciation: Intervention or Higher Interest Rates? Unpublished manuscript, University of California, Los Angeles. Mimeographed.

Lahiri, Amartya, and Carlos Végh. (2001b). Living with the Fear of Floating: An Optimal Policy Perspective. Unpublished manuscript, University of California, Los Angeles. Mimeographed.

Levy-Yeyati, Eduardo, and Federico Sturzenegger. (1999). Classifying Exchange Rate Regimes: Deeds vs. Words. Unpublished manuscript, Universidad Torcuato di Tella. Mimeographed.

Mendoza, Enrique. (2000). On the Benefits of Dollarization When Stabilization Policy Is Not Credible and Financial Markets Are Imperfect. Working paper no. 7824, National Bureau of Economic Research, Cambrdige, Mass.

Mishkin, Frederic. (1998). The Dangers of Exchange-Rate Pegging in Emerging Market Countries. *International Finance* 1: 81–101.

Mussa, Michael, Paul Masson, Alexander Swoboda, Esteban Jadresic, Paolo Mauro, and Andy Berg. (2000). *Exchange Rate Regimes in an Increasingly Integrated World Economy*. Washington, D.C.: International Monetary Fund.

Sachs, Jeffrey, and Felipe Larrain. (1999). Why Dollarization Is More Straitjacket than Salvation. *Foreign Policy* 116: 80–92.

3 Banking Crises in Emerging Markets: Presumptions and Evidence

Barry Eichengreen and
Carlos Arteta

3.1 Introduction

Each time there is a sudden decline in stock prices and the newspapers publish those photos of pensive investors gazing at the ticker in the window of a retail brokerage house, economists receive phone calls from journalists asking, "Could 'it' happen again?" Could the decline in asset valuations drag down the economy and lead to problems like those of 1929? The conventional answer is "Yes, but only if allowed to engulf the banking system." What made the Great Depression great was that declining asset prices and declining economic activity were allowed to disrupt the operation of financial intermediaries.[1] Loan defaults and depositor runs created problems on both the asset and liability sides of bank balance sheets. By setting the stage for banking panics and bank failures, they blocked a key channel supplying credit to the household and small-firm sectors. Firms starved of working capital were forced to limit production, and households were forced to compress their spending. Only when the authorities set aside other objectives and intervened to stabilize the banking system was the collapse of activity halted and the stage set for economic recovery.

This pattern is of more than historical interest, for today it is again the instability of banking systems that distinguishes economic crises from ordinary recessions. This contrasts with the immediately preceding period: the quarter century following World War II was one of tight financial regulation and control that left little scope for banking crises. There was only one banking crisis between 1945 and 1971 in the sample of twenty-one industrial and emerging markets considered by Bordo and Eichengreen (1999).[2] In contrast, the 1980s and 1990s were decades of financial liberalization and decontrol, developments that were necessary but not sufficient for banking crises. The IMF counts 54 banking crises in member countries between 1975 and 1997, and the World Bank lists an even larger number.[3]

The instability of banking systems is one way of understanding why the business cycle was more pronounced in the fourth quarter of the twentieth century than in the third.[4] In Latin America, the debt crisis of 1982 was preceded by significant financial liberalization and followed by serious banking problems (in Argentina, Colombia, Uruguay, Chile, and Peru, among other countries). Sharp drops in the ratio of deposits to GDP (on the order of 20 percent) created an atmosphere of credit stringency and contributed to the economic stagnation of the period. Finland, Sweden, and Norway experienced severe banking crises in the late 1980s and early 1990s (with resolution costs of 4 to 10 percent of GDP), along with recessions of unprecedented severity.[5]

Similar lessons can be drawn from the Latin American and Asian crises of the 1990s. The involvement of the banking system distinguishes the Mexican crisis of 1994–1995 from the Brazilian crisis of 1998–1999 and explains why Mexico's recession was more severe and its recovery longer delayed than Brazil's. That banking systems became engulfed explains the exceptional severity of the Asian crisis, and the relatively quick resolution of financial-sector problems explains Korea's relatively rapid and robust recovery, in contrast to chronic problems elsewhere in the region.

Thus what causes banking crises, in emerging markets and generally, has become a key question for policymakers, prompting the growth of a large empirical literature that has thus far not produced agreement on the answer. Among the leading suspects are lending booms, the exchange rate regime, destabilizing external factors, precipitous financial liberalization, inadequate prudential supervision, and weaknesses in the legal and institutional framework. Beyond this list of suspects, however, consensus does not extend. Contested questions include the following. Is it mainly internal or external factors that set the stage for banking crises? Are fixed or flexible exchange rates more likely to create or contribute to banking-sector problems? How important is domestic versus international financial liberalization? Does deposit insurance stabilize or destabilize banking systems? Should unusually severe business cycle downturns be regarded as the cause or consequence of banking crises?

In part, the absence of consensus answers reflects problems intrinsic to this type of empirical work. Since there is no agreed-upon list of crises, different investigators focus on different episodes; they measure the dependent variable differently. Since they are concerned with different settings, they differ in including or excluding advanced industrial economies, transition economies, and low-income African economies. Since there is no single way of measuring the explanatory variables and no agreement on what explanatory variables to include, they do not obtain the same results concerning the impact of the latter.

This is not to imply, however, that nothing can be said about the causes of banking crises. With sufficient sensitivity analysis it should be possible to determine which results are and are not robust. In this chapter we use such an approach in an attempt to determine what we know and what we don't know about the causes of banking crises in emerging markets. We employ a variety of different crisis-dating schemes, a variety of ways of measuring the independent variables, a variety of specifications, and a variety of estimators. To limit the field, we focus on emerging markets in the last twenty-five years.

3.2 The Literature

Table 3.1 summarizes the literature on emerging-market banking crises. It describes the approaches and findings of the principal contributions to the cross-country empirical literature.

The first systematic cross-country study of which we are aware is Demirgüç-Kunt and Detragiache 1997, which considered the role of macroeconomic and institutional variables in banking crises in sixty-five industrial and developing countries. They found that the risk of a banking crisis is heightened by macroeconomic imbalances (slow growth, high inflation) and inadequate market discipline (which they attribute to the presence of deposit insurance and weak institutions). Their 1998 follow-up considered in addition the role of financial liberalization and found that recent liberalization (as proxied by the removal of interest rate controls) further increased the likelihood of a banking crisis, but less so where the institutional environment (as proxied by the rule of law and the level of corruption) is strong. In a 2000 study they distinguished a variety of additional aspects of deposit insurance schemes (their funding, their coverage, etc.). Again

Table 3.1
Survey of systematic empirical studies on banking crises

Study	Main question(s)	Other question(s)	Sample and methodology
Demirgüç-Kunt and Detragiache 1997[c]	Determinants of systemic banking crises. Dating of crises.	Impact of deposit insurance, law enforcement.	65 developing and developed countries, 1980–1994. Multivariate logit.
Demirgüç-Kunt and Detragiache 1998[c]	Impact of financial (i.e., interest rates) liberalization on financial fragility. Dating of crises.	Impact of financial liberalization on financial development.	53 developing and developed countries, 1980–1995. Multivariate logit.
Demirgüç-Kunt and Detragiache 2000[c,f]	Impact of various explicit deposit insurance schemes on bank stability.	N/A	61 developing and developed countries, 1980–1997. Multivariate logit.
Eichengreen 2000[b]	In subsection, impact of exchange rate regime, type of peg, and duration of peg.	N/A	110 developing countries, 1975–1997. Multivariate probit.
Eichengreen and Rose 1998[a]	Impact of external conditions (industrial country interest rates and output growth).	Impact of debt composition and exchange rate regime.	105 developing countries, 1975–1992. Univariate graphical and multivariate probit analysis.
Frydl 1999[a,c,d,e]	Review of discrepancies among recent studies with regard to dating, length, and cost of crises.	Relation between crisis length and cost.	Four databases used in previous studies. OLS regressions of costs on length.
Glick and Hutchinson 1999[b,c]	Causes of banking and currency crises. Measure of individual and joint ("twin") occurrence of crises.	Whether each type of crisis provides information about the likelihood of the other.	90 industrial and developing countries, 1975–1997. Bivariate, multivariate, and simultaneous equation probit.

Table 3.1 (continued)

Explanatory variables	Main finding(s)	Other finding(s)
Growth, TOT, interest rates, credit, inflation, government deficit, depreciation, M2/reserves, GNP/capita, bank assets, deposit insurance, law and order.	Higher crisis probability if low growth, high inflation, high interest rates, deposit insurance, weak law and order.	N/A
Liberalization dummy, same variables as their 1997 paper, other institutional variables.	Financial liberalization increases probability of crisis (less when institutions are strong).	Financial liberalization improves financial development in some cases.
Various explicit deposit insurance schemes, same variables as their 1997, 1998 papers.	Explicit deposit insurance increases probability of crises (more under financial liberalization, weak institutional environment).	Adverse impact of deposit insurance is stronger if coverage extensive, scheme funded, scheme run by government (rather than private sector).
Same as Eichengreen and Rose 1998, plus definitions of "strong" pegs, duration of pegs.	Higher crisis probability if intermediate regimes, short-lasting pegs.	No impact of northern interest rates (suggesting unique nature of 1997 crises).
Northern interest rate, OECD growth, reserves, debt, current account, overvaluation, government budget, credit growth, exchange rate regime, GDP/capita growth.	Higher crisis probability if higher northern interest rates, low northern growth, more short-term debt.	No clear impact of exchange rate regime.
Crisis length, credit, output gap, interest rate. (Cost is dependent variable).	Important differences between timing, length, and cost of crises.	Some link between crisis length and forgone GDP.
GDP growth, inflation, financial liberalization. (Currency/banking crises dummy dependent variables.)	Twin crisis more common in emerging markets (mainly if financial liberalized).	Bank crises good leading indicator of currency crises. Converse not true.

Table 3.1 (continued)

Study	Main question(s)	Other question(s)	Sample and methodology
Gourinchas, Valdés, and Landerretche 1999[a,d]	In subsection, impact of lending booms and financial crises.	Identification of set of stylized facts surrounding lending booms.	91 developing and developed countries, 1960–1996. Univariate and bivariate analysis around lending booms.
Hardy and Pazarbasioglu 1998[d]	Identification of macro and financial variables as leading indicators.	Assessment of value of leading indicators in predicting Asian crisis.	38 developing and developed countries, 1980–1997. Multivariate logit.
Hutchinson 1999[b,c,d,f]	Determinants of crises, highlighting European experience.	Vulnerability of EU to systemic risk.	90 developing and developed countries, 1975–1997. Multivariate probit.
Hutchinson and McDill 1999[a,c,f]	Determinants of crises, highlighting Japanese experience.	Identification of leading indicators.	97 developing and developed countries, 1975–1997. Multivariate probit.
Kaminsky and Reinhart 1998[e]	Links between banking and currency ("twin") crises.	Common causes of crises.	20 developing and developed countries, 1970s–1995. Univariate, bivariate analysis.
Mendis 1998[a,c]	Effect of terms-of-trade shocks and capital flows, and interaction of exchange rate regime.	Other determinants of banking crises.	41 developing countries, 1970–1992. Multivariate logit model.
Rossi 1999[d]	Links among capital account liberalization, prudential regulation and supervision, and financial crises.	Development of new measures of liberalization and regulation and supervision.	15 developing countries, 1990–1997. Multivariate logit.

Table 3.1 (continued)

Explanatory variables	Main finding(s)	Other finding(s)
GDP gap, banking/currency crises, real interest rates, inflation, current account, RER, capital flows, short-term debt, TOT. (Credit/GDP dependent variable.)	Lending booms increase vulnerability to banking or balance of payment crisis.	Lending booms associated with output gains. Also, real interest rates higher, short-term debt higher.
GDP growth, consumption growth, investment growth, ICOR, deposit liability, credit, foreign liability, inflation, inflation rate, RER, import growth, TOT.	Higher crisis probability if GDP growth fall, inflation cycles, credit growth, capital inflows, high interest rates, ICOR fall, RER fall, adverse TOT shock.	Macro indicators of limited value for Asia. Difference between severe and full-blown crises.
GDP, inflation, exchange rate pressure, financial liberalization, plus new data on regulatory/financial environment.	Lower crisis probability if competent bureaucracy, legal enforcement, high accounting standards.	Model predicts low probability of distress in EMU countries.
Deposit insurance, financial liberalization, central bank independence, GDP growth, credit growth, interest rates, inflation, stock prices, government budget, M2/reserves, depreciation.	Higher crisis probability if asset prices decline, low growth, financial liberalization, deposit insurance, low central bank independence.	At crisis onset, Japan in stronger macro position. Real interest rates and asset prices good leading indicators.
M2 multiplier, credit., interest rates, TOT M2/reserves, deposits, export/import, RER, GDP, stock returns, government budget, etc.	Typically, banking crisis precedes currency crisis, and financial liberalization precedes banking crisis.	Common macro causes: credit boom, large capital Inflows, overvaluation—then recession.
TOT, capital flows, credit, M2/reserves, debt, inflation, RER, GDP growth, exchange rate regime.	Countries with flexible exchange rates able to lessen impact of TOT (but not capital flows).	GDP growth, debt, RER also have impact.
Control on inflows and outflows, prudential regulation, supervision, deposit safety (plus GDP growth, interest rates, inflation, M2/reserves, TOT, inflation, credit, GDP/capita, etc.).	Higher crisis probability if controls on outflows, more lax prudential supervision, and higher deposit safety.	Low GDP growth associated with crises.

Notes: [a] Uses Caprio and Klingebiel crisis dates. [b] Uses updated Caprio and Klingebiel crisis dates. [c] Uses Demirgüç-Kunt and Detragiache crisis dates. [d] Uses Lindgren, Garcia, and Saal crisis dates. [e] Uses other (less comprehensive) crisis dates. [f] Uses other sources to update/extend dates.

they concluded that explicit deposit insurance tends to increase banking fragility, more so where bank interest rates are deregulated and the institutional environment is weak. They also found that deposit insurance has a stronger adverse effect when its coverage is extensive, when it is funded, and when it is run by the government rather than the private sector, all of which the authors take as signs of moral hazard.

Several of these themes were pursued by Rossi (1999), who developed a longer list of institutional and regulatory variables by limiting his sample to fifteen developing countries.[6] However, Rossi's conclusions regarding the impact of domestic financial liberalization (proxied for by the level of domestic interest rates) contradicted those of Demirgüç-Kunt and Detragiache: where the level of deposit rates enters significantly, Rossi found that it has a negative sign, suggesting that liberalization reduces crisis risk. Deposit insurance enters with the same positive sign as in the Demirgüç-Kunt and Detragiache study, but the coefficient never differs from zero at the 95-percent confidence level.

Hardy and Pazarbasioglu (1998) expanded the range of macroeconomic indicators.[7] They too considered a relatively limited sample of countries (thirty-eight). Their main finding was that crisis risk rises when GDP growth rates fall, domestic credit growth is rapid, inflation is variable, and domestic interest rates and capital inflows are high.

The role of lending booms in setting the stage for banking crises has been a particular bone of contention. Gavin and Hausmann (1996) argued that lending booms have typically preceded banking crises in Latin America; Kaminsky and Reinhart (1998) verified this for their sample of twenty emerging markets, as did Gourinchas, Valdes, and Landerretche (1999) for a different sample of countries.[8] However, Caprio and Klingebiel (1996b) found little evidence of a link between lending booms and banking crises.

Eichengreen and Rose (1998) emphasized instead the role of external factors, finding that higher world interest rates and slower world growth strongly increase the probability of crises in emerging markets. On the other hand, they found little evidence of a connection between crises and the exchange rate regime. One of these authors (Eichengreen 2000) subsequently reestimated the Eichengreen-Rose model with five additional years of data. With the expanded time frame, the role of external factors turned out to be weaker (suggesting that there was something different about the 1997 crises).

The subsequent literature has proceeded in three directions. One strand distinguishes different parts of the world. Thus, Hutchison (1999) attempted to ascertain what is distinctive about Europe's banking crises, whereas Hutchison and McDill (1999) asked what was distinctive about the Japanese banking crisis. A second strand pursues the links between currency and banking crises. The pioneering study here, by Kaminsky and Reinhart (1999), concluded that banking crises contribute to currency crises (rather than the other way around) and that recent financial liberalization sets the stage for banking crises (à la Demirgüç-Kunt and Detragiache). Glick and Hutchison (1999) reached similar conclusions for a larger sample of countries: whereas banking crises predict currency crises, the converse is not true, and recent financial liberalization is the most powerful single predictor of banking-sector problems.

The third strand of work focuses on the connections between the exchange rate regime and external shocks. For a sample of forty-one developing countries, Mendis (1998) found that adverse external shocks are less likely to precipitate banking crises in countries with a flexible exchange rate regime. Less intuitively, he found that a flexible rate limits vulnerability to terms-of-trade (real) shocks but not shifts in capital flows (monetary) shocks.[9]

Thus only a limited degree of consensus has emerged from the recent literature. The role of lending booms is questioned. The predictive power of macroeconomic variables is contested. Whether deposit insurance weakens market discipline or provides insulation from depositor runs is disputed. The role of external factors and the exchange rate regime is uncertain. On the causes of banking crises in emerging markets, it is fair to say that the jury remains out.

3.3 Dating Banking Crises

One reason different authors obtain different results in studying the causes of banking crises is that they date crises differently. Whereas for currency crises it is possible to pinpoint crisis dates by constructing a numerical indicator of exchange market pressure (estimated as a weighted average of exchange rate changes, reserve changes, and where available, interest rate changes), quantitative measures of banking crises are more problematic. The value of nonperforming loans becomes available only with a lag, and even then official estimates of loan losses understate the problem. Because of the existence of deposit insurance and lender-of-last-resort intervention, depositor runs do not necessarily accompany banking-sector problems, making the change in the value of deposits a poor measure of banking-sector distress.

The typical approach, following Caprio and Klingebiel (1996a), is to use data on loan losses and the erosion of bank capital and make a judgment about whether a particular episode constitutes a crisis.[10] An episode is generally categorized as a crisis if there is evidence that most or all of the banking system's capital is eroded. Smaller, borderline banking crises in which only a subset of financial intermediaries is affected require a heavier dose of judgment.

Frydl (1999) compares five lists of crisis dates, those of Caprio and Klingebiel (1996b), Demirgüç-Kunt and Detragiache (1997), Dziobek and Pazarbasioglu (1997), Kaminsky and Reinhart (1998), and Lindgren, Garcia, and Saal (1996). In fact, not all of these studies warrant comparison, insofar as the Caprio and Klingebiel 1996 is the root source of many of the other lists.[11] In addition, the lists used in Kaminsky and Reinhart's widely cited study and Dziobek and Pazarbasioglu's follow-up are partial in coverage: the former considers only twenty countries and excludes crises in Africa, which account for a large number of episodes, whereas the latter, though not excluding Africa, considers only twenty-four countries, rendering its list of crisis dates of dubious utility for comparative purposes.

In this section we concentrate on the following crisis lists: the corrected and updated list in Caprio and Klingebiel 1999 (hereafter, CK-99 for short), that in Demirgüç-Kunt and Detragiache 1997 (hereafter, DKD-97), and that in Lindgren, Garcia, and Saal 1996 (hereafter, LGS-96). Initially, we consider crises through the end of 1995. These lists have the following features:

- CK-99 includes episodes from the mid-1970s to 1998. It divides crises into systemic and nonsystemic (i.e., smaller, borderline) events. It is based on published sources and interviews with experts familiar with particular episodes.
- DKD-97 includes episodes from 1980 to 1995. It does not distinguish systemic and nonsystemic crises. For a particular episode to be classified as a crisis, nonperforming assets as a share of total finan-

Table 3.2
Comparison of crises, 1980–1995

	DKD-97	CK-99	LGS-96	Common to all
Number of episodes	46	91	89	39
Average length	3.6	4.2	3.7	2.7

cial assets in the banking system must exceed 10 percent, the cost of a rescue operation must be at least 2 percent of GDP, banking-sector problems must result in the large-scale nationalization of banks, extensive bank runs must have taken place, and/or emergency measures (deposit freezes, prolonged bank holidays, generalized deposit guarantees) must have been enacted.

- LGS-96 covers the late 1970s to 1995. It distinguishes systemic episodes (also known as "crises") and nonsystemic ("other significant") episodes. The former are instances marked by runs or other substantial portfolio shifts, collapses of financial firms, or large-scale government interventions. The latter are episodes of unsoundness short of crises.

Table 3.2 compares the crisis dates in these three lists.[12] DKD-97 includes fewer crises than the others because its authors do not cover a number of countries included in the other studies, not because they identify fewer crises in countries that are common to all three data sets.[13]

The classification of crises into systemic and nonsystemic in CK-99 and LGS-96 (table 3.3) paints a different picture. Although the vast majority of episodes considered by CK-99 are classified as systemic crises, the majority in LGS-96 are classified as nonsystemic.

Although the comparison of dating schemes here considers only data through 1995, in analyzing the causes of banking crises it will be informative to include dates that come up as close as possible to the present.[14] For purposes of such analysis, we therefore use the updated CK-99 list, as well as an alternative series due to Glick and Hutchison (1999) (GH-99 for short). GH-99 supplements DKD-97 with CK-99 and, to a lesser extent, LGS-96 and national and international sources.

Table 3.4 compares CK-99 and GH-99, the two alternative lists available up through 1997. Since GH-99 draws on CK-99, it is not surprising that the two lists are highly correlated. With 2,231 common

Table 3.3
Comparison of crises, CK-99 and LGS-96 (distinction between systemic and nonsystemic), 1975–1995

	CK, systemic	CK, nonsystemic	LGS, systemic	LGS, nonsystemic	Common, systemic	Common, nonsystemic
Number of episodes	72	24	30	61	25	17
Average Length	4.3	3.5	4.1	3.4	3.9	3.4

Table 3.4
Comparison of crises, CK-99 and GH-99 (distinction between systemic and nonsystemic), 1975–1997

	CK, all	CK, systemic	CK, non-systemic	GH, all	GH, systemic	GH, non-systemic	Common, all	Common, systemic	Common, nonsystemic
Number of episodes	107	79	29	101	78	23	96	68	21
Average length	4.3	4.5	3.4	4.3	4.6	3.4	4.0	4.2	3.3

Note: The apparent discrepancy in the number of CK-99 crises reflects the fact that in Kenya a systemic crisis became nonsystemic (so there is an onset of a nonsystemic crisis but no corresponding additional number of total crises).

observations covering the years 1975–1997, the correlation of crisis dates in the two lists is 0.92. The correlation is lower when we separate systemic and nonsystemic crises (the respective correlations for the two subgroups are 0.85 and 0.82), indicating some disagreement about what constitutes a systemic crisis.

3.4 Data, Methodology, and Benchmark Results

Given the preceding, we focused on the updated Caprio and Klingebiel crisis dates through 1997.[15] In our baseline regressions, we considered only CK-99's systemic crises.[16] Although crisis dates for 122 developing countries can be constructed from CK-99, the availability of data on the independent variables limited us to 75.[17] There is good reason for thinking that banking crises in developing and developed countries differ. Banks account for a larger share of total assets of financial institutions in developing countries. The maturity of bank liabilities is typically shorter, supervision and regulation is typically less well developed, and opportunities to hedge external risk are fewer than in developed countries (Rojas-Suarez and Weisbrod 1996).

We partitioned the sample into crisis and noncrisis following Eichengreen, Rose, and Wyplosz 1996, constructing two-sided, three-year exclusion windows around each crisis to capture the observed persistence of banking crises. This gave us 78 crisis episodes and 2,248 noncrisis observations.[18]

All regressions included a standard list of macroeconomic variables: international reserves as a percentage of monthly imports, external debt relative to GNP, the current account relative to GDP, the government budget surplus relative to GNP, real exchange rate overvaluation, the ratio of M2 to reserves, the rate of domestic credit growth, the rate of growth of GNP per capita, the OECD growth rate, and a weighted average of interest rates in the advanced industrial countries.[19]

Figure 3.1 shows the behavior of these macroeconomic and financial variables around the crisis dates (denoted by the vertical lines). In each panel, the horizontal line is the mean for the noncrisis observations, and the values of the variables for the crisis cases are surrounded by two-standard-error bands. Some interesting patterns are evident. Growth rates declined in the period preceding the crisis (relative to the behavior of the typical noncrisis country), bottoming

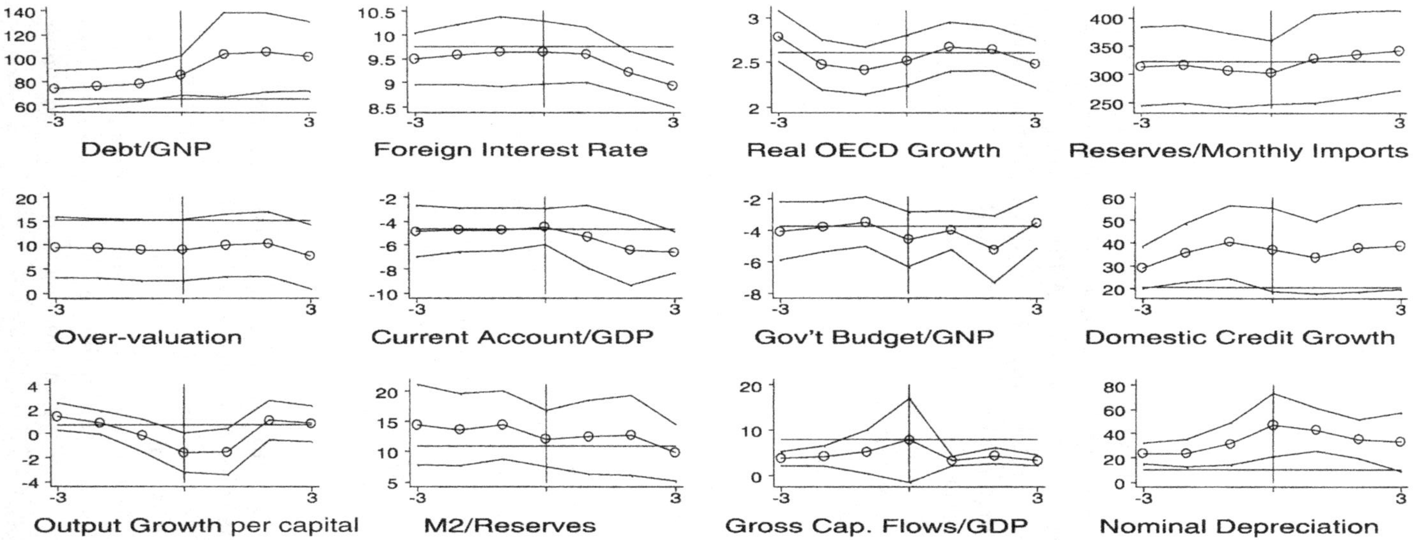

Figure 3.1
Macroeconomic and financial characteristics of banking crises. *Note:* Crisis onset (Caprio and Klingebiel); noncrisis mean marked. Data from 1975 to 1997. Scales and data vary by panel. Mean plus two-standard-deviation band; all figures are percentages. Movements three years before and after LDC bank crises.

out in the crisis year and the year subsequent. There is evidence of domestic credit booms preceding banking crises. On the other hand, although there is also some evidence of declining OECD growth in the run-up to crises, the overlap between the horizontal line and the two-standard-error bands makes it impossible to reject the hypothesis that OECD growth rates are no different in the run-up to crises than in tranquil periods.

We estimated probit regressions using maximum likelihood. All observations were weighted by per capita GNP.[20] In some cases it matters whether the explanatory variables are lagged. Consider, for example, the exchange rate regime. As Kaminsky and Reinhart (1996) have shown, banking crises often lead to currency crises that force a currency peg to be abandoned in favor of floating. Since the data on exchange rate regimes used by most authors are for the end of the calendar year, if the explanatory variables are not lagged, then one is likely to observe a contemporaneous correlation between floating and the incidence of banking crises and infer that floating causes banking-sector problems. In fact, floating could equally well be the result of banking-sector problems, as Kaminsky and Reinhart argued.[21] Or consider growth and banking crises. Previous investigators have found that a declining rate of economic growth is associated with an increased incidence of crises. Interpretation is problematic, however, because banking crises plausibly reduce the rate of economic growth. To minimize simultaneity, we lagged our explanatory variables by one year in all regressions reported below.[22]

Table 3.5 reports our basic regressions, in the first column for the full period through 1997, in the second column through 1992 for comparison with earlier studies.[23] Domestic credit booms are strongly associated with banking crises; this appears to be one of our most robust results. Low reserves (relative to the liabilities of the banking system, as proxied by M2) may be another symptom of rapid credit growth that sets the stage for crises.[24] In addition, the anomaly, noted by previous investigators, that budget *surpluses* rather than deficits are associated with banking crises was confirmed for both periods. This result appears to be driven, however, by the collinearity between the budget balance and other regressors like the debt/GNP and current account/GDP ratios. Indeed, the twin-deficits hypothesis suggests a strong positive correlation between the current account and the budget deficit, as was evident in our data.

Table 3.5
Banking crises: Benchmark regressions

	1975–1997	1975–1992
External debt/GNP	−0.009 (0.4)	0.017 (1.3)
Reserves/imports	0.001 (0.8)	0.001 (1.0)
Current account (%GDP)	0.159 (1.4)	0.063 (1.0)
Overvaluation	0.009 (0.4)	0.007 (0.4)
Budget balance (%GNP)	0.605 (3.5)	0.176 (2.0)
Domestic credit growth	0.056 (4.7)	0.028 (4.1)
Per capita output growth	−0.004 (0.0)	−0.020 (0.3)
M2/reserves	0.321 (4.1)	0.151 (3.6)
Northern interest rate	−0.216 (1.1)	0.365 (2.5)
Northern output growth	−1.271 (2.4)	−0.788 (2.2)
Number of observations	814	706
Pseudo R^2	0.163	0.231
Slopes [χ^2 test] (p value)	55.96 (0.0)	49.38 (0.0)

Note: Probit regressions estimated with maximum likelihood, weighted by GNP per capita. Derivatives (×100) reported for regressors; absolute z statistics (for no significant effect) in parentheses. Crisis is defined as Caprio and Klingebiel (1999) systemic episode.

Eliminating these regressors (and/or northern interest rates) eliminated the positive coefficient on the budget surplus. Thus, we are inclined to take this last result with a grain of salt.[25]

3.5 External Factors and Exchange Rate Regimes

The role of external factors has been a flashpoint in the literature on banking crises. Economists convinced of the need for changes in the international financial architecture have pointed to the sharp tightening of credit in the advanced industrial core and to slowdowns in OECD country growth as setting the stage for financial difficulties in emerging markets.[26] They point to the Volcker disinflation—the dramatic monetary tightening and recession in the United States in 1979–1981—as setting the stage for debt and banking problems in Latin America in 1982. They similarly point to monetary tightening in the United States in 1994 as setting the stage for the Mexican crisis. Others are inclined to dismiss this emphasis on external factors as an attempt to divert attention from policy problems in the emerging markets. They observe that it is harder to

Table 3.6
Banking crises across regimes, 1975–1997

	Fixed	Intermediate	Floating	Total
Tranquil	1,552	283	264	2,099
Banking crises	43	16	19	78
Total	1,595	299	283	2,177

Note: Pearson $\chi^2(2) = 14.3690$. Pr $= 0.001$.

point to external factors that could have contributed to Asia's difficulties in 1997.

Eichengreen and Rose (1998), in one of the first empirical studies of the issue, found a strong effect of external factors—OECD interest rates in particular, OECD growth rates to a lesser extent—on the probability of banking crises. However, they used data only through 1992. Updating these results through 1997, Eichengreen (2000) found less evidence of an OECD effect, possibly reflecting the fact that tightening global credit conditions (rising U.S. and European interest rates in particular) were less evident in the run-up to the Asian crisis in 1997 than in the episodes that preceded it (Eichengreen et al., 1998). There is a further complication, as Mendis (1998) notes: the impact of external factors will vary with the exchange rate regime, which may or may not insulate the domestic banking system from shocks, depending on the nature of the regime and of the shocks involved.

Some light can be shed on these questions by the coefficients in table 3.5 on growth and interest rates in the advanced industrial countries. For the period ending in 1992, we confirmed Eichengreen and Rose's (1998) result that higher northern interest rates and slower northern growth raise crisis risk. But when the sample was extended through 1997, the interest rate effect was weaker. This suggests that the banking crises of the mid-1990s have been different from those that preceded them: external factors (as proxied by the northern variables) have played a smaller role, internal factors a larger one.[27]

Table 3.6 shows that the incidence of crises is 3 percent when the exchange rate is fixed, 7 percent when it is floating, and 6 percent for intermediate regimes.[28] But does the role of the exchange rate regime remain once we control for other variables? There is some evidence in table 3.7 that fixed rates tend to be associated with a lower

Table 3.7
Banking crises and the exchange rate regime, 1975–1997

External debt/GNP	−0.016 (0.7)	−0.013 (0.6)	−0.016 (0.7)
Reserves/imports	0.002 (0.9)	0.002 (1.0)	0.002 (0.9)
Current account (%GDP)	−0.168 (1.6)	−0.159 (1.5)	−0.164 (1.5)
Overvaluation	0.011 (0.5)	0.017 (0.8)	0.015 (0.7)
Budget balance (%GNP)	0.548 (3.3)	0.553 (3.3)	0.539 (3.3)
Domestic credit growth	0.042 (3.7)	0.049 (4.4)	0.043 (3.8)
Per capita output growth	−0.035 (0.3)	−0.032 (0.3)	−0.040 (0.4)
M2/reserves	0.304 (4.2)	0.312 (4.2)	0.305 (4.3)
Northern interest rate	−0.102 (0.6)	−0.141 (0.8)	−0.107 (0.6)
Northern output growth	−0.977 (2.0)	−1.020 (2.0)	−0.947 (1.9)
Fixed regime	−3.525 (2.5)	—	−2.048 (1.2)
Intermediate regime	—	4.007 (2.6)	1.991 (1.1)
Number of observations	814	814	814
Pseudo R^2	0.183	0.182	0.186
Slopes [χ^2 test] (p value)	62.50 (0.0)	62.38 (0.0)	63.69 (0.0)

Note: Probit regressions estimated with maximum likelihood, weighted by GNP per capita. Derivatives (×100) reported for regressors; absolute z statistics (for no significant effect) in parentheses. Crisis is defined as Caprio and Klingebiel (1999) systemic episode.

incidence of banking crises and that intermediate regimes are associated with a higher one (floating rates being the omitted alternative in both cases). But when proxies for both fixed and intermediate regimes were included in the same equation, neither differed significantly from zero at standard confidence levels. Thus, neither effect was robust.[29] It would appear that countries with fixed rates and those with flexible rates are equally susceptible to banking crises. This is inconsistent with the beliefs of the "double-mismatch" school, according to which exchange rate fluctuations lead to banking-sector problems through their interaction with currency and maturity mismatches on financial institutions' balance sheets (Hausmann et al. 1999). But it is also inconsistent with the assertions of those who criticize soft pegs (like those that prevailed in Asia prior to its crisis) for encouraging the accumulation of unhedged exposures (Lindgren et al. 1999) and those critical of hard pegs and currency boards for hamstringing the lender-of-last-resort function (Wood 1999).[30]

To probe the robustness of this result, we redefined our measure of the exchange rate regime in variety of ways.[31] Reinhart (2000) questioned the IMF's official classification of exchange rate arrangements, observing that more than a few countries officially classified as having a floating rate limit the flexibility of their exchange rates in practice. Following Eichengreen and Rose (1998), we therefore included two measures of the actual stability/variability of the nominal rate: the first a dummy variable for cases in which the exchange rate changed by less than 5 percent in the previous year, the second an analogous dummy with a 10 percent variability cutoff. Adding these exchange rate stability measures to the benchmark specification for the same year as the dependent variable (that is, both the onset of the banking crisis and the rate of depreciation of the exchange rate are for the same calendar year), we found strong negative coefficients on currency stability (which differed from zero at the 99-percent confidence level in both cases).[32] But when the stability of the exchange rate was lagged a year, these effects disappeared: it is impossible to reject the null that the coefficients on these variables in fact equal zero at any reasonable confidence level.[33] This inclines us to interpret the relationship of exchange rate variability and banking crises in terms of reverse causality: banking crises force the abandonment of implicit or explicit currency pegs, as argued in the "twin-crisis" literature.[34]

As a further sensitivity check, we constructed a Frankel-Rose (1996) measure of currency crashes (a dummy variable that equals one when the first-difference of the log of the exchange rate exceeds 25 percent and the rate of depreciation has accelerated by at least 10 percent). Again, we found a stronger effect of currency crashes in the current year than of currency crashes in the preceding year, consistent with the view that the correlation reflects causality running from banking crises to currency crises rather than the other way around.[35] The implication is that the Indonesian syndrome, in which a currency collapse precipitates a banking collapse, is not all that common.[36]

Theory (and results reported in Mendis 1998) suggests that the association of the exchange rate regime with banking crises should depend on the source of shocks and, conversely, that the effects of shocks should vary with the exchange rate regime. Table 3.8 therefore analyzes the interaction of two measures of the severity of external shocks (net capital flows as a percentage of GDP, and the percentage change in the terms of trade) with the dummy for floating rates. When we used observations through 1992, these interaction terms entered with significant coefficients but implausible

Table 3.8
Banking crises, external shocks, and regimes

	1975–1997	1975–1992
External debt/GNP	−0.035 (1.1)	0.011 (0.7)
Reserves/imports	0.006 (2.1)	0.002 (0.9)
Current account (%GDP)	−0.092 (0.5)	0.135 (1.4)
Overvaluation	−0.003 (0.1)	0.006 (0.3)
Budget balance (%GNP)	0.637 (2.8)	0.163 (1.4)
Domestic credit growth	0.074 (4.3)	0.032 (3.5)
Per capita output growth	0.041 (0.3)	0.012 (0.2)
M2/reserves	0.557 (4.7)	0.248 (4.2)
Northern interest rate	−0.269 (1.1)	0.414 (2.4)
Northern output growth	−1.664 (2.4)	−0.958 (2.2)
Terms-of-trade (TOT) change	−0.044 (0.1)	−0.025 (0.8)
Net capital flows/GDP	0.447 (1.9)	0.056 (0.3)
Floating regime	−2.659 (0.9)	−1.665 (1.1)
TOT × Floating	0.168 (1.1)	0.160 (1.7)
Net Capital Flows × Floating	0.759 (0.9)	2.098 (2.7)
Number of observations	701	603
Pseudo R^2	0.181	0.294
Slopes [χ^2 test] (p value)	64.86 (0.0)	65.67 (0.0)

Note: Probit regressions estimated with maximum likelihood, weighted by GNP per capita. Derivatives (×100) reported for regressors; absolute z statistics (for no significant effect) in parentheses. Crisis is defined as Caprio and Klingebiel (1999) systemic episode.

signs; rather than helping to insulate the banking system from capital-account and terms-of-trade shocks, floating rates appear to do the opposite.[37] We are not inclined to place too much stock in these results, however, for these effects evaporated when we extended the data set through 1997.[38] And the dummy variable for floating-rate regimes entered in levels (as opposed to the interaction term) is insignificant regardless of time period. Although the conclusion of Gavin and Hausmann (1996, 29) that "when banking systems are fragile, some degree of exchange rate flexibility will reduce the likelihood that an averse shock will be transformed into a highly disruptive banking crisis" remains appealing on intuitive grounds, the evidence for it is weak.

The unavoidable conclusion is that contrary to assertions by the advocates of fixed and those of flexible rates alike, there is no stable association between the exchange rate regime and banking crises.

Table 3.9
Banking crises and domestic financial liberalization

	Not liberalized	Liberalized	Total
Tranquil	729	351	1,080
Banking crises	14	37	51
Total	743	388	1,131

Note: Pearson $\chi^2(1) = 34.6593$. Pr $= 0.000$.

Table 3.10
Banking crises and capital account openness, 1975–1997

	Not open capital	Open capital	Total
Tranquil	1,685	437	2,122
Banking crises	69	9	78
Total	1,754	446	2,200

Note: Pearson $\chi^2(1) = 3.8169$. Pr $= 0.051$.

3.6 Financial Liberalization

There are many exponents of the view that financial liberalization heightens the risk of banking crises. Table 3.9 shows a two-way partition of observations into cases of domestic financial liberalization/control and banking crises/periods of tranquility.[39] A Pearson chi-square test rejected the null that these distributions are the same and suggested that crises are more likely when domestic financial markets are liberalized.

But the evidence regarding capital account liberalization is weaker. Although banking crises have actually been more frequent when capital accounts are closed than when they are open (table 3.10), this difference only borders on statistical significance. The Pearson chi-square test rejected the null of equal distributions at the 94.9-percent (but not the 95-percent) confidence level.

Convincing conclusions require controlling for other determinants of crisis risk. The most widely cited source of evidence is Demirgüç-Kunt and Detragiache 1997, which found that recent liberalization (as proxied by the removal of interest rate controls) increases the risk of a banking crisis.[40] But these authors did not distinguish domestic from international financial liberalization (where critics of financial globalization point accusing fingers at the latter). Table 3.11 therefore adds to our baseline model dummy variables for both domestic

Table 3.11
Banking crises and financial liberalization, 1975–1997

External debt/GNP	−0.045 (1.6)	−0.059 (1.5)	−0.044 (1.7)	−0.047 (1.6)	−0.042 (1.2)	−0.036 (1.4)
Reserves/imports	0.004 (1.4)	0.006 (1.6)	0.004 (1.5)	0.002 (0.9)	0.004 (1.1)	0.002 (0.8)
Current account (%GDP)	−0.510 (3.3)	−0.575 (2.7)	−0.494 (3.4)	−0.582 (3.2)	−0.496 (2.5)	−0.613 (3.7)
Overvaluation	−0.006 (0.2)	0.002 (0.0)	−0.005 (0.2)	0.001 (0.0)	0.023 (0.6)	0.001 (0.0)
Budget balance (%GNP)	0.613 (3.1)	0.972 (3.5)	0.592 (3.1)	0.653 (3.3)	0.806 (3.3)	0.612 (3.6)
Domestic credit growth	0.038 (3.4)	0.067 (4.1)	0.037 (3.4)	0.040 (3.5)	0.064 (4.3)	0.043 (4.0)
Per capita output growth	−0.154 (1.1)	−0.118 (0.6)	−0.133 (1.0)	−0.182 (1.3)	−0.126 (0.7)	−0.110 (0.9)
M2/reserves	0.479 (4.4)	0.646 (4.1)	0.477 (4.5)	0.485 (4.2)	0.623 (4.4)	0.409 (4.2)
Northern interest rate	0.344 (1.5)	−0.289 (1.0)	0.355 (1.6)	0.288 (1.3)	0.112 (0.4)	0.318 (1.6)
Northern output growth	−0.691 (1.1)	−1.882 (2.4)	−0.680 (1.2)	−0.669 (1.0)	−1.604 (2.0)	−0.573 (1.0)
Open capital account	−2.131 (1.4)	—	2.612 (0.6)	—	—	—
Domestic financial liberalization	10.638 (5.0)	—	11.706 (5.0)	11.127 (4.9)	—	3.810 (1.5)
Open Capital × Domestic Financial Liberalization	—	0.064 (0.0)	−3.361 (1.4)	—	—	—
Gross capital flows/GDP	—	—	—	0.077 (0.3)	—	−1.191 (2.0)
Gross Capital Flows × Domestic Financial Liberalization	—	—	—	—	1.192 (4.6)	1.477 (2.3)
Number of observations	598	598	598	572	572	572
Pseudo R^2	0.275	0.168	0.28	0.273	0.232	0.293
Slopes [χ^2 test] (p value)	92.37(0.0)	56.63 (0.0)	94.14 (0.0)	89.22 (0.0)	75.76 (0.0)	95.67 (0.0)

Note: Probit regressions estimated with maximum likelihood, weighted by GNP per capita. Derivatives (×100) reported for regressors; absolute z statistics (for no significant effect) in parentheses. Crisis is defined as Caprio and Klingebiel (1999) systemic episode.

financial liberalization (proxied for by deposit rate decontrol) and an open capital account. The former enters with a strong positive coefficient that differs from zero at the 99-percent confidence level, confirming Demirgüç-Kunt and Detragiache's finding that domestic financial liberalization heightens crisis risk, presumably by facilitating risk taking by intermediaries.[41]

In contrast, the dummy variable for capital account liberalization displays a zero coefficient when entered in levels and when its interactions with domestic liberalization are examined.[42] To be sure, the binary measure of capital account openness constructed from the IMF's *Annual Report on Exchange Arrangements and Exchange Restrictions* is a blunt measure of external liberalization. An alternative is to focus on outcome- rather than policy input–based measures and to substitute gross capital flows as a percentage of GDP (with the numerator constructed as the sum of inflows and outflows, both in absolute-value terms) as a measure of external liberalization. When entered in levels, this measure had no significant impact on crisis risk. Strikingly, however, when the interactions of capital flows and domestic financial liberalization were examined, they entered with a positive coefficient that differed from zero at the 95-percent confidence level. We got the same result when we instead examined the interaction of domestic financial liberalization with *net* capital inflows—that is, inflows net of outflows.[43] This suggests an interpretation in terms of Hellmann, Murdock, and Stiglitz's (2000) hypothesis that external liberalization allows banks entitled to engage in price competition for deposits to lever up their bets.[44]

3.7 Deposit Insurance

Many economists would argue that the extent of deposit insurance risks depends on the nature of the financial safety net and the quality of supervision and regulation. Some (e.g., Demirgüç-Kunt and Detragiache) would argue that deposit insurance increases crisis risk by weakening market discipline and encouraging excessive risk taking. Others (e.g., Gropp and Vesala [2000]) would insist that deposit insurance plays a stabilizing role by removing the depositor panic problem and that this dominates any adverse effect on market discipline.

In table 3.12 there is no obvious difference in the frequency of crises in countries with and without deposit insurance.[45] But

Table 3.12
Banking crises and deposit insurance, 1975–1997

	No deposit insurance	With deposit insurance	Total
Tranquil	736	131	867
Banking crises	42	8	50
Total	778	139	917

Note: Pearson $\chi^2(1) = 0.0291$. Pr = 0.864.

Demirgüç-Kunt and Detragiache (1997, 2000) concluded on the basis of their regression analysis that deposit insurance heightens crisis risk. Strikingly, we find the opposite in table 3.13. That Hutchison (1999) and Rossi (1999), for their part, reported insignificant coefficients for deposit insurance underscores that there is no unique view on this issue. Also striking is that the Hutchison and McDill (1999) moral-hazard variable—the interaction of deposit insurance with domestic financial liberalization—has no consistent effect, according to the table.[46]

Two factors appear to account for the difference between our table 3.13 results and those of Demirgüç-Kunt and Detragiache: we considered different countries, and we used a different deposit insurance series. The preceding results used the CK-99 crisis dates, which are available for a substantially larger set of developing countries and a longer period. When we limited the sample to developing countries included in Demirgüç-Kunt and Detragiache (2000) and followed their deposit insurance coding, we were able to replicate their finding of a positive and significant coefficient on deposit insurance.[47] But when we substituted our preferred measure of deposit insurance (from GH-99), this coefficient no longer differed significantly from zero at standard confidence levels.[48] Although the two series for deposit insurance are almost identical for the countries and years they have in common (their correlation is 0.99), their coverage differs: the GH-99 deposit insurance series is available for fifty-six developing countries, whereas the DKD-2000 deposit insurance series is available for only forty-one.[49] In other words, considering data for more countries—which are available when we use the GH-99 deposit insurance series and the CK-99 crisis dates, both of which are available for more countries than their DKD-2000 counterparts—weakened the result.[50]

Table 3.13
Banking crises, deposit insurance, and institutional quality, 1975–1997

External debt/GNP	−0.056 (1.5)	−0.113 (2.2)	−0.116 (2.3)	−0.118 (2.3)	−0.077 (1.7)	−0.083 (1.7)	−0.118 (2.9)	−0.111 (2.9)
Reserves/imports	0.003 (1.0)	0.003 (0.8)	0.003 (0.8)	0.003 (0.7)	0.003 (0.7)	0.007 (1.5)	0.002 (0.6)	0.002 (0.5)
Current account (%GDP)	−0.708 (3.3)	−1.022 (3.7)	−1.024 (3.7)	−1.016 (3.7)	−0.832 (2.8)	−0.989 (3.1)	−0.859 (4.2)	−0.826 (4.2)
Overvaluation	0.045 (1.1)	0.051 (1.2)	0.059 (1.4)	0.063 (1.5)	0.068 (1.4)	0.022 (0.5)	0.013 (0.4)	0.016 (0.5)
Budget balance (%GNP)	0.989 (3.6)	0.774 (2.5)	0.808 (2.7)	0.807 (2.6)	1.260 (3.4)	1.229 (3.2)	0.520 (2.4)	0.506 (2.5)
Domestic credit growth	0.069 (4.0)	0.068 (3.8)	0.069 (3.9)	0.069 (3.9)	0.080 (3.8)	0.078 (3.5)	0.047 (3.6)	0.044 (3.5)
Per capita output growth	0.004 (0.0)	0.079 (0.4)	−0.095 (0.5)	−0.097 (0.5)	−0.098 (0.4)	−0.100 (0.4)	−0.069 (0.4)	−0.060 (0.4)
M2/reserves	0.507 (3.3)	0.424 (2.5)	0.425 (2.5)	0.425 (2.5)	0.781 (3.5)	0.850 (3.6)	0.350 (2.5)	0.342 (2.6)
Northern interest rate	−0.339 (1.2)	−0.388 (1.2)	−0.412 (1.3)	−0.402 (1.3)	−0.251 (0.7)	−0.381 (1.0)	0.176 (0.7)	0.198 (0.8)
Northern output growth	−1.602 (2.1)	−1.699 (2.0)	−1.698 (2.0)	−1.695 (2.0)	−1.856 (1.9)	−2.247 (2.2)	−0.506 (0.7)	−0.467 (0.7)
Deposit insurance	−4.643 (2.3)	−4.388 (2.1)	−3.353 (0.5)	—	−9.131 (2.2)	—	—	—
Institutional environment	—	−1.131 (0.9)	—	—	—	—	−0.739 (0.7)	—
Deposit Insurance × Institutions	—	—	−4.838 (0.2)	−1.610 (2.0)	—	—	—	—
Domestic liberalization	—	—	—	—	—	—	—	5.221 (1.3)
Deposit Insurance × Liberalization	—	—	—	—	10.780 (1.1)	−3.857 (1.2)	—	—
Institutions × Liberalization	—	—	—	—	—	—	2.587 (4.2)	1.100 (1.1)
Number of observations	465	365	365	365	425	425	395	395
Pseudo R^2	0.228	0.265	0.261	0.26	0.212	0.187	0.328	0.333
Slopes [χ^2 test] (p value)	61.60 (0.0)	60.06 (0.0)	59.32 (0.0)	59.10 (0.0)	58.33 (0.0)	51.41 (0.0)	81.60 (0.0)	82.93 (0.0)

Note: Probit regressions estimated with maximum likelihood, weighted by GNP per capita. Derivatives (×100) reported for regressors; absolute z statistics (for no significant effect) in parentheses. Crisis is defined as Caprio and Klingebiel (1999) systemic episode.

The effect of adding OECD countries, in which deposit insurance is more prevalent, turned out to be more complex.[51] If we used the DKD-2000 crisis list for both developed and developing countries together with our preferred GH-99 deposit insurance measure, the coefficient on deposit insurance again turned positive and significant.[52] But this result was sensitive to weighting observations by GNP per capita, as we did in most of our analyses.[53] Weighted regression placed particularly heavy weight on the OECD countries, which appear to be driving these results. In unweighted regressions, the significant coefficient on deposit insurance vanished, regardless of the crisis list used.[54]

Thus, there is at least as much evidence that deposit insurance has favorable effects—that it provides protection from depositor panics—as that it destabilizes banking systems by weakening market discipline in emerging markets.[55] But neither effect was robust in our results. Probably the most judicious conclusion is that there is no consistent effect. Deeper investigation also provides a reminder that small differences in coding, sample, and estimation can have an important impact on results. Even significant coefficients should not be overinterpreted, in other words.

3.8 Institutional Quality

The argument that crisis risk is greatest where institutions are weak is straightforward and intuitive. Where supervision and regulation are weak, banks will have the most scope to indulge in excesses.[56] Where contract enforcement is poor, banks are most likely to be left holding the bag when credit boom turns to credit bust, because loans go bad and because of the difficulty of seizing collateral.[57]

But does the evidence support this presumption? Table 3.13 also addresses the hypothesis that stronger domestic institutions reduce crisis risk.[58] We proxy institutional quality using an index of law and order that is available for fifty-two countries.[59] Since this index runs from zero to six, with larger values indicating stronger institutions, we anticipated a negative coefficient. Although the coefficient obtained was indeed negative, it did not differ significantly from zero at standard confidence levels. An alternative measure, reliability of contract enforcement, yielded only a slightly stronger coefficient (with a t statistic of 1.6).[60]

We next considered the interaction of institutional quality with deposit insurance, the argument being that moral hazard and the erosion of market discipline should be most pronounced where institutions are weak. Disappointingly, neither deposit insurance nor the product of deposit insurance and rule of law entered with a coefficient that differed significantly from zero at standard confidence levels. When we included only the interaction term, however, the coefficient was significantly different from zero at standard confidence levels. And when we substituted contract enforcement for rule of law, the coefficient remained negative (and the *t* statistic rose to 2.41). There is some support, in other words, for the hypothesis that the interaction of weak institutions and deposit insurance is a source of moral hazard.

In parallel with the literature on deposit insurance, it has been argued that weak domestic institutions magnify the risks of financial liberalization. We tested this argument by examining the interaction of deposit insurance with institutional quality. We found no support for the hypothesis when we used, as a proxy for institutional quality, respect for law and order, the measure available for the largest number of developing countries. When we proxied institutional development using the quality of contract enforcement and limited the analysis to the smaller country sample that is usable in this case, the results were somewhat more supportive of the argument: the interaction of institutional quality and domestic liberalization entered with the expected negative coefficient (so long as the dummy variable for domestic liberalization was also included) but fell short of statistical significance at standard confidence levels.[61]

We used sensitivity analysis to identify the source of the differences between our results and those of previous investigators. It appears that weighting of observations and treatment of OECD countries is key. When the sample was limited to the developing countries in DKD-2000, the law and order index displayed a pleasing negative sign and significant coefficient. Although we continued to get a negative coefficient when we added observations for OECD countries, the addition of an OECD dummy (which entered negatively) reduced the coefficient on the institutional index to insignificance.[62] Moreover, once we used unweighted observations, the coefficient on the institutional quality variable became uniformly insignificant regardless of the crisis list used, of whether OECD countries were included, and of the presence or absence of the OECD dummy. These results convince us that findings for institutional quality are fragile and that implications for policy should be drawn with caution.

3.9 Conclusions and Implications

What have we learned from running 10,000 regressions? One way of organizing the results is to distinguish the robust from the fragile. Among the robust causes of banking crises in emerging markets are rapid domestic credit growth, large bank liabilities relative to reserves, and deposit rate decontrol. This suggests that bank stability in emerging markets is at risk when macroeconomic and financial policies combine with financial deregulation to create an unsustainable lending boom. Monitoring borrowers becomes more difficult when the volume of lending rises rapidly; hence, the quality of loans declines. Macroeconomic policies conducive to rapid credit growth and financial overheating generally (allowing bank liabilities to grow large relative to international reserves) set the stage for these problems. Domestic interest rate liberalization, which allows banks to compete for deposits, finances these unsustainable lending activities, and the associated reduction in franchise values encourages the pursuit of risky activities. There is also some indication that external liberalization that is allowed to give rise to large inflows further heightens those risks, especially when domestic financial institutions are allowed to compete for deposits on price.

These results should resonate with the European audience for which this chapter was written. In all three Nordic countries experiencing banking crises in the early 1990s, for example, the crisis was preceded by liberalization of banks' funding sources and very significant deregulation-related credit booms. In Norway, the ratio of bank loans to GDP increased from 40 percent in 1984 to 65 percent in 1988. The surge in lending occurred later in Finland and Sweden but was equally dramatic, with the same ratio rising between 1984 and 1990 from 55 to 98 percent in Finland and from 41 to 58 percent in Sweden. In all three cases the increase in funding opportunities and reduction in franchise values (coming on top of inadequate levels of capitalization) encouraged the rapid growth of bank lending.[63] In all three cases there followed a credit-financed surge in capital formation and a deterioration in the current account balance, neither of which proved sustainable (see Lehmussaari 1990). In all three cases there was also a reluctance to tighten monetary conditions despite the sharp growth of lending and private indebtedness.

On the other hand, there is little evidence of any particular relationship between the exchange rate regime and banking crises. Different results obtain for different specifications and different classifications of exchange rate regimes. We suspect that those who have imputed a strong effect of the exchange rate regime on banking-sector stability may have inverted cause and effect. There is little reason to think that a particular exchange rate regime—be it a free float, a currency board, or something else—will magically dissolve the problem of banking-sector instability.

Another fragile finding is that the weaker is the institutional environment, the greater are the risks of financial liberalization. Although the logic for this argument is clear, the evidence for it is not robust. Whether this lack of robustness reflects the crude nature of proxies for these institutions, their incomplete country coverage, or the secondary role of contract enforcement and the rule of law is clearly an important topic for further investigation.

Similarly, the evidence that deposit insurance, by weakening market discipline, heightens crisis risk in emerging markets is of questionable robustness. There is at least as much evidence that deposit insurance reduces crisis risk by solving the depositor run problem than there is of its encouraging crises by weakening market discipline. Again, this is a question deserving of additional research. But until such research is completed, either argument should be made with circumspection.

Appendix 3.1 Data Sources

As explained in the text, we began with data for 122 developing (nontransitional) countries. In practice, missing values limited the sample to the following 75 countries: Argentina, Bangladesh, Barbados, Belize, Benin, Botswana, Brazil, Burkina Faso, Burundi, Cameroon, Chile, Colombia, Republic of Congo, Costa Rica, Cote d'Ivoire, Dominican Republic, Ecuador, Arab Republic of Egypt, Fiji, Gabon, Gambia, Ghana, Guatemala, Guinea-Bissau, Guyana, Haiti, Honduras, Hungary, India, Indonesia, Islamic Republic of Iran, Jamaica,

Kenya, Republic of Korea, Lesotho, Madagascar, Malawi, Malaysia, Mali, Malta, Mauritania, Mauritius, Mexico, Morocco, Nepal, Nicaragua, Niger, Nigeria, Oman, Pakistan, Panama, Papua New Guinea, Paraguay, Peru, the Philippines, Rwanda, Senegal, Seychelles, Sierra Leone, Solomon Islands, South Africa, Sri Lanka, St. Vincent and the Grenadines, Sudan, Swaziland, Syrian Arab Republic, Thailand, Togo, Trinidad and Tobago, Tunisia, Turkey, Uruguay, Venezuela, Zambia, and Zimbabwe.

Dependent Variables

Banking Crises Dates for Comparison Purposes

- Caprio and Klingebiel Banking Crisis Dates (CK-99). Source: Caprio and Klingebiel 1999.
- Glick and Hutchison Banking Crisis Dates (GH-99). Sources: Glick and Hutchison 1999; Hutchison 1999; Hutchinson and McDill (personal communication).
- Demirgüç-Kunt and Detragiache Banking Crises Dates (DKD-97). Source: Demirgüç-Kunt and Detragiache 1997, 1998.
- Demirgüç-Kunt and Detragiache Banking Crises Dates (DKD-2000). Source: Demirgüç-Kunt and Detragiache 2000.
- Lindgren, Garcia, and Saal Banking Crisis Dates (LGS-96). Source: Lindgren, Garcia, and Saal 1996.

Banking Crises Dates Used as Dependent Variables in Probit Regressions

- Lead of Caprio and Klingebiel Banking Systemic Crisis Dates (CK-99) (default dependent variable).
- Lead of Glick and Hutchison Banking Systemic Crisis Dates (GH-99) (alternative dependent variable for sensitivity analysis).
- Lead of Dermirgüç-Kunt and Detragiache Banking Crisis Dates (DKD-2000) (alternative dependent variable for sensitivity analysis).

Independent Variables for Probit Regressions

Unless otherwise noted, source for all data is World Bank 1999a.

Macroeconomic ("Core") Regressors

- Total external debt/GNP (percentage). Source: World Bank 1999b.
- Gross international reserves/months of imports (percentage).
- Current account balance/GDP (percentage).
- Real exchange rate overvaluation, defined as deviation from time-averaged country-specific real exchange rate [i.e., log (price level)/(U.S. price level * nominal exchange rate with US$) * 100].
- Budget balance/GNP (percentage), defined as budget balance divided by GNP (both in current local currency) * 100.
- Domestic credit growth (percentage), defined as the first-difference of the log of net domestic credit (in current local currency) * 100.
- Output per capita growth (percentage), defined as the first-difference of the log of per capita GNP (in 1995 US$) * 100.
- M2/reserves (percentage).

External Factors

- Northern interest rates (percentage), defined as weighted average of short-term interest rates from the United States, Germany, Japan, France, the United Kingdom, and Switzerland, the weights being proportional to the fraction of debt denominated in the relevant currencies. Sources: International Financial Statistics (for short-term rates), World Bank 1999b (for share of debt).
- Northern output growth (percentage), defined as the first-difference of the log of real OECD output (GNP in constant US$) growth.

Exchange Rate Regime

- Fixed regime, a dummy for fixed exchange rate regimes against a particular currency, a basket of currencies, or Special Drawing Rights (including soft pegs, currency boards, and dollarized systems). Source: IMF *Annual Report on Exchange Arrangements and Exchange Restrictions* (various issues).
- Intermediate regime, a dummy for limited flexibility (against a single currency or a cooperative arrangement) or a managed float with a preannounced path for the exchange rate. Source: IMF *Annual Report on Exchange Arrangements and Exchange Restrictions* (various issues).

• Floating regime, a dummy for managed float with no pre-announced path for the exchange rate or for independent floating. Source: IMF *Annual Report on Exchange Arrangements and Exchange Restrictions* (various issues).

External Shocks

• Terms-of-trade shocks (percentage), defined as the first-difference of the log of the terms-of-trade index in goods and services (1995 = 100).

• Net private capital flows/GDP (percentage).

• Interaction term of terms-of-trade shocks and floating regime.

• Interaction term of net private capital flows/GDP and floating regime.

Financial Liberalization

• Open capital account, a dummy for the absence of capital account controls. Source: IMF *Annual Report on Exchange Arrangements and Exchange Restrictions* (various issues).

• Domestic financial liberalization, a dummy for the absence of interest rate ceilings. Sources: Demirgüç-Kunt and Detragiache 1997, 1998, as updated to 1997 by Glick and Hutchison 1999.

• Interaction term of open capital account and domestic financial liberalization.

• Gross private capital flows/GDP (percentage), as a proxy for open capital account.

• Interaction term of gross private capital flows/GDP and domestic financial liberalization.

Institutional Variables

• Deposit insurance, a dummy for the presence of an explicit deposit insurance scheme. Source: Kyei 1995, as updated by Glick and Hutchison 1999.

• Institutional environment, measured by an index for law and order (default, ranging from zero to six, where a higher value denotes a better institutional framework) or an index for contract enforcement (alternative index, ranging from zero to four, where a higher value denotes a better institutional framework). Source: Business environment risk intelligence for contract enforcement, *International Country Risk Guide* for law and order, as gathered by Demirgüç-Kunt and Detragiache (1997, 1998).

• Interaction term of deposit insurance and institutional environment.

• Interaction term of deposit insurance and domestic financial liberalization.

• Interaction term of institutional environment and domestic financial liberalization.

Appendix 3.2 Results for Alternative Crisis Dates

In this appendix we document the robustness of our conclusions to alternative sources of crisis dates, reporting two tables that use Glick and Hutchison's dates in place of those of Caprio and Klingebiel. Table A3.1 shows the results for external factors, exchange rates and their interaction; table A3.2 shows the results for financial liberalization; and table A3.3 shows the results for the regulatory and institutional environment.

Table A3.1
Banking crises, external factors, and exchange rates, 1975–1997

External debt/GNP	−0.022 (0.8)	−0.027 (1.0)	−0.026 (1.0)	−0.027 (1.0)	−0.053 (1.5)
Reserves/imports	0.001 (0.3)	0.001 (0.4)	0.001 (0.4)	0.001 (0.4)	0.004 (1.4)
Current account (%GDP)	−0.204 (1.6)	−0.213 (1.8)	−0.207 (1.7)	−0.210 (1.7)	−0.146 (0.8)
Overvaluation	0.023 (0.8)	0.022 (0.8)	0.029 (1.1)	0.027 (1.0)	0.017 (0.5)
Budget balance (%GNP)	0.664 (3.6)	0.618 (3.4)	0.613 (3.4)	0.606 (3.4)	0.652 (2.8)
Domestic credit growth	0.059 (4.7)	0.049 (3.9)	0.054 (4.4)	0.050 (4.0)	0.083 (4.6)
Per capita output growth	−0.022 (0.2)	−0.051 (0.4)	−0.056 (0.4)	−0.060 (0.5)	−0.025 (0.2)
M2/reserves	0.316 (3.8)	0.307 (3.9)	0.310 (3.9)	0.308 (3.9)	0.537 (4.4)
Northern interest rate	−0.423 (2.0)	−0.328 (1.6)	−0.349 (1.7)	−0.329 (1.6)	−0.608 (2.2)
Northern output growth	−0.955 (1.7)	−0.733 (1.4)	−0.725 (1.3)	−0.687 (1.3)	−1.234 (1.8)
Peg regime	—	−2.650 (1.8)	—	−1.116 (0.6)	—
Intermediate regime	—	—	3.437 (2.1)	2.368 (1.1)	—
Floating regime	—	—	—	—	−4.671 (1.6)
Terms-of-Trade (TOT) change	—	—	—	—	0.011 (0.2)
Net capital flows/GDP	—	—	—	—	0.542 (2.1)
TOT × Floating	—	—	—	—	0.260 (1.5)
Net Capital Flows × Floating	—	—	—	—	1.472 (1.5)
Number of observations	767	767	767	767	664
Pseudo R^2	0.162	0.172	0.175	0.176	0.188
Slopes [χ^2 test] (p value)	54.41 (0.0)	57.71 (0.0)	58.68 (0.0)	59.04 (0.0)	66.85 (0.0)

Note: Probit regressions estimated with maximum likelihood, weighted by GNP per capita. Derivatives (×100) reported for regressors; absolute z statistics (for no significant effect) in parentheses. Crisis is defined as Glick and Hutchison (1999) systemic episode.

Table A3.2
Banking crises and liberalization, 1975–1997

External debt/GDP	−0.060 (2.1)	−0.071 (1.8)	−0.055 (2.0)	−0.059 (2.0)	−0.057 (1.5)	−0.052 (1.9)
Reserves/imports	0.004 (1.3)	0.005 (1.4)	0.004 (1.3)	0.003 (0.9)	0.004 (1.2)	0.002 (0.8)
Current account (%GDP)	−0.613 (3.9)	−0.677 (3.0)	−0.578 (3.9)	−0.634 (3.6)	−0.576 (2.8)	−0.674 (4.0)
Overvaluation	−0.009 (0.3)	−0.005 (0.1)	−0.007 (0.3)	−0.004 (0.2)	0.016 (0.4)	−0.003 (0.1)
Budget balance (%GDP)	0.630 (3.2)	1.065 (3.6)	0.592 (3.2)	0.631 (3.3)	0.843 (3.3)	0.599 (3.5)
Domestic credit growth	0.041 (3.6)	0.074 (4.3)	0.039 (3.6)	0.041 (3.7)	0.068 (4.5)	0.043 (4.0)
Per capita output growth	−0.206 (1.5)	−0.184 (0.9)	−0.171 (1.3)	−0.217 (1.5)	−1.808 (1.0)	−0.159 (1.2)
M2/reserves	0.440 (4.0)	0.618 (3.8)	0.436 (4.1)	0.442 (4.0)	0.606 (4.2)	0.394 (4.0)
Northern interest rate	0.077 (0.3)	−0.639 (2.0)	0.105 (0.5)	0.043 (0.2)	−0.172 (0.6)	0.095 (0.5)
Northern output growth	0.093 (0.2)	−1.240 (1.5)	0.021 (0.0)	−0.024 (0.0)	−1.042 (1.3)	−0.013 (0.0)
Open capital account	−1.681 (1.1)	—	4.097 (0.9)	—	—	—
Domestic financial liberalization	11.715 (5.2)	—	13.025 (5.1)	11.648 (5.0)	—	5.436 (2.0)
Open Capital × Domestic Financial Liberalization	—	0.804 (0.3)	−3.416 (1.5)	—	—	—
Gross capital flows/GDP	—	—	—	0.069 (0.3)	—	−0.979 (1.6)
Gross Capital Flows × Domestic Financial Liberalization	—	—	—	—	1.191 (4.6)	1.214 (1.9)
Number of observations	588	588	588	572	572	572
Pseudo R^2	0.289	0.169	0.294	0.29	0.237	0.303
Slopes [χ^2 test] (*p* value)	96.62 (0.0)	56.69(0.0)	98.54 (0.0)	94.36 (0.0)	77.09 (0.0)	98.56 (0.0)

Note: Probit regressions estimated with maximum likelihood, weighted by GNP per capita. Derivatives (×100) reported for regressors; absolute z statistics (for no significant effect) in parentheses. Crisis is defined as Glick and Hutchison (1999) systemic episode.

Table A3.3
Banking crises, deposit insurance, and institutional quality, 1975–1997

External debt/GDP	−0.066 (1.6)	−0.131 (2.5)	−0.134 (2.5)	−0.136 (2.5)	−0.086 (2.0)	−0.104 (1.9)	−0.149 (3.2)	−0.137 (3.2)
Reserves/imports	0.003 (0.9)	0.003 (0.8)	0.003 (0.7)	0.003 (0.7)	0.002 (0.4)	0.007 (1.4)	0.001 (0.4)	0.001 (0.3)
Current account (%GDP)	−0.777 (3.4)	−1.122 (3.9)	−1.125 (3.9)	−1.115 (3.9)	−0.835 (3.0)	−1.125 (3.3)	−1.008 (4.7)	−0.939 (4.7)
Overvaluation	0.047 (1.1)	0.052 (1.2)	0.059 (1.3)	0.063 (1.4)	0.075 (1.6)	0.017 (0.3)	0.013 (0.4)	0.018 (0.6)
Budget balance (%GDP)	1.012 (3.7)	0.754 (2.5)	0.787 (2.6)	0.787 (2.6)	1.191 (3.5)	1.245 (3.1)	0.467 (2.2)	0.434 (2.2)
Domestic credit growth	0.073 (4.1)	0.072 (3.9)	0.072 (4.0)	0.073 (4.0)	0.082 (4.0)	0.084 (3.6)	0.049 (3.6)	0.043 (3.6)
Per capita output growth	−0.029 (0.2)	0.030 (0.1)	0.046 (0.2)	0.047 (0.2)	−0.150 (0.6)	−0.176 (0.7)	−0.161 (0.9)	−0.141 (0.9)
M2/reserves	0.506 (3.2)	0.400 (2.4)	0.401 (2.4)	0.402 (2.4)	0.698 (3.4)	0.843 (3.4)	0.276 (1.8)	0.259 (1.9)
Northern interest rate	−0.584 (1.9)	−0.680 (2.0)	−0.699 (2.1)	−0.684 (2.0)	−0.437 (1.2)	−0.667 (1.6)	−0.059 (0.2)	−0.024 (0.1)
Northern output growth	−1.286 (1.6)	−1.279 (1.5)	−1.274 (1.5)	−1.288 (1.5)	−1.083 (1.2)	−1.755 (1.7)	0.350 (0.5)	0.380 (0.6)
Deposit insurance	−5.057 (2.5)	−4.663 (2.2)	−4.256 (0.6)	—	−13.344 (2.1)	—	—	—
Institutional quality	—	1.015 (0.8)	—	—	—	—	−1.077 (1.0)	—
Deposit Insurance × Institutions	—	—	−0.201 (0.1)	−1.708 (2.1)	—	—	—	—
Domestic liberalization	—	—	—	—	—	—	—	7.366 (1.9)
Deposit Insurance × Liberalization	—	—	—	—	38.669 (1.6)	−3.104 (0.9)	—	—
Institutions × Liberalization	—	—	—	—	—	—	2.908 (4.5)	0.840 (0.9)
Number of observations	461	360	360	360	421	421	382	382
Pseudo R^2	0.226	0.266	0.263	0.262	0.222	0.179	0.337	0.347
Slopes [χ^2 test] (p value)	61.50 (0.0)	60.63 (0.0)	60.02 (0.0)	59.65 (0.0)	61.12 (0.0)	49.29 (0.0)	83.77 (0.0)	86.37 (0.0)

Note: Probit regressions estimated with maximum likelihood, weighted by GNP per capita. Derivatives (×100) reported for regressors; absolute z statistics (for no significant effect) in parentheses. Crisis is defined as Glick and Hutchison (1999) systemic episode.

Appendix 3.3 Further Sensitivity Analyses

Table A3.4
Baseline regression: Sensitivity analysis of estimation method, 1975–1997

	Robust estimation	Clustered estimation	Unweighted estimation
External debt/GDP	−0.009 (0.3)	−0.009 (0.3)	0.020 (1.2)
Reserves/imports	0.001 (0.7)	0.002 (0.6)	0.002 (0.9)
Current account (%GDP)	−0.159 (1.2)	−0.159 (1.1)	0.023 (0.2)
Overvaluation	0.009 (0.2)	0.009 (0.2)	0.015 (0.5)
Budget balance (%GDP)	0.605 (3.0)	0.605 (3.0)	0.372 (2.6)
Domestic credit growth	0.056 (3.6)	0.056 (2.9)	0.044 (3.3)
M2/reserves	−0.004 (0.0)	−0.004 (0.1)	−0.091 (0.9)
Per capita output growth	0.321 (3.9)	0.321 (2.9)	0.154 (3.6)
Northern interest rate	−0.216 (0.7)	−0.216 (0.7)	0.101 (0.5)
Northern output growth	−1.271 (2.8)	−1.271 (3.2)	−0.866 (1.7)
Number of observations	814	814	814
Pseudo R^2	0.163	0.163	0.111
Slopes [c^2 test] (p value)	53.61	47.26	33.39

Note: Probit regressions estimated with maximum likelihood. First two columns are weighted by GNP per capita. Derivatives (×100) reported for regressors; absolute z statistics (for no significant effect) in parentheses. Crisis is defined as Caprio and Klingebiel (1999) systemic episode. Robust estimation uses robust standard errors. Clustered estimation uses robust standard errors adjusted for clustering of within-country observations.

Table A3.5
Banking crises and exchange rate stability, 1975–1997

	Using current values of regressors			Using lagged values of regressors		
|Exchange rate change| < 5%	−3.783 (3.0)	—	—	1.492 (1.2)	—	—
|Exchange rate change| < 10%	—	−5.689 (4.0)	—	—	0.893 (0.63)	—
Exchange rate crash	—	—	−1.984 (1.1)	—	—	0.402 (0.2)
Number of observations	843	843	843	814	814	814
Pseudo R^2	0.219	0.239	0.195	0.167	0.165	0.163
Slopes [c^2 test] (p value)	78.88	85.95	70.20	57.28	56.36	55.98

Note: Probit regressions estimated with maximum likelihood, weighted by GNP per capita. Ten baseline regressors included in the estimation but not reported. Derivatives (×100) reported for regressors; absolute z statistics (for no significant effect) in parentheses. Crisis is defined as Caprio and Klingebiel (1999) systemic episode.

Table A3.6
Banking crises, deposit insurance, and institutional quality, 1975–1997: Sensitivity analysis using different crisis definitions and country groups

	DKD-2000 LDCs only		CK-99 LDCs and OECDs		DKD-2000 LDCs and OECDs	
Deposit insurance	−0.108 (0.0)	−6.851 (1.3)	0.202 (1.0)	0.266 (2.0)	1.879 (2.1)	1.884 (2.4)
Institutional quality	—	−22.585 (2.0)	—	−0.130 (2.6)	—	−0.870 (2.4)
Number of observations	214	156	849	714	464	464
Pseudo R^2	0.224	0.237	0.356	0.429	0.236	0.275
Slopes [c^2 test] (p value)	35.92	30.28	62.40	62.85	32.80	38.10

Note: Probit regressions estimated with maximum likelihood, weighted by GNP per capita. First two columns: Ten baseline regressors included in the estimation but not reported. Last four columns: Seven regressors (ten baseline regressors minus debt/GNP, northern interest rates, and OECD output growth) included in the estimation but not reported. Derivatives (×100) reported for regressors; absolute z statistics (for no significant effect) in parentheses. DKD-2000: Crisis is defined as Demirgüç-Kunt and Detragiache (2000) episode. CK-99: Crisis is defined as Caprio and Klingebiel (1999) systemic episode.

Table A3.7
Banking crises, deposit insurance, and institutional quality, LDCs and OECDs, 1975–1997: Sensitivity analysis using different crisis definitions and OECD dummy

	CK-99 LDCs and OECDs			DKD-2000 LDCs and OECDs		
OECD dummy	−1.642 (2.4)	−1.233 (2.3)	0.009 (0.0)	−2.283 (1.3)	−5.783 (2.0)	−0.542 (0.2)
Deposit insurance	—	0.294 (1.6)	0.265 (1.9)	—	2.185 (2.4)	1.943 (2.3)
Institutional quality	—	—	−0.132 (1.6)	—	—	−0.754 (1.1)
Number of observations	1253	849	714	566	464	464
Pseudo R^2	0.237	0.386	0.429	0.188	0.266	0.275
Slopes [c^2 test] (p value)	58.75	67.68	62.85	31.73	36.86	38.15

Note: Probit regressions estimated with maximum likelihood, weighted by GNP per capita. Seven regressors (ten baseline regressors minus debt/GNP, northern interest rates, and OECD output growth) included in the estimation but not reported. Derivatives (×100) reported for regressors; absolute z statistics (for no significant effect) in parentheses. DKD-2000: Crisis is defined as Demirgüç-Kunt and Detragiache (2000) episode. CK-99: Crisis is defined as Caprio and Klingebiel (1999) systemic episode.

Notes

We are grateful to Gerard Caprio, Asli Demirgüç-Kunt, Enrica Detragiache, Geoffrey Garrett, Atish Ghosh, Reuven Glick, Michael Hutchinson, Daniela Klingebiel, and Jason Sorens for making their data available to us. We thank Enrica Detragiache, Maria Soledad Martinez-Peria, and seminar participants at the Inter-American Development Bank, the Dubrovnik Conference organized by the Croatian National Bank, and the Harvard Institute for International Development for very useful comments. All errors are our own.

1. Notably in the United States, but also in other countries. The role of bank failures in the U.S. depression is emphasized by Friedman and Schwartz (1963) and Bernanke (1983). Their role in the depression in other countries is the subject of Bernanke and James 1991 and Grossman 1994.

2. In Brazil in 1963 (Bordo and Eichengreen 1999, appendix table 1).

3. See IMF 1998 and, for World Bank estimates, Caprio and Klingebiel 1996a. We discuss these at length below.

4. Of course, one can also argue the opposite: that the increasing severity of recessions, occurring for independent reasons, was responsible for the growing frequency of banking crises. Economic historians have argued for this direction of causality, as in Gorton 1991 and Calomiris and Gorton 1991.

5. With GDP growth in Finland, the most dramatic case, swinging from +5 percent in 1989 to −8 percent in 1991. To be sure, the banking crisis was not the only factor involved in either Finland or Sweden (the collapse of Soviet trade and of property prices also belong on any respectable list), but it was a major one (Jonung, Soderstrom, and Stymne 1996).

6. And to the period 1990–1997. The countries in Rossi's sample are Argentina, Brazil, Chile, Colombia, India, Indonesia, Israel, Korea, Malaysia, Mexico, Peru, the Philippines, South Africa, Thailand, and Venezuela.

7. Their objective was to construct an early warning system, so the institutional variables are of relatively little interest, given that these change only slowly over time.

8. Honohan (1997) similarly found that domestic lending booms predict subsequent banking crises.

9. Standard theory predicts the opposite.

10. Typically, the judgments of the authors are supplemented by the judgments of country economists at the International Financial Institutions (like IMF, WB Group, etc.) and national experts. This same approach is used by Bordo and Eichengreen (1999) in constructing historical banking-crisis dates.

11. Caprio and Klingebiel (1999) have recently corrected some discrepancies in their earlier list and updated it through 1998.

12. For consistency, only nontransition developing countries are considered. To be precise, table 3.2 and its sequels consider the year of onset of each crisis, since these data sets typically provide a span of years during which each crisis persisted.

13. For instance, DKD-97 counts forty-six developing-country crises between 1980 and 1995, whereas CK-99 counts sixty-nine developing-country systemic crises in the same

period. In the countries that overlap, they differ in only nine episodes. If we redefine CK-99 to include both systemic and nonsystemic crises, there are only three discrepancies between DKD-97 and CK-99 in the countries and years that overlap.

14. Given the controversy surrounding the causes of the Asian crises.

15. Where results differ when alternative measures of the dependent variable are used, we report these discrepancies in appendices 3.2 and 3.3 and in subsequent footnotes.

16. It turns out that the results of estimating the baseline model are robust to redefining the dependent variable as all CK-99 crises (including the so-called nonsystemic ones).

17. We add OECD countries to the sample where previous studies and our own sensitivity analysis suggest that such an extension of the country sample is important.

18. When (in appendix 3.2) we substitute GH-99, we have 77 crisis episodes and 1,657 noncrisis observations. For purposes of this exercise, "crisis" means year of onset. Thus if a crisis lasts more than one year, we consider only the year of its onset and disregard the subsequent observations.

19. This is the same baseline model used in Eichengreen and Rose 1998, in which the specification is more fully justified. For purposes of this chapter, we exclude Korea and Mexico from the OECD classification, despite the fact that they entered the OECD toward the end of the sample period.

20. Following Eichengreen and Rose 1998. This procedure attaches more weight to middle-income developing countries, which is sensible given data quality considerations. In practice, regressions using unweighted observations yield similar results. Although we report unadjusted standard errors for ease of comparison with other studies, we also computed heteroskedasticity-robust (Huber-White) standard errors, which differed little in practice. We also estimated robust standard errors adjusted for the clustering of within-country observations (thus relaxing the assumption of within-country independence), again obtaining similar results. The robustness of the baseline results to these alternatives is documented in table A3.4. Unless noted otherwise in subsequent footnotes, subsequent regressions were similarly insensitive to the use of these alternative estimators.

21. We pursue this point in section 3.5.

22. A final reason for lagging the independent variables one period is that crises tend to be recognized with a lag. The results, aside from the examples mentioned in this paragraph, are generally robust to substitution of the alternative lag structure. Where this is not the case, we note this in subsequent footnotes.

23. Although we refer to "coefficients," for ease of interpretation we report dF/dx, the change in the probability of a crisis given a change in the regressor, evaluated at the mean of the regressor, except when dealing with binary independent variables, which show the effect of a discrete change from zero to one in the value of the dummy. A constant term is included in all equations but not reported in the tables. As mentioned above, we also ran the probit regressions with contemporaneous values of the explanatory variables (instead of first lags). We reached similar conclusions, with the exception of output growth, which is negative and significant, underscoring the problem of reverse causality between output fall and crisis onset.

24. Previous studies reporting similar findings can be criticized on the grounds that reserve losses are as plausibly a consequence as a cause of banking crises (given the findings of the twin-crisis literature). Since this result continues to come through strongly when we lag the independent variables by one period, we are skeptical that all we are picking up is reverse causality.

25. Although the current account balance/GDP ratio is insignificant in the baseline regressions, it is actually significant (and intuitively negative) in many regressions.

26. See, for example, Calvo, Leiderman, and Reinhart 1993, Goldstein and Turner 1996, and Taylor and Sarno 1997. The literature on this subject is reviewed in Eichengreen and Fishlow 1998.

27. This post-1992 change also emerges when we use GH-99 as the alternative source of our dependent variable (see table A3.1).

28. We can decisively reject that its incidence is the same across these three regimes.

29. Unweighted, robust, and clustered estimates also yielded coefficients insignificantly different from zero regardless of whether the "fixed" and "intermediate" dummies are included together. We also substituted the GH-99 crisis dates for CK-99; reassuringly, the findings again carry over (as shown in table A3.1). The evidence that fixed rates are associated with a lower incidence of crises is more robust if we end the sample in 1992, but as table 3.7 shows, this effect was not robust when we used data through 1997.

30. The incidence of banking crises in a number of the hard-peg countries in our sample (notably Argentina and Panama) and the fact that a number of floating-rate countries (India, for example) have been immune from serious banking crises raises questions about both assertions. The econometric evidence indicates that these exceptions are prevalent enough to lead to rejection of both hypotheses.

31. We report these results in appendix table A3.5.

32. Eichengreen and Rose (1998) reported the same finding.

33. And the point estimates are now positive, not negative.

34. See, e.g., Kaminsky and Reinhart 1999, Rossi 1999, and Glick and Hutchison 1998.

35. Although neither effect was significant at standard confidence levels (see table A3.5).

36. As Glick and Hutchison (1999) put it, "the occurrence of banking crises provides a good leading indicator of currency crises in emerging markets.... The converse does not hold, however, as currency crises are not a useful leading indicator of the onset of future banking crises" (1).

37. As suggested by Hausmann et al. (1999).

38. In addition to the first-difference of the log of terms of trade, and following Mendis (1998), we also experimented with the deviations of the long-term trend (i.e., time-averaged mean) country-specific terms-of-trade index. We again obtained insignificant results.

39. The liberalization dummy was lagged one period relative to the crisis dates, paralleling the procedure we followed in the multiple regressions.

40. Kaminsky and Reinhart (1998) similarly reported that financial liberalization preceded banking crises in eighteen of the twenty-five crisis cases in their sample.

41. When we used the Glick and Hutchison crises (in table A3.5), the domestic financial liberalization dummy was even more strongly significant, documenting the robustness of this result. These conclusions are robust to alternative estimation methods (which take the clustering of observations into account, do not weight by GNP, and calculate robust standard errors). The literature suggests a number of explanations for this association of financial liberalization with the risk of banking crises. Bank credit managers accustomed to a controlled financial environment may not possess the skills needed to evaluate additional sources of credit and market risk. The intensification of price competition may pressure banks to undertake riskier activities. Although interest rate decontrol might not seem like the ideal empirical proxy for financial liberalization, Hellmann, Murdock, and Stiglitz (2000) showed that allowing banks to compete for deposits on price in an environment characterized by insurance guarantees can lead to a reduction in franchise values and a significant increase in risk taking by financial intermediaries. Our results support their intuition.

42. This confirms a result obtained by Rossi (1999) for a much more limited list of countries and years. Since capital account liberalization creates pressure for greater exchange rate flexibility, we worried that the capital account liberalization measure might also be picking up the effects of the exchange rate regime. We therefore added a dummy for floating rates to the regressions discussed in the text, but since the additional variable was never significant and did not alter the coefficients on the liberalization measures, we ended up excluding it.

43. As in our analysis of Mendis's hypothesis, above.

44. A complementary interpretation, advanced by Calvo and Goldstein (1996), is that capital account liberalization heightens crisis risk by making it easier for depositors fearful for the stability of the banking system to substitute foreign for domestic assets. A rival interpretation, that financial stability is threatened by external liberalization prior to domestic financial decontrol and the removal of implicit guarantees—the Goldstein (1998)–Dooley (2000) interpretation of the Asian crisis—receives little support in literature.

45. In this case, the Pearson chi-square test fails to reject the null of equal distributions at standard confidence levels.

46. The effect was somewhat stronger when we used the GH-99 crisis dates, as in table A3.3, but only in some specifications, and we are still unable to reject the null of a zero coefficient at standard confidence levels.

47. Result not reported in this chapter. This coefficient was insignificant, however, when we did not weight the observations, as emphasized below. We used Demirgüç-Kunt and Detragiache's crisis dates, though the choice between DKD-97 and CK-99 was inconsequential once we limited the sample to the subset of developing countries considered by Demirgüç-Kunt and Detragiache. Hence, from that point onward, we used the same crisis list as Demirgüç-Kunt and Detragiache 2000 (hereafter, DKD-2000). Although DKD-2000 includes crises up to 1997, it actually covers fewer countries than DKD-97. Nevertheless, we prefer DKD-2000 because the inclusion of the recent Asian crises provides information that is lost when the sample ends in 1995 and because this is the crisis list used by Demirgüç-Kunt and Detragiache in their paper dealing exclusively with deposit insurance. (Reassuringly, using DKD-97 and DKD-

2000 yielded similar results, except when, for sensitivity purposes, we added industrial countries and an OECD dummy—a point to which we return below. Given the number of robustness checks we undertake in this section, we do not report the regressions using DKD-97.)

48. As shown in table A3.6.

49. There are only three discrepancies between the two deposit insurance series—for Argentina in 1992, 1993 and 1994, for which DKD-2000 codes deposit insurance as present but GH-99 codes it as absent. The fact is that Argentina abolished an extremely broad and generous deposit insurance scheme in 1992 and then reinstituted a limited one (funded by the private sector) in 1995 (Calomiris and Powell 2000). DKD-2000 does not include Argentina in their sample, whereas we do. This is another reason why we prefer the GH-99 deposit insurance series.

50. As mentioned before, the differences between our results and Demirgüç-Kunt and Detragiache's appear to reflect the larger sample of countries and years we use: whereas DKD-2000 has thirty-four emerging-market crises in the period 1980–1997, CK-99 has seventy-six emerging-market systemic crises in the same period. In all, there are eight discrepancies between the crisis coding in DKD-2000 and CK-99's systemic crises (the variant considered here) for countries and years that overlap. Six are cases in which DKD-2000 codes crises and CK-99 codes *nonsystemic* crises. But when we used all CK-99 crises as the dependent variable (and not just the systemic crises), eliminating three fourths of the discrepancies in the coding of the dependent variable, the results we reported in the text were unchanged. Therefore, it is not discrepancies in what is considered a crisis, but rather differences in country and year coverage between the two lists of crisis dates, that explain the differences in results. Note that although the regressions reported in DKD-97 and DKD-2000 have more observations, ours have more crises. The main reason we have fewer non-crisis observations is our three-year, two-sided exclusion window, which Demirgüç-Kunt and Detragiache do not use.

51. Out of 1,326 developing-country observations, only 225 have deposit insurance; on the other hand, out of 504 developed-country observations, 322 have deposit insurance.

52. See the fifth column of table A3.6. Using the joint LDC/OECD sample required us to drop the debt/GNP ratio and the "northern" variables (industrial-country interest rates and OECD output growth). Table A3.6 (third through sixth columns) and table A3.7 include the remaining seven regressors (although we do not report their coefficients). If we use the CK-99 systemic crises, the coefficient on deposit insurance weakens, as reported in the third in column of table A3.6.

53. As noted elsewhere, most of our other results were insensitive to this weighting scheme. The effect of deposit insurance was an important exception.

54. The sensitivity of the results for deposit insurance to the inclusion of OECD countries and their weighting suggested that an OECD dummy should be added to see whether this affects the deposit insurance coefficient. There is weak evidence that OECD countries are less likely to suffer banking crises, ceteris paribus, as reported in table A3.7. This OECD dummy performs poorly when we use DKD-97 (not reported) instead of DKD-2000, reflecting the relatively large number of emerging-market crises after 1995. More importantly, the DKD deposit insurance result obtained even after the OECD dummy was included. However, when we used unweighted regres-

sions (again, not reported), any significant coefficient of deposit insurance vanished, whereas the coefficient of the OECD dummy still displayed a marginal significance.

55. This same result obtains whether or not we lag the independent variable(s).

56. Thus, Drees and Pazarbasioglu (1998, 21) emphasize that in the Nordic countries "little emphasis was placed at the time of deregulation on strengthening and adapting prudential safety-and-soundness regulations to the new competitive environment, in particular in the areas of real estate and foreign currency lending."

57. As Goldstein and Turner (1996, 24) put it, "If the legal system makes it difficult to seize or to transfer the collateral behind delinquent loans, or for debtors to pledge collateral for bank loans, or to adjudicate cases of corporate or individual bankruptcy, then both banks' credit losses and the cost of borrowing for firms will be (abnormally) high."

58. In addition to the destabilizing effects of deposit insurance, Demirgüç-Kunt and Detragiache also found that crises are less likely when the institutional environment is strong. See Demirgüç-Kunt and Detragiache 1997, 1998, 2000.

59. This series is available for 1985–1995 in our data set. To cover the entire 1975–1997 period, we used time-averaged values per country for this index in our regression analysis. In fact, using the original series (i.e., without time-averaging the values) yielded very similar results (not reported), since these indices change slowly over time.

60. We again used time-averaged values for the series. When we used the GK-99 crises, the contract enforcement variable performed more strongly, consistently displaying the expected negative sign and differing from zero at standard confidence levels. One should be cautious not to overinterpret this result, since the contract enforcement index is available only for a limited sample of twenty-four countries for the period 1980–1995.

61. Does this last pair of results reflect differences in how the two measures capture the quality of the relevant institutions or differences in country sample? To get at this, we reestimated our equations for financial liberalization and institutions using rule of law as a measure of institutional quality while limiting the sample to the smaller number of countries for which we also have data on contract enforcement. (In this smaller sample of developing countries, the correlation of the two [time-averaged] measures of institutional quality was 0.57. When we included industrial as well as developing countries, the correlation rose to 0.74.) The results were unchanged; in other words, the country coverage of the two indices is not driving the difference in results.

62. As the third and sixth columns of appendix table A3.7 show. The correlation between the OECD dummy and the law and order index was 0.82. In other words, there are fewer banking crises in OECD countries where institutions are stronger. But OECD countries plausibly differ in other respects as well, some of which can be even more difficult to measure. Thus, dummying out the OECD countries robs the institutional-quality index of much of its explanatory power.

63. "Fearing that they could lose ground in the vigorous competition touched off by liberalization, many banks, in particular some large ones, pursued aggressive lending policies as a premptive response and were prepared to accept higher risk. In this context, the aggressive lending behavior of the Finnish savings banks following a loss

of market share in the early 1980s may not be surprising in hindsight" (Drees and Pazarbasioglu 1998, 20).

References

Bernanke, Ben. (1983). Nonmonetary Effects of the Financial Crisis in the Propagation of the Great Depression. *American Economic Review* 73: 257–76.

Bernanke, Ben, and Harold James. (1991). The Gold Standard, Deflation, and Financial Crisis in the Great Depression: An International Comparison. In R. Glenn Hubbard (ed.) *Financial Markets and Financial Crises*, 33–68. Chicago: University of Chicago Press.

Bordo, Michael, and Barry Eichengreen. (1999). Is Our Current International Financial Environment Unusually Crisis Prone? In David Gruen and Luke Gower (eds.), *Capital Flows and the International Financial System*, 18–75. Sydney: Reserve Bank of Australia.

Calomiris, Charles, and Gary Gorton. (1991). The Origins of Banking Panics: Models, Facts, and Bank Regulation. In R. Glenn Hubbard (ed.), *Financial Markets and Financial Crises*, 109–73. Chicago: University of Chicago Press.

Calomiris, Charles, and Andrew Powell. (2000). Can Emerging Market Bank Regulators Establish Credible Discipline? The Case of Argentina, 1992–1999. Working Paper no. 7715, National Bureau of Economic Research, Cambridge, Mass.

Calvo, Guillermo, and Morris Goldstein. (1996). Crisis Prevention and Crisis Management after Mexico: What Role for the Official Sector? In Guillermo Calvo, Morris Goldstein, and Eduard Hochreiter (eds.), *Private Capital Flows to Emerging Markets after the Mexican Crisis*, 233–292. Washington, D.C.: Institute for International Economics.

Calvo, Guillermo, Leo Leiderman, and Carmen Reinhart. (1993). Capital Inflows and Real Exchange Rate Appreciation in Latin America: The Role of External Factors. *IMF Staff Papers* 40: 108–51.

Caprio, Gerard, Jr., and Daniela Klingebiel. (1996a). Bank Insolvencies: Cross-Country Experience. Policy research working paper no. 1620, World Bank, Washington, D.C.

Caprio, Gerard, Jr., and Daniela Klingebiel. (1996b). Bank Insolvency: Bad Luck, Bad Policy, or Bad Banking? Paper presented at the Annual World Bank Conference on Development Economics, Washington, D.C., April.

Caprio, Gerard, Jr., and Daniela Klingebiel. (1999). Episodes of Systematic and Borderline Financial Crises. Unpublished manuscript, World Bank, Washington, D.C.

Demirgüç-Kunt, Asli, and Enrica Detragiache. (1997). The Determinants of Banking Crises: Evidence from Developing and Developed Countries. Working paper no. WP/97/106, International Monetary Fund, Washington, D.C.

Demirgüç-Kunt, Asli, and Enrica Detragiache. (1998). Financial Liberalization and Financial Fragility. Working paper no. WP/98/83, International Monetary Fund, Washington, D.C.

Demirgüç-Kunt, Asli, and Enrica Detragiache. (2000). Does Deposit Insurance Increase Banking System Stability? Working paper no. WP/00/3, International Monetary Fund, Washington, D.C.

Dooley, Michael P. (2000). A Model of Crises in Emerging Markets. *Economic Journal* 110: 256–72.

Drees, Burkhard, and Ceyla Pazarbasioglu. (1998). The Nordic Banking Crises: Pitfalls in Financial Liberalization? Occasional paper no. 161, International Monetary Fund, Washington, D.C.

Dziobek, Claudia, and Ceyla Pazarbasioglu. (1997). Lessons from Systemic Bank Restructuring: A Survey of 24 Countries. Working paper no. 97/161, International Monetary Fund, Washington, D.C.

Eichengreen, Barry. (2000). When to Dollarize. Unpublished manuscript, University of California, Berkeley.

Eichengreen, Barry, and Albert Fishlow. (1998). Contending with Capital Flows: What Is Different about the 1990s? In Miles Kahler (ed.), *Capital Flows and Financial Crises*, 23–68. Ithaca: Cornell University Press.

Eichengreen, Barry, Donald Mathieson, with Bankin Chada, Auhe Jansen, Laura Kodres, and Sunil Sharma. (1998). Hedge Funds and Financial Market Dynamics. Occasional paper, no. 166, International Monetary Fund, Washington, D.C.

Eichengreen, Barry, and Andrew Rose. (1998). Staying Afloat When the Wind Shifts: External Factors and Emerging-Market Banking Crises. Working paper no. 6370, National Bureau of Economic Research, Cambridge, Mass.

Eichengreen, Barry, Andrew Rose, and Charles Wyplosz. (1996). Exchange Market Mayhem: The Antecedents and Aftermath of Speculative Attacks. *Economic Policy* 21: 249–312.

Frankel, Jeffrey, and Andrew Rose. (1996). Currency Crashes in Emerging Markets: An Empirical Treatment. *Journal of International Economics* 41: 351–66.

Friedman, Milton, and Anna Schwartz. (1963). *A Monetary History of the United States, 1863–1960*. Princeton: Princeton University Press.

Frydl, Edward. (1999). The Length and Cost of Banking Crises. Working paper no. WP/99/30, International Monetary Fund, Washington, D.C.

Gavin, Michael, and Ricardo Hausmann. (1996). The Roots of Banking Crises: The Macroeconomic Context. In Ricardo Hausmann and Liliana Rojas-Suarez (eds.), *Banking Crises in Latin America*, 27–63. Baltimore: Johns Hopkins University Press.

Glick, Reuven, and Michael Hutchison. (1999). Banking and Currency Crises: How Common Are Twins? Unpublished manuscript, Federal Reserve Bank of San Francisco and University of California, Santa Cruz.

Goldstein, Morris. (1998). *The Asian Financial Crisis*. Washington, D.C.: Institute for International Economics.

Goldstein, Morris, and Philip Turner. (1996). Banking Crises in Emerging Economies: Origins and Policy Options. Economic papers no. 46, Bank for International Settlements, Basel, Switzerland.

Gorton, Gary. (1991). Banking Panics and Business Cycles. in N. F. R. Crafts, N. H. Dimsdale, and S. Engerman (eds.), *Quantitative Economic History*, 221–51. Oxford: Clarendon.

Gourinchas, Pierre-Olivier, Rodrigo Valdés, and Oscar Landerretche. (1999). Lending Booms: Some Stylized Facts. Unpublished manuscript, Princeton University, Princeton, N.J., and Central Bank of Chile, Santiago, Chile.

Gropp, Reint, and Jukka Vesala. (2000). Deposit Insurance and Moral Hazard: Does the Counterfactual Matter? Unpublished manuscript, European Central Bank, Frankfort am Main, Germany.

Grossman, Richard. (1994). The Shoe that Didn't Drop: Explaining Banking Stability during the Great Depression. *Journal of Economic History* 54: 654–82.

Hardy, Daniel, and Ceyla Pazarbasioglu. (1998). Leading Indicators of Banking Crises: Was Asia Different? Working paper no. WP/98/91, International Monetary Fund, Washington, D.C.

Hausmann, Ricardo, Michael Gavin, Carmen Pages-Serra, and Ernesto Stein. (1999). Financial Turmoil and the Choice of Exchange Rate Regime. Unpublished manuscript, Inter-American Development Bank, Washington, D.C.

Hellmann, Thomas, Kevin Murdock, and Joseph Stiglitz. (2000). Liberalization, Moral Hazard in Banking and Prudential Regulation: Are Capital Requirements Enough? *American Economic Review* 90: 147–65.

Honohan, Patrick. (1997). Banking System Failures in Developing and Transition Economies: Diagnosis and Prediction. Working paper no. 39, Bank for International Settlements, Basel, Switzerland.

Hutchison, Michael. (1999). European Banking Distress and EMU: Institutional and Macroeconomic Risks. Unpublished manuscript, University of California, Santa Cruz.

Hutchison, Michael, and Kathleen McDill. (1999). Are All Banking Crises Alike? The Japanese Experience in International Comparison. NBER Working paper no. 7253, National Bureau of Economic Research, Cambridge, Mass.

International Monetary Fund (IMF). (various years). *Annual Report of Exchange Arrangements and Exchange Restrictions*. Washington, D.C.: IMF.

International Monetary Fund (IMF). (1998). Financial Crises: Characteristics and Indicators of Vulnerability. *World Economic Outlook* (May): 74–97.

International Monetary Fund (IMF). (2000). *International Financial Statistics*, Washington, D.C.: IMF.

Jonung, Lars, Hans Tson Soderstrom, and Joakim Stymne. (1996). Depression in the North: Boom and Bust in Sweden and Finland, 1985–1993. *Finnish Economic Papers* 9: 55–71.

Kaminsky, Graciela, and Carmen Reinhart. (1998). The Twin Crises: The Causes of Banking and Balance-of-Payments Problems. *American Economic Review* 89: 473–500.

Kyei, Alexander. (1995). Deposit Protection Arrangements: A Survey. Working paper no. WP/95/134, International Monetary Fund, Washington, D.C.

Lehmussaari, Olli-Pekka. (1990). Deregulation and Consumption: Saving Dynamics in the Nordic Countries. *IMF Staff Papers* 37: 71–93.

Lindgren, Carl-Johan, Tomas J. T. Balino, Charles Enoch, Anne-Marie Gulde, Marc Quintyn, and Leslie Teo. (1999). Financial Sector Crisis and Restructuring: Lessons from Asia. Occasional paper no. 188, International Monetary Fund, Washington, D.C.

Lindgren, Carl-Johan, Gillian Garcia, and Matthew I. Saal. (1996). *Bank Soundness and Macroeconomic Policy*. Washington, D.C.: International Monetary Fund.

Mendis, Chandima. (1998). External Shocks and Banking Crises in Small Open Economies: Does the Exchange Rate Regime Matter? Unpublished manuscript, Center for the Study of African Economies, Oxford, England.

Reinhart, Carmen. (2000). The Mirage of Floating Exchange Rates. *American Economic Review* 90, no. 2: 65–70.

Rojas-Suarez, Liliana, and Steven Weisbrod. (1996). Banking Crises in Latin America: Experiences and Issues. In Ricardo Hausmann and Liliana Rojas-Suarez (eds.), *Banking Crises in Latin America*, 3–21. Baltimore: Johns Hopkins University Press.

Rossi, Marco. (1999). Financial Fragility and Economic Performance in Developing Countries: Do Capital Controls, Prudential Regulation and Supervision Matter? Working paper WP/99/66, International Monetary Fund, Washington, D.C.

Taylor, Mark, and Lucio Sarno. (1997). Capital Flows to Developing Countries: Long- and Short-Term Determinants. *World Bank Economic Review* 11: 451–70.

Wood, Geoffrey. (1999). Great Crashes in History: Have They Lessons for Today? *Oxford Review of Economic Policy* 15: 98–109.

World Bank. (1999a). *World Development Indicators*. Washington, D.C.: World Bank.

World Bank. (1999b). *Global Development Finance*. Washington, D.C.: World Bank.

4 International Financial Crises: The Role of Reserves and SDR Allocations

J. Onno de Beaufort Wijnholds and Arend Kapteyn

4.1 Introduction

The nature of international financial crises has changed markedly in recent decades. The changes are mirrored by a wealth of currency crisis models, ranging from Krugman's (1979) "first-generation model" to more recent models of multiple equilibria and those emphasizing balance sheet effects. The latter half of the 1990s, in particular, has highlighted the importance of international financial markets. Starting with the Mexican crisis in 1995, termed the first crisis of the twenty-first century by the then–IMF Managing Director Michel Camdessus, and later Asia, Russia, and Brazil, drastic reversals of capital flows wreaked havoc in emerging markets. Clearly, the capital account of the balance of payments has become a major vehicle for vulnerability, if not a source of vulnerability in its own right.

In analyzing the impact of the enormously increased importance of international financial markets at the country level, the traditional distinction between only two categories, the industrial and developing countries, has become outdated. The countries traditionally classified as developing have very large differences with respect to their ability to attract private foreign capital. Hence it is desirable to make a distinction between low-income developing countries and emerging-market countries. The low-income developing countries generally have no access to financial markets. They are eligible for credits from the IMF's Poverty Reduction and Growth Facility (formerly the Enhanced Structural Adjustment Facility or ESAF) at highly subsidized rates of interest. Since these countries are not major debtors to the private sector, they do not figure in international financial crises as such (though they may be affected by the fallout) and will not be part of the analysis of this chapter.

We focus our analysis here on the emerging-market countries, which have generally made important progress in their economic development and are striving to graduate to the status of industrial countries. The countries in this increasingly important group, encompassing a large part of Latin America, several Asian countries, and a number of Eastern European countries, as well as South Africa, are large importers of private capital. They are also the most important borrowers from the IMF and have figured prominently in recent international financial crises.

Much of the global architecture debate concerning emerging-market financial crises has revolved around the following issues: the extent of moral hazard created by large-scale official involvement, the bailout of banks and other market participants by the IMF, the need to "bail in" the private sector, the need for increased transparency, the adoption of standards and codes to guide best practices in emerging-market countries, the improvement of statistics, and the appropriate exchange rate regime for emerging-market countries.[1] An underplayed aspect in the debate is the role that reserve policies of the emerging-market countries can play in crisis prevention, to which special attention will be accorded in this chapter.

Devoting (fresh) attention to the size of countries' international reserves is important for four reasons. First, we currently have no commonly accepted framework for assessing reserve adequacy for emerging-market countries. The heyday of the reserve adequacy literature dates back to the 1960s and 1970s, when the focus was mainly on import-based (variability) measures. Scant attention was given to the importance of (short-term) capital flows and, for instance, capital flight. There is thus a clear need to update our approach in light of the changed global circumstances. This would assist monetary authorities in assessing what level of reserves is "optimal" for smoothing adjustment and creating a buffer stock against crises. Second, reserves in various ratios with other economic variables have turned out to be a useful crisis predictor, as borne out by the flurry of literature on crisis prediction and early-warning systems that started to emerge in the mid-1990s. Third, reserve targets are an important factor in calculating financing gaps under IMF programs and, as such, determine the size of Fund arrangements.[2] The degree of judgment used in determining those reserve targets has become problematic, especially as regards emerging-market countries. For developing countries a rule of thumb of three months of imports is often used as a target level, but for emerging-market countries the argumentation varies.[3] Fourth, reserve levels are used as a trigger for "private-sector involvement." That is, if reserve levels are projected to fall because of large net capital outflows and the financing gap reaches such dimensions that the IMF cannot or will not—for instance, out of moral hazard considerations—close it with its own resources, it will not wait until a country's reserves have been completely depleted. Rather, a predetermined "floor" for net international reserves, a standard feature in Fund arrangements, will serve as a trigger for debt rescheduling.[4] Where that floor is set is of no small concern to private-sector creditors.

The chapter is organized as follows. Section 4.2 provides a brief overview of the literature on reserve adequacy. Earlier major contributions to the literature are highlighted, followed by a description of newly proposed rules of thumb for reserve adequacy in the aftermath of the Asian crisis. In section 4.3 we propose our own reserve adequacy benchmark and provide data on how this benchmark relates to the actual reserve positions of emerging markets. The costs of holding reserves are also treated in this section. Whether a large special drawing right (SDR) allocation is the solution for dealing with systemic financial crises is discussed in section 4.4, followed by conclusions in section 4.5.

4.2 A Brief Review of the Literature on Reserve Adequacy

Three developments stand out in the reserve adequacy literature of the last fifty years. First, the focus on money-based measures of adequacy, which were prevalent prior to World War II, has largely disappeared, with the exception of that used in the context of currency board arrangements. Second, reserve adequacy of individual countries, in the post–World War II period, has come to be defined almost entirely in terms of trade and trade variability. Third, research has highlighted the importance of different levels of development (and market access) among countries, and different types of exchange rate regimes, in explaining different levels of demand for reserves. Studies singling out the role of capital account vulnerability in explaining reserve demand have been largely absent.

4.2.1 *The Shift to Trade-Related Measures of Adequacy*

The importance of reserves for mitigating external vulnerability gained increasing attention after World War II, under the influence of the Great Depression and the writings of John Maynard Keynes. This was reflected in the Keynes plan for an international clearing union in which the bancor quotas, the proposed main source of liquidity, would be related to the value of trade. The importance of external vulnerability was also recognized in the quota formulas in the IMF Articles (which won out over Keynes's bancor proposals), in which export variability was one of the five variables used to calculate each member's ability to contribute, voting rights, and entitlement to IMF resources. Triffin (1947) went further and argued that the demand for reserves should normally be expected to grow in line with trade (i.e., in a linear fashion) so that the reserves/imports ratio could be taken as a measure of reserve adequacy.[5]

The IMF was first asked in 1953, by the United Nations, to conduct a study on the adequacy of reserves (see IMF 1953). The IMF staff argued that adequacy was not a simple matter of an arithmetic relationship. Rather, it was related to the efficiency of the international credit system, the realism of the existing pattern of exchange rates, the appropriateness of monetary and fiscal policies, policy objectives, and the stage of development of countries.[6] Much of that holds true today. A somewhat less-qualified approach was followed five years later (IMF 1958), with the IMF staff stating that "foreign trade is the largest item in the balance of payments. It is therefore *natural* that in the first place reserves should be compared with a country's trade figures" (17, italics added). The 1958 study substantiated this assertion with the observation that an analysis of the data showed that countries in general appeared to achieve annual reserves/imports ratios of between 30 and 50 percent. It qualified this observation by saying that such a ratio could, at best, give only a preliminary indication of adequacy. Triffin (1960) criticized this minimum benchmark, as 30 percent (i.e., four months of import cover) would be too low given the economic circumstances of countries around or below those levels. In his view, a 35-percent reserves/imports ratio was a minimum.

Heller (1966) was the first to analyze the needed level of reserves in terms of a rational optimizing decision, defining the optimal reserve level at that point where marginal utility equals marginal cost. He highlighted the precautionary motive for holding reserves, with the benefit of holding reserves stemming from the ability to smooth consumption and production in case of a balance-of-payments deficit. Importantly, however, he also included an analysis of the opportunity cost for holding the reserve buffer. His assumption was that the rate of return on reserves had to be compared with the social return on capital, which he proxied using a rough average of long-term government bond yields of a range of countries (estimated at around 5 percent). In Heller's model, the demand for reserves was thus determined by the cost of adjusting to the external imbalance, the opportunity cost of holding reserves, and the probability that a need for reserves of a given magnitude would arise.[7] Heller argued that his approach led to a more reliable and consistent index of reserve adequacy then a simple reserves/imports ratio.

Subsequent studies, like Heller's, went beyond the earlier casual empiricism of finding simple reserve/import ratios and generally focused on four main variables affecting the demand for reserves: external payments variability, the marginal propensity to import, a scale variable such as output or imports, and opportunity cost. The variability measure was generally uncontested, it being assumed that the demand for reserves was positively associated with the fluctuations in the balance of payments. Different measures have been used to measure variability, with variability being defined in terms of either reserves or export receipts, but in essence there have been no major disagreements.[8] Empirically, the variability variable also held up.

More debated on theoretical grounds was the rationale to use the marginal propensity to import (usually proxied by the *average* imports as a share of GDP) in the reserve demand function. On theoretical grounds it was unclear whether the propensity to import should have a positive or negative effect. In a Keynesian model, reserves are built up by a contraction in imports; thus a negative relationship would be expected (e.g., Heller 1966). To the extent, however, that a high import/GDP ratio reflected openness, and thus more vulnerability, a positive relationship could be expected (Cooper 1968; Iyoha 1976). Frenkel (1978) developed a model that allowed for expenditure switching rather than expenditure reduction that, also empirically, yielded significant results. More openness was associated with a higher demand for reserves.

The main question surrounding the scale variable was whether economies of scale were present. The key point here is that reserves finance not flows, but payments imbalances. Whether or not reserves thus grow with world trade hinges entirely on whether imbalances in payments can be expected to grow in proportion to international transactions. Implicitly, this is the assumption behind using a reserves/imports ratio for reserve adequacy. Polak (1970) noted that the evidence was mixed, but that the ratio of the rates of growth of payments fluctuations to trade is unlikely to be below unity (or say, 0.8). Other studies (e.g., Oliviera 1971 and Officer 1976) argued that the elasticity of reserves with respect to imports is significantly below unity.

Probably the most difficult challenge has been finding an adequate measure of opportunity cost that can withstand empirical scrutiny. Alternative measures proposed have included per capita income (presumably capital is scarcer in developing countries and therefore the opportunity cost higher), net foreign indebtedness (another measure of capital scarcity), the government bond yield, and the spread between the government bond yield and short-term interest rates (to reflect the fact that reserves also generate investment income). Despite these efforts, the various proxies that had been tried for opportunity cost had, as Williamson put it in 1973, met with a uniform lack of success. One explanation for the lack of explanatory value of opportunity cost variables could be that central banks are extremely risk-averse regarding reserve shortfalls (Grimes 1993).[9]

In addition to the four main variables discussed above, mention should be made of two other main findings in the reserve adequacy literature that are pertinent to what follows. First, reserve demand was found to be influenced by the type of exchange regime. After the breakdown of the Bretton Woods system, attention focused on assessing the demand for reserves generated by the move to more flexible exchange rate regimes. Heller and Khan (1978) found that for industrial countries there had indeed been a downward shift in reserves, even if the shift had not been very significant, but for non-oil developing countries, the demand for reserves seemed to have increased. The latter finding seemed to reflect the fact that these countries retained pegged regimes even after the collapse of Bretton Woods. To the extent that countries were floating, the float was anything but free, and overall uncertainty and payments variability had increased. Frenkel (1983) later found further evidence that the move to floating had reduced the demand for reserves, although the effect for developed and industrial countries had been more pronounced than that for developing countries.

Second, studies generally found that the behavior of developing countries differed significantly from that of industrial countries, with external variability being a more important factor of reserve demand for the former. Lizondo and Mathieson (1987) found that the debt crisis of the early 1980s had produced a similar structural break in the demand for reserves as the collapse of the Bretton Woods system. The sensitivity to payment imbalances and openness had increased for developing countries, but it had declined for industrial countries. They hypothesized that this finding reflected the relative degree of market access for the two groups. Related to this, but more generally, several studies (Heller and Khan 1978; Eichengreen and Frankel 1996) postulated that there can be no presumption that the advent of capital mobility either raises or lowers the demand for reserves. On the one hand, capital mobility allows countries to finance at least a portion of external deficits by borrowing abroad. On the other hand, it assumes that capital mobility is not a source of vulnerability in its own right. A high degree of capital mobility could, for instance, increase exchange rate variability.

Although there exists a rich literature on reserve adequacy, most of it dates from before the 1980s. Interest in the subject waned as much of the industrial world moved to floating exchange rates and the level of reserves became largely demand determined for countries with easy access to the vastly expanded international financial markets. Moreover, the emergence of a multiple-reserve currency system removed the so-called Triffin dilemma.[10]

Not only is much of the literature on reserves dated, but it is also clear that many of the often ingenious theoretical contributions in the field of assessing reserve adequacy suffer from a lack of operational value. That is, they have not provided much guidance on what level of reserves would be adequate for a particular country. This has made them of limited use for actual assessments of reserve adequacy. Hence, the IMF has continued to rely quite heavily on the imperfect, yet readily available, ratio of reserves to imports, although more recently this has been complemented by so-called vulnerability indicators in the country reports that are presented to the IMF Executive Board. Appendix 4.1 shows the development of the reserves/imports ratio over the last twenty-five years for emerging-market countries. The crude rule of thumb that reserves have to equal at least three months of imports has lost much of its relevance, as openness and external vulnerability are no longer defined merely in terms of trade shocks. Its significance is nowadays mainly limited to countries at an early stage of development that have no significant access to international financial markets.

4.2.2 New Reserve Adequacy Measures: Post–Asia Crisis

One of the lessons that has been drawn from the Asian financial crisis is that countries' vulnerability to the withdrawal of capital in that crisis could have been reduced by better management of their asset and liability position—in other words, better reserves and debt management. These developments have stimulated a renewed interest in the question of reserve adequacy, especially for emerging-market countries.

It is increasingly recognized that it is necessary to take into account the vastly increased importance of capital flows for emerging-market economies and to relate the size of reserves to a country's short-term external debt (Greenspan 1999). This ratio appears to be the most relevant single indicator of reserves for countries that borrow in international financial markets. Building on Sachs, Tornell, and Velasco 1996 and using variables from the early-warning system model developed by the IMF staff, Bussière and Mulder (1999) concluded that higher liquidity can significantly decrease countries' vulnerability to external shocks in the face of weak domestic fundamentals. Their research suggests full coverage of total short-term external debt as a practical rule for reserve adequacy for individual countries, with the proviso that the real exchange rate is not seriously overvalued and that the current account deficit is modest. Deviations would call for higher reserve levels. Feldstein (1999), who observed that judging reserve adequacy in terms of imports "ignores the fact that currency crises are about capital flows, not trade financing" (104), also supports the notion that large reserves reduce countries' vulnerability to financial crises and increase confidence in their currencies. He adds, however, that when currencies are overvalued, protection through reserves requires much larger reserves than have traditionally been held by emerging-market countries. Fischer (1999) pointed out that countries holding very large reserves have coped better with the financial crises of recent years than others. He also expects that countries will draw from these crises the lesson that they should hold much larger reserves than before, and he cites the case of Korea, where a rapid buildup of reserves can be observed.

Two concrete proposals for minimum benchmarks for reserve adequacy have been put forward that could serve as new rules of thumb. First, Pablo Guidotti, the former deputy minister of finance of Argentina, is credited with being the first to propose that countries should manage their external assets and liabilities in such a way as to be capable of living without foreign borrowing for up to one year.[11] This implies, at a minimum, that foreign exchange reserves should exceed scheduled external amortization for one year.

The second proposal, put forward by Alan Greenspan, chairman of the Federal Reserve Board of the United States, is to complement the "Guidotti rule" with two enhancements. The first of these would be to have an additional rule that the average maturity of a country's external liabilities should exceed a certain threshold, such as three years (see Greenspan 1999). The second enhancement would be to have a "liquidity-at-risk" standard under which a country's external liquidity position would be calculated over a wide range of possible outcomes, taking into account the full set of external assets and liabilities. An appropriate level of reserves would then be one that provides a high probability (say, 95 percent) that external liquidity will be sufficient to avoid new borrowing for one year. This methodology is similar to the value-at-risk methodology used by commercial banks.

This shift in emphasis toward analysis of the need for reserves of emerging-market countries in terms of the potential for capital outflows is apposite. In our view, however, the Guidotti–Greenspan suggestions could usefully be improved upon. First, their proposals seem to focus entirely on an "external drain" on a country's reserves, disregarding the fact that there is also usually an "internal drain" (i.e., capital flight by residents). This is a factor that needs to be added. Secondly, the Greenspan proposal for a liquidity-at-risk approach could be simplified to make it operational. In the following analysis, leading to an estimate of what constitutes adequate reserves for twenty-one emerging-market countries, we build upon the suggestions by Guidotti and Greenspan.

4.3 Adequate Reserves for Emerging-Market Countries: A New Minimum Benchmark

The question of whether emerging-market countries should hold larger international reserves than they hitherto have held is a complex one that requires making assumptions with regard to exchange rate policies, controls on capital flows, and the magnitude of potential official financing packages. Dealing with these matters in a purely analytical approach would require a comprehensive model and an analysis of many variables. Looking at everything, however, is tantamount to looking at nothing. Rather than attempting to take that route, we choose here a less-elaborate but fully quantifiable approach based on key reserve need indicators. These indicators are refined to capture better the specific circumstances of countries, such as their exchange rate regime and the degree of risk of capital flight. The exercise results in estimates of a range of adequate reserves for twenty-one emerging-market countries. Finally, considerations of the costs of holding reserves are taken into account.

Several matters have to be clarified before we can proceed with the approach envisaged. First of all, we acknowledge that there is no single optimal exchange rate regime for emerging-market countries, let alone for all countries. There is, however, strong evidence that pegged exchange rates have become much more risky in a world with mobile capital. Indeed, several emerging-market countries have in recent years abandoned their pegs and adopted floating rates. Although such a regime change reduces the need for holding reserves as such, care should be taken not to infer that floaters require few reserves. Apart from the need to maintain a certain level of reserves for strategic reasons (the age-old "war chest"), countries tend to manage the float of their exchange rate. There has hardly been a country in modern times that over an extended period has adhered to a fully free, or "clean," float,[12] including even the United States, which has intervened in the foreign exchange market from time to time despite the fact that it has no exchange rate objective. At the other end of the spectrum are a number of countries that adhere to a currency board regime. Hong Kong is the prime example of an area where various economic and political factors provide strong arguments for such an approach. We therefore distinguish three groups of countries when assessing the adequacy of their reserves: those with (managed) floating exchange rates; those with pegged rates, including bands and crawls; and those with a currency board.

Although many emerging-market economies have liberalized parts of their external financial relations in recent years, most retain a mixed system of restrictions and freedom as regards capital movements, as clearly described in Williamson and Mahar 1998 and IMF 1999b. Although a country's degree of control over capital transactions is relevant for assessing its need for reserves, we assume that the differences among most emerging-market countries on this score are not all that big.[13] Where such differences may be significant, we point this out in qualitative terms (there are obvious difficulties of quantification as regards the overall degree of control over capital flows). It should also be emphasized that with the development of modern technology and new financial instruments, countries find it increasingly hard, in the absence of a huge and dirigiste foreign exchange control apparatus, to avoid capital flight during a crisis. In extreme cases of capital controls, in which the exchange of currency is for instance prohibited, capital flight would likely still occur, but this would not necessarily show up in the reserves figures. We disregard such extreme cases in what follows. We also disregard the possibility of debt defaults or moratoria, which would be another way of protecting reserves. We assume that neither capital controls nor debt defaults constitute a working assumption of central banks in deciding on reserve adequacy levels. We discuss below to what extent capital flight could have an effect on reserves, taking into account that some forms of capital flight (e.g., nonrepatriation of capital or underinvoicing of exports) need not affect the official reserves (other than that reserves would have been higher without the capital flight).

Another potentially major factor influencing reserve adequacy is the availability of official financial support. If a country can rely on ready access to credit from the International Monetary Fund and friendly central banks, it can feel justified in keeping relatively modest reserves. The same is true if countries can rely on contingent credit lines from the private sector. In practice, however, countries have been very reluctant to come to the IMF, partly because some perceive such an action as signaling a crisis; because there is a political cost in asking for financial help and economic advice from an outside organization; and because the conditionality associated with Fund programs, though necessary, is often politically painful. In other words, we do not believe in significant debtor moral hazard, nor do we believe that countries conduct reserve management policy taking into account possible IMF reserve supplements, which in any case have to be repaid.[14]

As for private contingent reserve supplements, the market for these seems rather thin. Only a few countries have negotiated such lines, and there are questions as to their additionality (i.e., they may be at the cost of other credit to an economy because of offsetting transactions, dynamic hedging, or country exposure limits of creditors) (see IMF 1999a). Moreover, contingent credit lines with commercial banks were not renewed after Mexico's use of them in the fall of 1998. Banks seemed to awaken to the fact that the lines would be drawn, and bank exposure increased, precisely when they were seeking to reduce it. We assume that although emerging-market countries could reduce their need for holding reserves somewhat through arrangements with the private sector, they will be reluctant to place a strong reliance on such arrangements, even if they can obtain them. The situation appears to be different for an advanced capital-importing country like Canada, where relatively low reserves are supplemented by special arrangements and ready access to financial markets.[15]

4.3.1 A Simple Benchmark for Reserve Adequacy

To ascertain whether the reserve holdings of emerging-market countries are broadly adequate in light of the considerable potential for capital outflows, we present a relatively simple benchmark for reserve adequacy for twenty-one countries. These countries are the largest emerging-market countries that enjoy more or less uninterrupted access to international financial markets.[16]

For many of the emerging-market countries, gross international reserves have grown considerably in the 1990s, as can be ascertained from the charts in appendix 4.1. There is, however, a distinct dip for most emerging-market countries in 1997, reflecting the financial crisis in Asia and its subsequent spread to other countries. Reserves declined strongly in Brazil and Russia in 1998 when both countries came under speculative attack and had to abandon their fixed-rate regime. Korea's reserves showed a spectacular increase as it recovered from the 1997–1998 crisis, reflecting the lesson mentioned by Fischer (1999) as well as the country's aversion to going through the experience of a sharp financial crisis ever again. China's rapid earlier reserve accumulation has slowed in recent years but is still at a very high level in absolute terms as compared to that of other countries,[17] whereas Hong Kong's reserves have declined slightly since 1997.

As a first step toward assessing reserve adequacy we look at three indicators (table 4.1). Although we put no great store in the reserves/imports ratio, the first indicator, we do note the low coverage for Mexico, Russia, and South Africa. It should be borne in mind that Mexico's important border trade with the United States proba-

Table 4.1
Reserve adequacy indicators: Emerging-market countries, end-1999

	Reserves/ imports (weeks of imports)	Reserves/M2 (percentage)	Reserves/short-term external debt (percentage)
Floating rates			
Brazil	37	24	83
Chile	49	20	200
Colombia	37	25	134
Czech Republic	23	29	225
India	38	12	327
Indonesia	57	32	126
Korea	32	22	162
Mexico	11	21	119
Peru	67	67	131
Philippines	21	37	145
Russia	11	29	70
South Africa	12	6	43
Thailand	35	21	206
Average	33	27	152
Pegged rates			
China (mainland)	49	10	655
Hungary	20	40	154
Malaysia	24	27	336
Poland	28	37	316
Turkey	30	24	93
Venezuela	43	53	235
Average	33	32	298
Currency boards			
Argentina	53	25	62
Hong Kong	28	25	103
Average	41	25	82

Sources: All data IFS, except for R/STED ratio, which is from the Joint BIS/IMF/OEDC World Bank Statistics on External Debt; data for imports in the Reserves/Import ratio is c.i.f., except for that for Brazil, the Czech Republic, and Peru, which is on an f.o.b. basis due to availability.

bly contributes to a high import content of exports. Russia and South Africa are major gold producers and do not hold large amounts of foreign exchange reserves. Because of valuation problems as well as the diminishing role of monetary gold, we have excluded gold from our calculations of reserves. Emerging-market countries tend to hold modest amounts of gold in their reserves.[18]

Turning to the second indicator, the reserves/M2 ratio (R/M2) several studies related to the research on early warning systems (EWSs) that started to come to fruition after the Mexico crisis of 1995 indicate that the ratio of reserves to broad money supply is a predictor of financial crises.[19] Thus with higher levels of R/M2 the probability of a crisis is reduced. Calvo (1996), for instance, argued that the ratio of reserves to the broad money supply is the appropriate standard for reserve adequacy for countries with a pegged exchange rate. Other studies that found R/M2 (defined either as a "level" or "the change in") to be a significant variable in predicting crises were Esquivel and Larraín 1998; Kaminsky, Lizondo, and Reinhart 1997; Frankel and Rose 1996; and Sachs, Tornell, and Velasco 1996.[20] Care should be taken in interpreting the EWS results. The models tend to produce many false crisis prediction signals, use very different techniques, and perform significantly better in-sample than out-sample (i.e., predicting a crisis that still has to happen). Nevertheless, the results seem to bear out that M2 is a natural measure for assessing the potential demand for foreign assets from domestic sources. It is also noteworthy to add that the EWS regressions show reserves themselves to be a reliable predictor of crises.

The data do indicate slightly higher ratios of reserves to M2 for countries with pegged exchange rates on average, consistent with the premise that their central banks attach more concern to possible internal demand for their reserves (see also appendix 4.2 for a more elaborate table with R/M2 ratios). The low figures for China (and also India) probably reflect the dearth of alternative financial investment instruments in these countries and therefore a relatively large money supply. The two currency board cases do not show any unusual feature. For them full coverage of the monetary base is of course the immediate target. However, given the inflexibility of a currency board regime and the risk of loss of confidence when reserves are seen as dangerously low, a considerable surplus over base money coverage seems to be necessary (see also Rojas-Suárez and Weisbrod 1995).

The third indicator, which we consider to be the most important one for emerging market economies, relates reserves to short-term external debt (STED), defined as debt with a remaining maturity of less than one year. Again, several EWS studies that have specified the ratio of reserves to short-term external debt (R/STED) have found low levels of this variable to lead to an increased probability of crisis (Bussière and Mulder 1999; Rodrik and Velasco 1999; Berg et al. 1999). Examination of this indicator across countries in general shows the expected result, that is, a (much) higher ratio of reserves to short-term external debt for countries with pegged rates or bands than for countries operating a floating-rate regime. The unweighted average for the floaters was 152 percent at the end of 1999; it was almost double that (298) for the peggers. Very comfortable reserve positions are indicated for China, India, Malaysia, Poland, the Czech Republic, Venezuela and Thailand. Among the floaters quite low levels of R/STED can be seen for Russia, Brazil, Colombia, and Indonesia, all of which had to abandon their pegs in 1998–1999 and turned to the IMF. South Africa also has a very low ratio. For a number of years it pursued a policy of intervening in the forward exchange market for large amounts, enabling it to support its currency despite a lack of foreign exchange reserves. In this way it built up a large net open forward position, which it has started to reduce in recent years.

Among the countries with a pegged rate or a crawling rate or band, only Turkey has an R/STED below 100 percent. After long negotiations it reached agreement with the IMF in the latter part of 1999 for a standby credit of $4 billion, specifically intended to strengthen its gross reserves. Among this group the ratio for Hungary is also substantially below the average. Finally, the figures for the two currency board cases prima facie look on the low side. The fact that the short-term external liabilities of the banking system partly reflect the purely interbank relationships of a financial center appears to explain Hong Kong's rather modest level of R/STED. It should be noted that a significant part of Argentina's banking system is owned by foreign-headquartered institutions, which artificially inflates its debt figures, possibly quite substantially so. Argentina also has private contingent credit lines that could be taken into account.[21]

It is also useful to examine how the R/STED indicator of reserve adequacy has developed over the past years (see table 4.2, and also

Table 4.2
Reserves as a percentage of short-term external debt

	1990	1991	1992	1993	1994	1995	1996	1997	1998	1999
Floating rates										
Brazil[a]	34	35	85	94	122	128	106	89	92	83
Chile[a]	148	198	172	171	184	172	179	153	176	200
Colombia[a]	186	226	201	197	140	124	137	123	110	134
Czech Republic				343	329	327	242	168	161	225
India	37	75	103	175	233	194	232	265	312	327
Indonesia[a]	55	52	54	53	51	46	48	43	91	126
Korea[a]	73	54	60	63	58	54	45	31	131	162
Mexico[a]	55	69	77	78	15	52	58	85	99	119
Peru	52	118	128	190	283	184	161	156	128	131
Philippines	29	84	102	147	146	106	109	53	94	145
Russia[a]				60	21	65	42	39	44	70
South Africa			13	16	20	27	9	32	32	43
Thailand[a]	151	128	123	108	90	76	76	62	117	206
Average	82	104	102	130	130	120	111	100	122	152
Pegged rates or bands										
China (mainland)	335	316	122	116	227	262	333	358	449	655
Hungary	42	136	180	252	189	239	165	142	121	154
Malaysia	475	314	379	304	338	246	206	124	266	336
Poland	137	88	92	89	246	505	451	463	420	316
Turkey[a]	78	62	70	49	70	103	114	88	87	93
Venezuela	175	191	168	171	162	144	298	251	230	235
Average	207	184	168	164	205	250	261	238	262	298
Currency boards										
Argentina	65	56	66	77	64	55	59	63	63	62
Hong Kong	19	21	24	24	23	26	34	51	84	103
Average	42	38	45	51	44	41	47	57	74	82

Source: Joint BIS/IMF/OECD/World Bank Statistics on External Debt; all debt data are stocks at year end on a residual maturity basis.

[a] Countries that underwent a change of exchange rate regime in the period shown. Exchange rate classification is on the basis of the situation at end-1999.

appendix 4.3, which reproduces the table as a set of figures). What stands out is that for most countries with a low level of R/STED, a financial crisis ensued and that the affected countries turned to the IMF for financial support. The major exception, Turkey, did not suffer from a full-fledged financial crisis, as it approached the IMF before confidence was seriously eroded.

Perhaps the most striking examples of how low levels of reserve adequacy, as indicated by low R/STED ratios, go hand in hand with an external financial crisis are provided by the main actors in the Asian financial crises: Indonesia, Korea, and Thailand, but also the Philippines, and to a lesser extent Malaysia. In Indonesia an already unfavorable ratio declined further to a level of only 43 percent in 1997, whereas in Korea the decline was even sharper, with the ratio falling to a level of only 31 percent by the end of 1997. In Thailand, where the Asian crisis originated in the summer of 1997, a relatively comfortable level of R/STED was almost halved between 1993 and 1997. Had these developments been clearly highlighted before the Asian crisis, the IMF and other relevant parties would have been better forewarned about the impending problems, especially in Korea, where they were least expected. What about Malaysia, which managed to avoid having to turn to the IMF? It clearly had a much better starting position than the three Asian countries most affected by the crisis. Although Malaysia's short-term external debt more than doubled between 1994 and 1997, as was the case in the three crisis countries, its relatively high level of reserves before the onset of the Asian crisis appears to have protected it from more serious damage.[22] In the meantime, all Asian countries shown in table 4.2 have experienced a sharp improvement in their R/STED ratios, led by Korea, where a quadrupling took place in only one year. On average, the five Asian countries most affected by the crisis saw their R/STED ratio rise by 132 percentage points since 1997.

Russia is another example in which a strong decline in the R/STED indicator foreshadowed a serious collapse. With a relatively weak starting level of around 70 percent, the Russian coverage of short-term external debt fell to a level of 40 percent in 1997. Given its continuing difficulties with capital flight, R/STED for Russia has remained dangerously low. In sharp contrast to this is the experience of China, which had absorbed into its reserves a significant share of the huge capital inflows it enjoyed during the early and middle 1990s. It succeeded in maintaining a stable exchange rate during the Asian financial crisis despite many calls for a devaluation of the yuan.

The evidence provided here strongly suggests that countries holding large international reserves, especially relative to their short-term debt obligations in foreign currency, are much less prone to suffer from financial crises than those with relatively low reserves. The R/STED ratio stands out as the most appropriate indicator of reserve adequacy for emerging-market countries. For countries with floating exchange rates, a level of reserves that fully covers their foreign debt obligations with a maturity of up to a year would seem to be a prudent minimum to aim for.[23] Although the one-year rule is perhaps somewhat arbitrary, aside from the empirical support it receives in EWS regressions, it is conceptually similar to the stress tests used by financial institutions to analyze exposure to large market movements. In view of the rather weak standing of a number of these countries in international financial markets, as reflected, for instance, by an unfavorable investment grade, they would seem well advised to aim for a more comfortable level of reserves than 100 percent of STED. Such countries run a distinct risk that they could be cut off from the capital markets for more than a year. Moreover, they have to take into account the risk of capital flight by residents. Even if they are prepared to have the exchange rate take some of the strain, emerging-market countries are generally not prepared to allow a free fall of their currency even for short periods. For countries that operate a currency peg of one kind or another, more stringent requirements are clearly in order. Defending the peg in the face of a financial crisis will require a larger buffer of foreign exchange than for countries practicing a managed float.

This brings us to our suggested benchmark for the adequacy of reserves for the main emerging-market countries. Starting from the minimum of full coverage of short-term external debt, we add a rough estimate of the potential for capital outflow stemming from residents (table 4.3). Residents will require domestic liquidity to enable them to purchase the foreign currency that allows capital flight. It is therefore logical to assume that a certain fraction of the broad domestic money supply provides an indication of the potential for capital flight. Obviously the risk that residents will wish to convert domestic into foreign liquidity in times of lack of confidence will be greater for countries with a currency peg than for floaters. Since emerging market countries tend to practice managed floating,

Table 4.3
Estimated adequate and actual reserves (end-1999, billions of U.S. dollars)

	STED	Fraction of M2[a]	Country risk index	Adequate reserves $[a + (b \times c)]$	Actual reserves
Floating rates	*a*	*b*	*c*	*d*	*e*
Brazil	41.9	8.3–16.5	0.66	47.3–52.8	34.8
Chile	7.2	7.4–14.7	0.31	9.5–11.8	14.4
Colombia	5.7	3.2–6.4	0.53	7.4–9.1	7.6
Czech Republic	5.7	2.0–4.0	0.36	6.4–7.1	12.8
India	10.0	12.7–25.5	0.42	15.3–20.7	32.7
Indonesia	21.0	4.1–8.2	0.71	23.9–26.9	26.4
Korea	45.8	13.8–27.7	0.36	50.8–55.8	74.0
Mexico	26.7	3.7–14.7	0.51	30.5–34.2	31.8
Peru	6.7	0.7–1.4	0.52	7.0–7.4	8.7
Philippines	9.1	1.7–3.4	0.40	9.8–10.4	13.2
Russia	12.1	1.4–2.8	0.78	13.2–14.3	8.5
South Africa	14.6	3.8–7.7	0.52	16.6–18.6	6.4
Thailand	16.5	7.2–14.3	0.40	19.4–22.2	34.1
Pegged rates or bands					
China (mainland)	24.1	144.8–289.6	0.43	86.3–148.6	157.7
Hungary	7.1	2.3–4.6	0.43	8.1–9.1	11.0
Malaysia	9.1	11.4–22.9	0.36	13.2–17.3	30.6
Poland	7.8	6.7–13.4	0.35	10.1–12.5	24.5
Turkey	25.0	9.0–18.0	0.62	30.5–36.1	23.3
Venezuela	5.2	2.2–4.3	0.54	6.4–7.5	12.3
Currency boards					
Argentina	42.6	4.6–9.2	0.55	45.1–47.6	26.3
Hong Kong SAR	93.9	17.7–35.3	0.33	99.7–105.5	96.2

Sources: Same as table 4.1, plus the Economist Intelligence Unit for the country risk index.

[a] For countries with floating rates or currency boards: 5 to 10 percent of M2; for countries with pegged rates or bands: 10 to 20 percent of M2.

however, the central bank will also have to hold foreign exchange against the risk of some drain on the reserves in countries with a flexible exchange rate. How much of a country's broad money supply could be mobilized against reserves to finance capital flight is very difficult to ascertain (see appendix 4.4). De Gregorio et al. (1999) argue that "if residents are inclined to flee in response to developing financial difficulties, the whole of the money supply (M1 or even wider aggregates) has to be covered by foreign reserves to prevent the collapse of the exchange rate regime and the financial system" (15). In our view, however, this is too extreme. It is hard to see how in a relatively short span of time the entire money supply could be mobilized against reserves. Moreover, with rising marginal costs of reserves, optimal reserve levels would presumably not need to cover the entire money supply.

We have assumed that for countries with a peg the fraction of domestic money to be covered by reserves could be between 10 and 20 percent of M2 (we use M2 since there are standardized IMF data for this magnitude). In some cases these fractions may be too low, but we wish to avoid presenting figures that would clearly go beyond a minimum level of adequacy for most of the countries examined. For countries with floating exchange rates we assume that no more than between 5 and 10 percent of M2 would be mobilized against reserves in a relatively short time span. For countries operating a currency board we assume the same, in view of the confidence that one could normally expect to stem from the operation of a solid currency board. Appendix 4.4 provides a rationale for these chosen percentages. For instance the standard deviation of the R/M2 ratio over the last ten years falls within the 5–10 percent range for eight out of thirteen countries with floating exchange rates. For countries with a fixed exchange rate, half the countries have a standard deviation of the R/M2 ratio that falls within the 10–20 percent range.

We take the analysis a step further by recognizing that not all emerging-market countries are equally susceptible to the risk of capital flight. Countries with good economic, financial, and political fundamentals obviously run a smaller risk of residents' "voting with their money" than countries where the potential for instability is significant. To incorporate this element, we adjust the fraction of M2 (between 10 and 20 percent for peggers and between 5 and 10 percent for floaters) for an index of country risk (the third column in table 4.3). For this we use *The Economist*'s country risk index (Economist Intelligence Unit 1999), which takes into account seventy-seven different indicators, ranging from monetary and fiscal policy to political stability.[24] The index is expressed on a scale of 100, with Russia seen as the riskiest country among the countries included in our table and Chile as the least risky. The adjustment factor thus obtained (i.e., the fraction of broad money multiplied by the country risk index) is added to the amount of STED from column 1, which produces our estimates in the range of adequate reserves for emerging-market countries (the fourth column in the table). These are then compared to the actual level of reserves (the fifth column). If one wanted to take up the suggestion in note 23 to require, in addition, reserve cover for that part of the current account deficit not covered by foreign direct investment, one could add the amounts shown in appendix 4.5.

We are aware that the estimates of reserve need provided here may be subject to challenges on several grounds. Indeed, such estimates should be seen as indicating a rough order of magnitude. Nevertheless, an exercise such as this appears useful, since mere qualitative expressions such as "reserves are too small" or "more than adequate" are too vague for policy purposes. No doubt further useful refinements could be made to the calculations, but this would require quite specific country knowledge. National authorities would be in the best place to undertake such an exercise. We do feel that the approach followed here could be a useful starting position from which countries could examine the adequacy of their reserve positions. If they have arranged contingent credit lines with the private sector and are confident that these can be fully relied upon in an emergency, these should be taken into account. We are aware of only quite limited credit lines of this nature for emerging-market countries at present. In fact Mexico no longer relies on this instrument, having last used it in the fall of 1998. Mexico did announce a package of new contingent funding in 1999 that undoubtedly provides it with considerable comfort on top of its reserves, which at the end of 1999 were just inside the minimum-adequacy range.

Our benchmark range for adequate reserves deviates substantially from actual reserve levels in a number of cases. Among the peggers, only in Turkey did reserves fall short of calculated adequate reserves. As mentioned, Turkey turned to the IMF in 1999 to borrow reserves. As regards floaters, the largest shortfalls are found in the case of Russia and South Africa, and to a lesser extent, Brazil. The picture is modified somewhat when monetary gold is included. It is unlikely, however, that relatively large amounts of gold could be sold at short notice to combat a financial crisis without severely depressing the price of gold. The gold lease market has added liquidity to the gold market, but the amount of liquidity is rather small in size. Hence, we do not think that adding gold at full market value would do justice to the actual reserve ease of Russia and South Africa.

Our benchmark estimates, which do not err on the side of caution, partly in view of the costs of holding reserves (discussed in the next subsection), also show a few cases in which reserves appear to be quite comfortable. This is the case for India, where actual reserves are almost double the estimated midpoint of the adequacy range, as well as for the Czech Republic, Malaysia, Poland, Thailand, and Venezuela. In view of China's still elaborate capital controls, the adjustment factor (10 to 20 percent of M2) may be on the high side. Even so actual reserves exceeded the upper band of the adequacy range. On the other hand, the M2 range of 5 to 10 percent could well be on the low side for Russia, where capital flight has been a continuous headache since the breakdown of the Soviet Union. Russia's M2 converted into dollars has been quite small since the sharp devaluation of the ruble in August 1998. There may well be scope for more capital outflows via the liquidation of other assets or other more obscure channels, as recent history seems to suggest.

Other countries with comfortable reserve levels are Korea, where the external position has dramatically turned around in the last two years, Chile, Hungary, and the Philippines. Reserve levels for Indonesia, Mexico, and Colombia fall just within the adequacy range. Argentina, operating a currency board since 1991 while comfortably covering base money with its reserves, falls short of the Guidotti rule, that is, full coverage of its short-term external debt. However, Argentina established a contingent credit line of $6.1 billion with commercial banks in late 1996 that has been rolled over but not used so far. It makes sense to take into account this line when evaluating Argentina's reserve position (and, as noted, its debt figures may be artificially inflated). Finally, Hong Kong, where a currency board has been in place since 1983, holds reserves somewhat smaller than our estimate of an adequate level. However, the short-term external debt average requirement seems to be too severe in cases where a large part of it constitutes interbank positions in a financial center.

4.3.2 *The Costs of Holding Reserves*

Most emerging-market economies borrow on international financial markets on a regular basis, bringing in foreign exchange to the country through loans taken up by either the government or the private sector, including interbank financing. Borrowing costs differ widely, however, depending on the creditworthiness of the debtor as well as the type and maturity of the loan. Reserves are of course invested by the central banks managing them. Although yields will vary according to the type of investment, the range of outcomes will tend to be much narrower across countries than in the case of borrowing, since central banks tend to stick to assets with a high degree of liquidity. This is necessary to ensure that intervention demands can be met at short notice and without suffering major losses due to, for instance, an intervening decline in bond rates. This implies that the net costs of obtaining reserves for emerging-market countries is mainly due to the difference in borrowing costs.

The external debt profiles of emerging-market countries show considerable differences. Whereas some countries have been able to place large amounts of international bonds, others have relied more on loans from foreign banks. The large Latin American countries have been users of both instruments. Some countries have matched increases in their reserves with short-term external borrowing. This is the cheapest way of obtaining foreign exchange, and in the absence of a high country risk premium, the net cost of holding reserves can be quite modest. As emphasized earlier, however, in times of crisis, rollover problems can occur. Hence, a broader spectrum of external borrowing will make countries less vulnerable with respect to rollovers. Nevertheless, a degree of short-term external borrowing can be an acceptable means of strengthening reserves, if in fact the proceeds are held as reserves by the central bank.[25]

Take, for instance, a country with reserves of $5 billion and a short-term external debt of $10 billion. The coverage is only 50 percent. If the country decides to borrow an additional $5 billion of short-term funds and invests all of it as liquid reserves, it will increase its cover ratio to 67 percent. Assuming a margin of 100 basis points in net borrowing costs, the total annual cost to the country of holding reserves of $10 billion will be only $100 million. If, however, the country decides that it does not want to be vulnerable to a sudden cessation of further short-term borrowing, and it succeeds in borrowing the required $5 billion in bond markets, its cost will be considerably higher. Typically an emerging-market country with an average credit rating has to pay around 300 to 400 basis points above the interbank rate. Thus the insurance against a sudden withdrawal of capital would add some $200 million to $300 million a year to the budgetary outlays of the country in our example. Whether such an insurance premium is excessive is difficult to judge. It very much depends on the probability of a financial crisis and the macroeconomic cost (and from the point of view of the sitting government, the political cost) of having to take abrupt adjustment measures. Typically countries use a blend of borrowing instruments, reflecting trade-offs of this nature.

Obviously for countries with low creditworthiness, the cost of borrowing in bond markets can be very high, if they can obtain such funds at all. Examples are Russia and Turkey before the summer of 1998, which had to pay spreads of 400–700 basis points (yield spread measured as the difference between the bond yield at issue and the prevailing yield for industrial-country government bonds in the same currency and of comparable maturity). Countries like Korea can, however, currently obtain bond financing at around 200 basis points above the interest rate on U.S. Treasury bonds. Syndicated bank loans, once the dominant form of international financing, tend to be less expensive but harder to obtain for emerging-market countries since the Asian crisis. Bonds with shorter maturities or notes can also be an attractive and relatively inexpensive vehicle for these countries. The main point here is that it is not accurate to generalize, as some authors do, that borrowing to strengthen reserves is quite costly for emerging-market countries, assuming that such borrowing is all done in long-term bond markets. Feldstein (1999), for instance, calculates that if Mexico borrows an additional $30 billion to double its reserves, the cost would be $1.8 billion or 0.5 percent of its GDP per year. Assuming borrowing in accordance with Mexico's external debt profile, where bank loans (a portion of which have a short maturity) outstrip bond borrowing, the cost would be considerably lower.[26]

One way to mitigate the cost of borrowing to build up reserves is to invest the proceeds in higher-yielding assets. In fact, over the last decade or so, central banks have increased the range of assets in which they invest their reserves to obtain a higher return. There are limits to this development, however, as reserves by their nature have to be sufficiently liquid to serve their purpose. Reserves should not be confused with government investment accounts.[27] There may also be legal limitations with respect to the types of asset in which a central bank can invest its reserves. Feldstein (1999), however, suggests that emerging-market countries should invest part of their reserves in equity. This is unsound advice. Although yields will tend to rise with such a strategy, so will volatility. Reserves need to be liquid in a broad sense; that is, not only must it be possible to liquidate reserve assets readily (and this would be true for blue chip stocks), but the holder must also be able to rely on their value. The second requirement is not met with respect to stocks (or long-term bonds). Indeed, according to the IMF's definition of reserve assets, these should be liquid and marketable. "Marketable" assets refer to those that can be bought, sold, and liquidated with minimum cost and time and for which there are willing sellers and buyers (IMF 1999b). To our knowledge central banks have refrained from investing in equity; they are not investment agencies and should not take on the degree of risk that goes with investment in the stock market.

Returning to the question of whether holding larger reserves under conditions of increased capital mobility is optimal for emerging-market countries, we consider the following. The "insurance premium" to be paid for better protection against the shocks of financial crises equals the net borrowing costs, as measured by the average gross borrowing cost and the yield obtained on reserve assets. The policymakers of emerging-market countries have to make conscious judgments on the trade-off involved. It is our impression that the minimum estimates of adequate reserves presented in the previous section will generally prove to be acceptable in terms of the costs involved to the twenty-one countries included in our sample. In other words, the countries for which inadequate reserves are indicated should, preferably gradually, borrow prudently to strengthen their reserves, either from the markets or temporarily from the IMF. The cost of "regular" borrowing from the Fund is considerably lower than that of turning to the market,[28] but IMF financing is of course meant to be temporary and is subject to policy conditionality.

A final consideration that we have is that whereas holding inadequate reserves can leave a country dangerously exposed to shocks, an excessive build up of reserves is also to be avoided. Holding very large amounts of reserves, even if financed at relatively attractive terms, can be a considerable drain on a country's budget. Moreover, and probably more importantly, a very high degree of reserve ease can affect countries' willingness to adjust to changing circumstances (see Rojas-Suárez and Weisbrod 1995 and Polak 1970). Huge reserves can effectively remove the external constraint as regards countries' policy choices, which may lead to laxity in macroeconomic policies or the prolonged defense of overvalued exchange rates. Such policy mistakes can turn out to be quite costly in the long run. The question arises as to whether some countries, in the aftermath of the negative experience of the Asian crisis, now seek to build up reserves beyond what can be considered ample.

4.4 SDRs to the Rescue?

Special drawing rights in the IMF were introduced in the late 1960s to deal with the problem of a possible shortage of international reserves. The exact language of the decision on SDR was much debated to ensure that a fiduciary creation of liquidity by means of SDR allocations would not degenerate into the provision of "easy money." Article XVIII of the IMF Articles of Agreement stipulates that SDR allocations shall be limited to supplementing existing reserves "to meet the long-term global need" for international reserves. This language has been subject to endless interpretation, usually in order to find a reason for a new allocation for SDRs in situations in which there was no obvious shortage of overall international liquidity, that is, on a *global* scale. The SDR section in the Fund's articles also stipulates that decisions concerning allocations require an 85 percent majority of the voting power, thereby providing the United States, and also combinations of like-minded smaller countries, with a de facto veto over such decisions.

Having suggested in the previous section that a number of emerging-market countries would be well advised to build up their foreign exchange reserves to decrease their vulnerability to costly external shocks, the question arises as to whether an SDR allocation would be appropriate to finance such a buildup. Since there are no convincing signs of a *global* shortage of international reserves, the case for an SDR allocation, which is distributed on the basis of member countries' quotas, is very hard to make. Although the increase in the mobility of international capital appears to have enlarged the need for reserves of emerging-market countries, it may well have lowered it for industrial countries. Capital-importing countries among the advanced economies have enjoyed easy access to international financial markets, even in times of international stress. This has generally made it possible for them to hold relatively low levels of reserves. Moreover, the countries of the European Monetary Union presently have a considerably smaller need to hold reserves than when they still operated separate currencies. In fact the reserves of the EMU zone appear to be much larger than any foreseeable intervention needs to support the euro.

4.4.1 Systemic Threats and SDRs

Circumstances can arise in which international liquidity can dry up in large parts of the world, threatening a collapse of the international financial system. During the tense period following the collapse of the Russian ruble in the summer of 1998, some expressed fears that contagion in financial markets could become so widespread that consequences of a *systemic* nature could arise. In that light, thought was given to the possibility of allocating a very large amount of SDRs to alleviate the threat of insufficient liquidity in a large number of financial markets, possibly including those of some industrial countries. Leaving aside the question of interpretation of the Fund's articles, it could be envisaged that a widespread financial crisis, commonly perceived as a systemic threat, could generate the 85 percent majority required among the Fund's Board of Governors to allow an SDR allocation, essentially as a *safety net* in order to ward off the risk of a *global* financial crisis.

After the financial tensions of 1998 ebbed, a number of proposals to institutionalize this safety net feature of the SDR emerged. Some of these have been worked out in some detail and merit careful attention.[29] Lipton (2000) notes that although an SDR allocation could in principle be agreed upon quickly in a crisis, this is unlikely to happen. Since SDRs are allocated according to countries' quotas in the IMF, the bulk of such an allocation will be directed to industrial countries, which are not the ones most likely to suffer from a reserve shortage in a crisis. Lipton therefore proposes a two-step procedure encompassing an allocation of SDRs, with the largest countries depositing their share into a trust fund that would serve as a last line of defense whenever the international financial system faces a "dire threat." Lipton mentions $300 billion as the possible size of the allocation, which would yield a pool of $205 billion in the trust fund if all twenty-five countries participating in the New Arrangements to Borrow agree to deposit their allocations. Activation of the pool would require a finding, based on a supermajority vote of the participants in the trust fund, that there is a systemic threat. Lipton also proposes that the participants, rather than the IMF, become the direct creditors of the borrowing countries, so that there would not be a new IMF facility. He sees this as an additional means of ensuring conservative management of the trust fund. The pool would lend freely in a crisis and at a penalty rate but would retain constructive ambiguity concerning activation to limit moral hazard.

A similar approach has been recommended by an independent task force (of which Lipton was a member) sponsored by the U.S. Council on Foreign Relations, with Morris Goldstein acting as project director (see Independent Task Force 1999). Although the task force advocated smaller IMF-led rescue packages than those put together between 1995 and 1999, to limit moral hazard, it saw a need for a backup facility to deal with systemic crises as distinct from country crises. The task force was especially concerned about instances of financial contagion, the victims of which are subject to a weakening of their external position, for reasons largely beyond their control, that is expected to be temporary. It has in mind a *contagion facility* that would not require a Fund program; that is, it would be without policy conditions. This facility would replace two existing Fund facilities: the supplementary reserve facility and the contingent credit line (CCL). It would be funded by a (presumably very large) one-time SDR allocation. Only developing countries could use the facility, and activation would require a supermajority among creditors. As in the Lipton proposal, the contributing countries would be taking the credit risk, not the IMF. The task force notes that an important advantage of financing the contagion facility with newly allocated SDRs is that it does not require approval from national legislatures for funding when a crisis is underway (a particular problem for the United States given Congress's general reluctance to provide additional resources to the IMF). Goldstein also claims that the new facility would not involve borrower moral hazard, as it would be triggered only by widespread contagion rather than by policy mistakes in the borrowing countries and by charging a market interest rate and requiring short repayment maturities.

The problem that we see with these proposals is that they change the source of the moral hazard associated with large-scale financial rescue operations rather than diminishing it. By advocating smaller packages in the case of country crises, the task force intends to reduce creditor moral hazard, which has been much criticized following the large rescue packages beginning with Mexico in 1995. The existence of a large pool of resources, however, in the form of a systemic backup facility, financed through liquidity creation instead of out of creditor countries' reserves or budgets, could well provide private-sector creditors with the feeling that whenever there appears to be a threat to the system, there will be a bailout. The mere existence of a backstop pool of perhaps $200 billion is likely to make international lenders less cautious than they would otherwise be. Although requiring supermajority decision making would reduce the risk of too easily declaring a particular crisis to be systemic,[30] politicians and market participants are likely to exert pressure to use a contagion facility every time a crisis emerges that is not confined to a particular (smaller) country. Whereas Lipton leaves open the role of conditionality in his proposal, Goldstein explicitly rules out setting policy conditions in conjunction with use of the contagion facility, although there would apparently be eligibility criteria. Setting up an unconditional facility, funded by liquidity creation (declaring it a "one-time" SDR allocation might not convince everybody) is also bound to engender significant borrower moral hazard, something that is largely absent where conditional lending is involved. All in all, these proposals therefore do not put to rest the moral hazard problem; if anything they seem to aggravate it.

An important consideration in these proposals appears to be the desire to be able to mobilize additional liquidity quickly in a crisis without having to obtain authorization from the U.S. Congress. Although this is an understandable reaction to the difficult process of securing funding for the IMF, especially in the United States, but also in a few other countries, it raises the question whether such a "short-track" approach would be the most desirable route. National legislatures may be difficult to deal with as regards international financial matters, but in our view there is wisdom in requiring them to ratify national funding of contributions to international financial institutions.[31] By circumventing them through an exceptional use of the SDR mechanism, an important—albeit sometimes unpredictable—check on the expansion of lending by international organizations would be undone.

Moreover, systemic threats do not necessarily have to be dealt with only by the IMF, either directly or through a one-step-removed contagion facility. Central banks have a long tradition of providing liquidity support both in domestic and international financial crises. Instead of providing SDRs as under the Lipton/task force proposal, which would not be the liquidity of choice of countries in a crisis, central banks would provide immediately usable hard currencies. Hence, rather than using the SDR mechanism for purposes for which it was not intended (crisis financing rather than meeting the long-term global need for reserves), the Fund could, in partnership with major central banks, devise a means of obtaining sufficient liquidity to stem a major crisis threatening the international financial system. Two possible approaches come to mind: short-term lending to the IMF by major central banks in their own currencies (dollars, euros, yen, and possibly sterling and Swiss francs), and alternatively, short-term loans provided by these central banks to borrowing countries in parallel with IMF credits.[32] Given the vast money-creating powers of major central banks, there need be no doubt that the liquidity necessary to combat an international crisis could be made available. However, in line with the principle of constructive ambiguity and to avoid as much moral hazard as possible, it would not be desirable to spell out in any detail the nature of such an international lender-of-last-resort function.

In conclusion, although the SDR mechanism could potentially play a safety net role for the international financial system when it is under threat, we believe that institutionalizing this feature, for instance, in the form of a contagion facility, is undesirable. Creditor moral hazard is unlikely to be reduced by such an innovation, and borrower moral hazard could be expected to become significant. In situations in which the resources of the IMF are insufficient to meet a truly systemic threat, a role can be envisaged for the major central banks.

4.5 Conclusions

The severe international financial crises witnessed since the mid-1990s have generated a debate on the so-called global financial architecture, focusing on both crisis prevention and crisis resolution. Many proposals have been put forward concerning crisis prevention, and quite a few are being developed or implemented under the aegis of the IMF. These include greater transparency and improved data collection, codes of conduct for fiscal and monetary policy, strengthened surveillance of member countries' performance and policies, and the creation of a new facility, the CCL, which has not been used so far. What has been underplayed in the prevention debate is the role of holding adequate reserves in crisis-prone countries. It is striking to observe that emerging-market countries that held relatively large reserves withstood the recent financial crises considerably better than those with only modest reserves. This lesson seems to have been learned, in that many emerging-market countries have been strengthening their reserves in the aftermath of the Asian and Russian financial crises.

It is one thing to state that higher reserves offer better protection against contagion and crises, but quite another to indicate with any precision what levels can be considered adequate but not excessive. The traditional adequacy measure, expressed in terms of months of imports, has lost most of its relevance, particularly for emerging-market countries that generally rely on private capital inflows to balance their external accounts. We propose an alternative, relatively simple, and operational benchmark for reserve adequacy, building on the approach that relates the level of reserves to the size of STED. Although we consider it necessary for countries to hold reserves that fully cover STED, we believe that such a level would still provide insufficient protection in a confidence crisis. In addition to the external drain on foreign exchange reserves that results from the nonrollover of STED, there tends to be an internal drain on account of capital flight by residents. This second element can be captured by assuming that a fraction of broad money can flow out in a relatively short period. We distinguish in this regard between countries with floating exchange rates and those with fixed regimes, including crawling pegs and bands. The fraction of broad money that could readily flow out is assumed to be considerably higher for countries with a fixed-rate regime than for floaters, whose exchange rate movements will absorb part of the effect of the outflow.

In a further refinement, especially to allow for better cross-country comparisons, we adjust the fraction of broad money susceptible to quasi-immediate outflow with a country risk factor. Clearly the risk of capital flight by residents is closely related to the riskiness with which the country is perceived. Hence for countries, such as Russia, with high financial and political risk, the capital flight component of the reserve adequacy benchmark is commensurately higher than for low-risk countries such as Chile. To avoid the suggestion of precision, we express the minimum benchmark for reserves in terms of a range. Calculations are presented for twenty-one of the larger emerging-market countries.

Although there is a strong case for accumulating adequate reserves in emerging-market countries, one should not overlook the costs involved. For countries having access to international financial markets, the costs consist of the difference between the interest paid on external borrowing and the yield obtained on the investment of the proceeds. We argue that it is not necessary to accumulate reserves only through borrowing on bond markets, which generally carries the highest cost, but that syndicated bank loans and in some cases also limited amounts of short-term borrowing can also be part of countries' borrowing strategies. For those emerging-market countries in which reserves fall short of the estimated minimum benchmark range, we believe that the cost of reaching an adequate level is reasonable. It can be viewed as an insurance premium to provide a degree of protection against financial crises. It is also emphasized, however, that in some cases countries may have a tendency to accumulate excessive reserves. Not only will this entail a considerable cost, but it could also lead to a laxity in macroeconomic policies in the future, as the external constraint is effectively removed.

Finally, we examine whether a large allocation of SDRs would be an appropriate response to a financial crisis of systemic proportions. A proposal to have larger countries, which would receive the bulk of an SDR allocation, deposit their share in a contagion facility that could be activated in times of severe crises is discussed. We conclude that such an approach merely shifts the source of moral hazard involved in large rescue packages but does not diminish it. A better response to a truly global financial crisis would be combining liquidity support from the IMF with that from the major central banks. In line with the principle of constructive ambiguity, and to minimize moral hazard, no rules should be spelled out in advance concerning such operations.

Appendix 4.1 Reserve Developments in Emerging-Market Countries

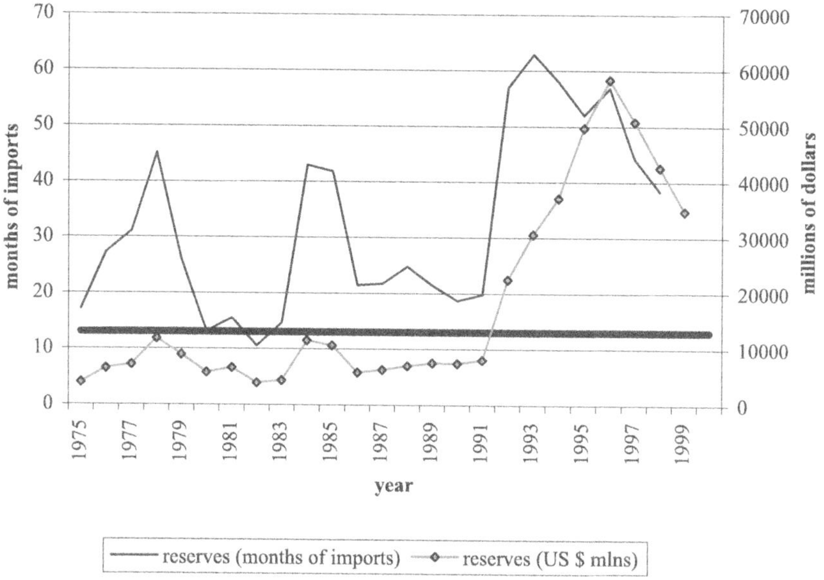

Figure A4.1
Brazil

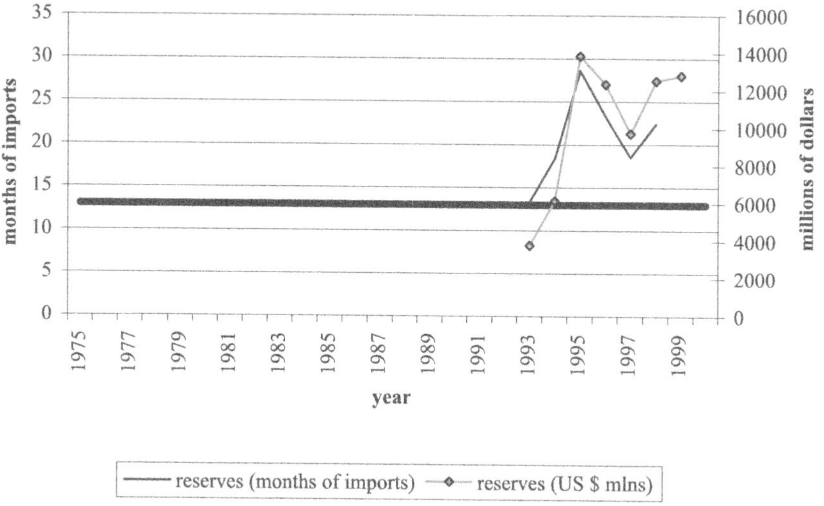

Figure A4.2
Czech Republic

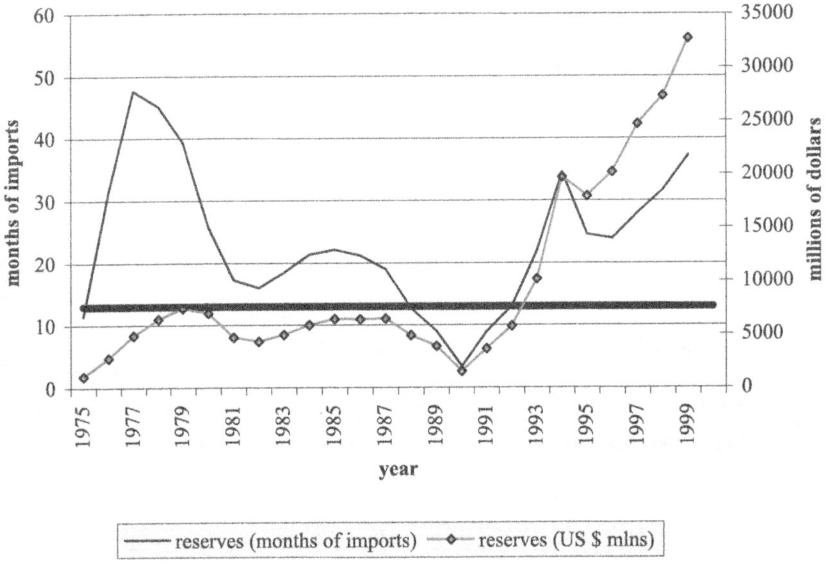

Figure A4.3
India

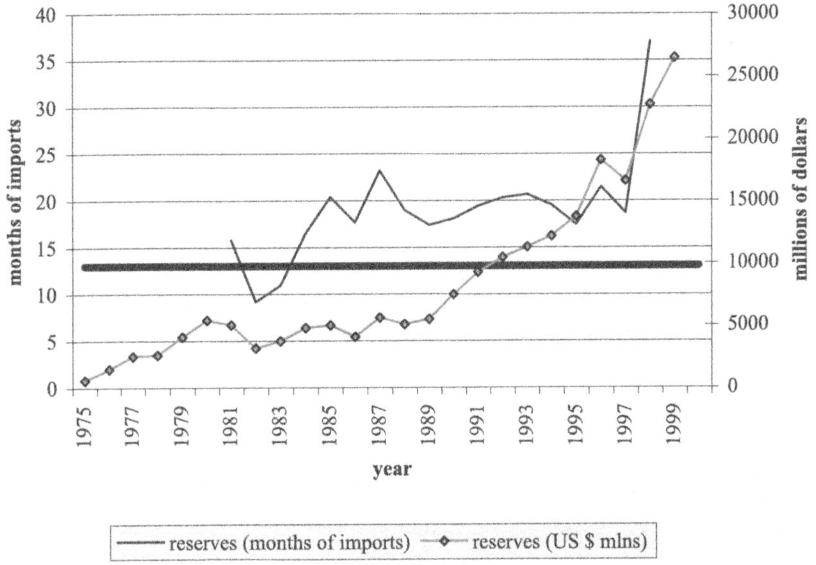

Figure A4.4
Indonesia

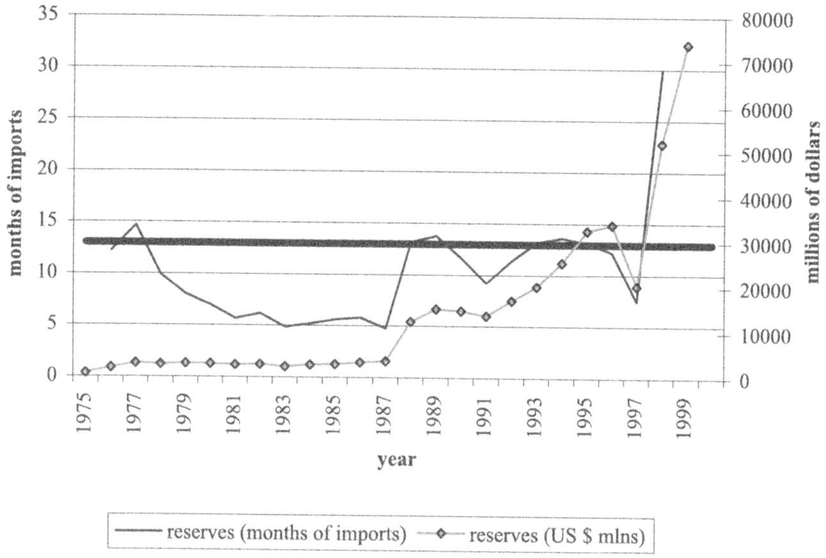

Figure A4.5
Korea

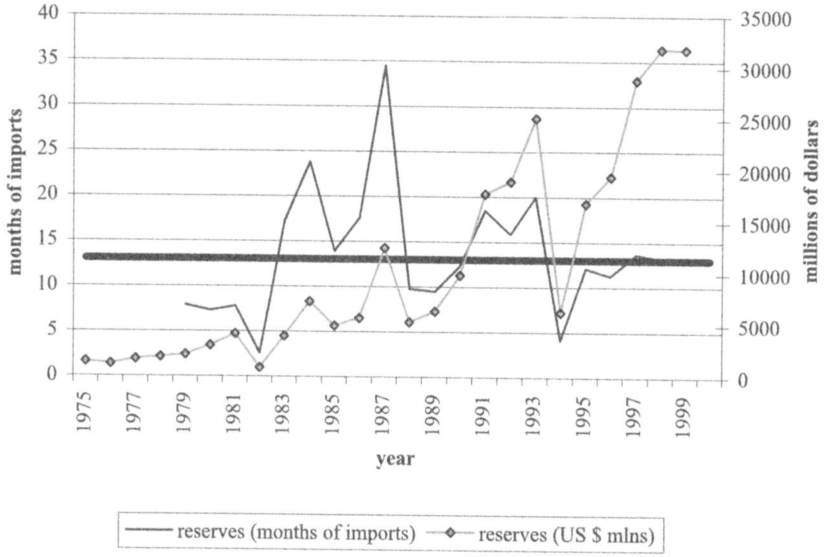

Figure A4.6
Mexico

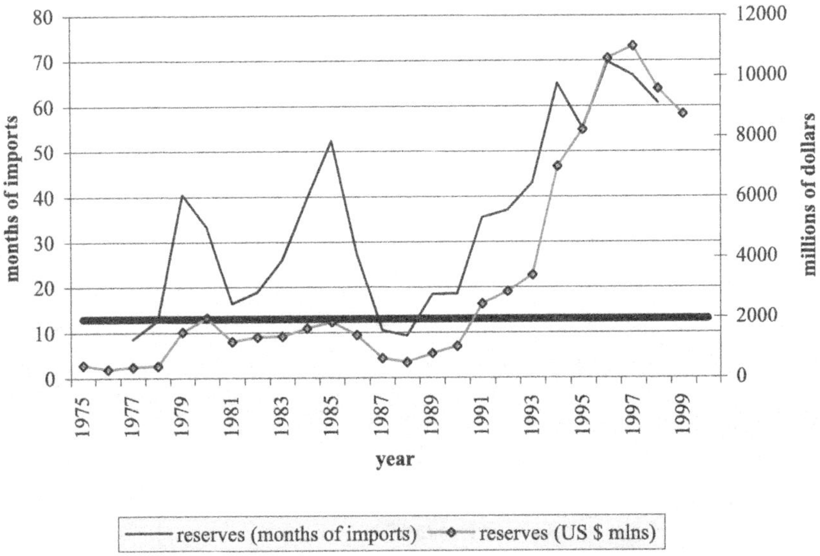

Figure A4.7
Peru

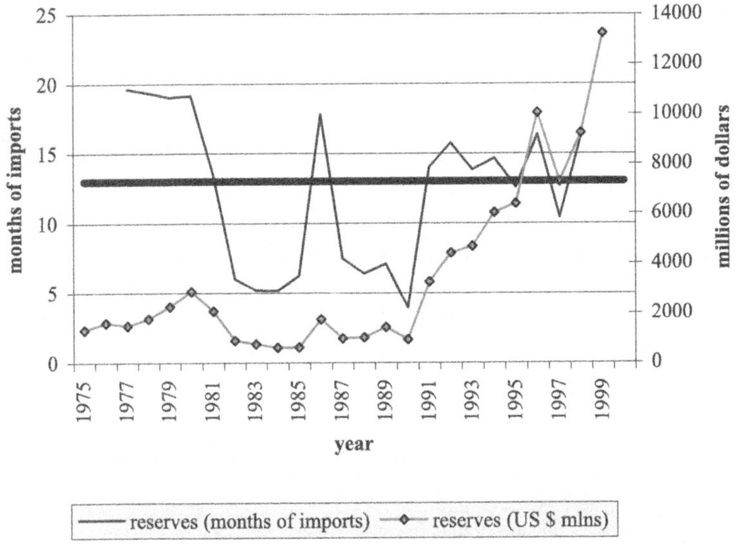

Figure A4.8
The Philippines

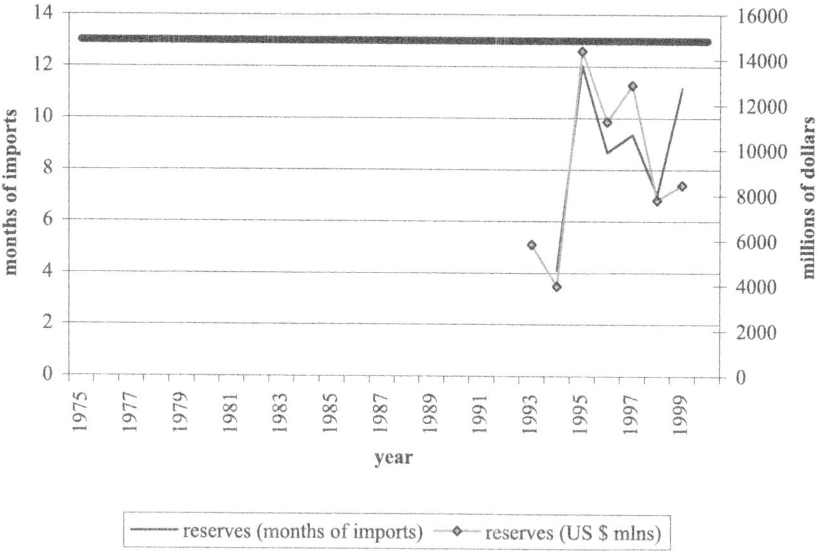

Figure A4.9
Russia

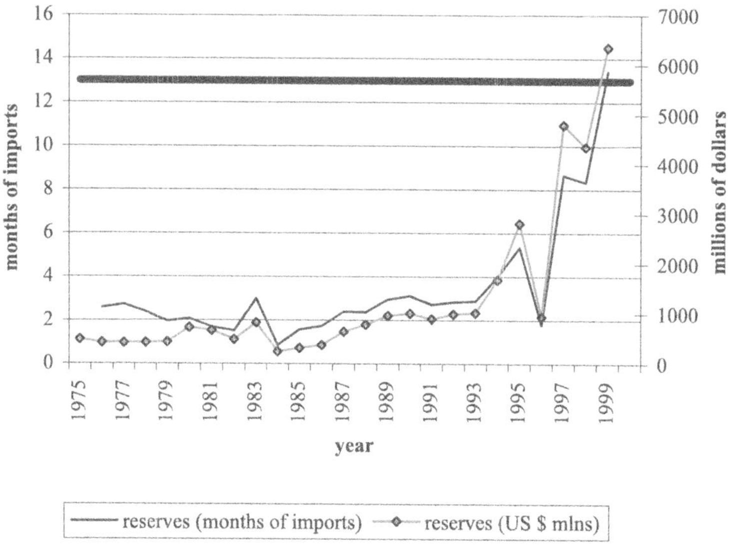

Figure A4.10
South Africa

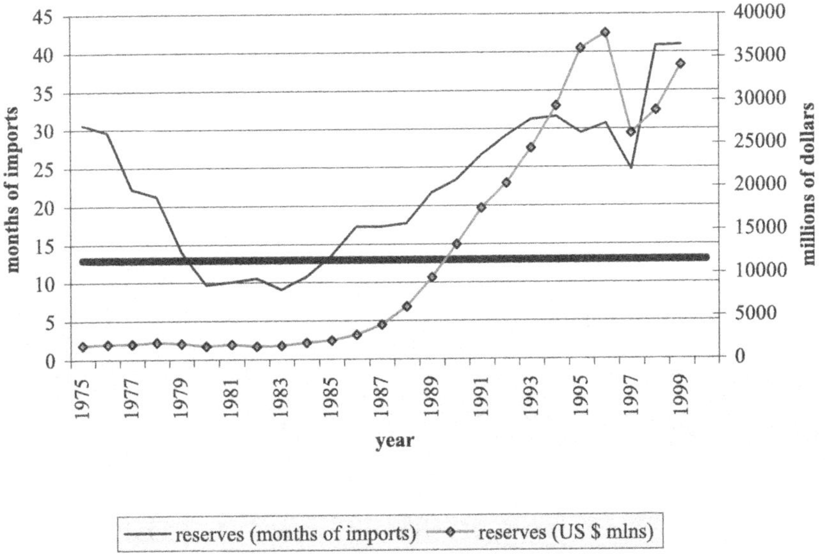

Figure A4.11
Thailand

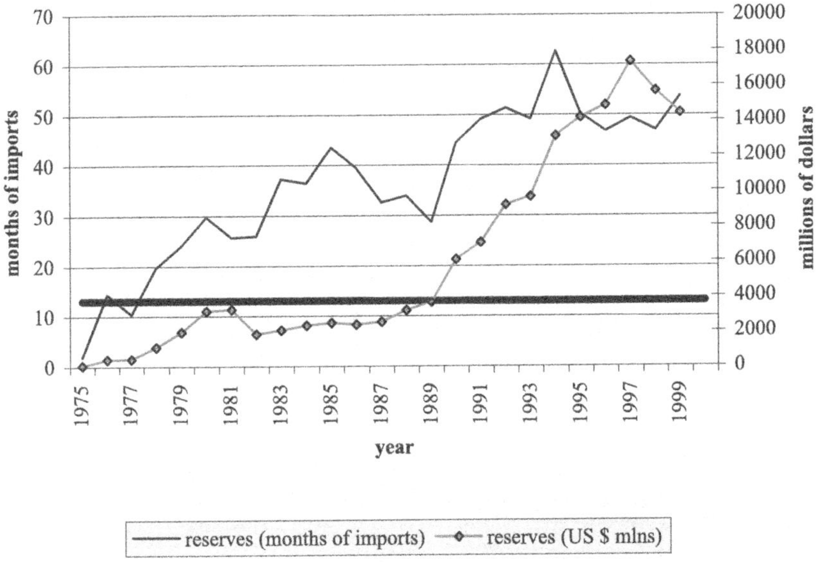

Figure A4.12
Chile

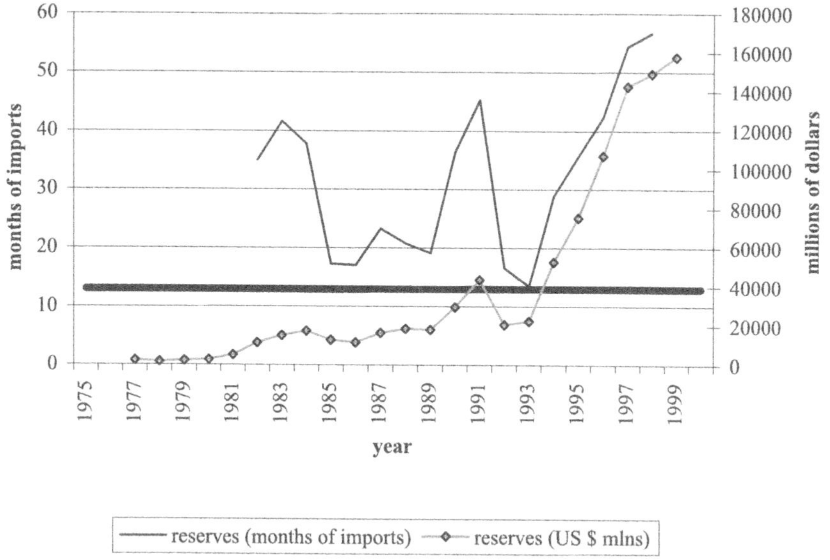

Figure A4.13
China

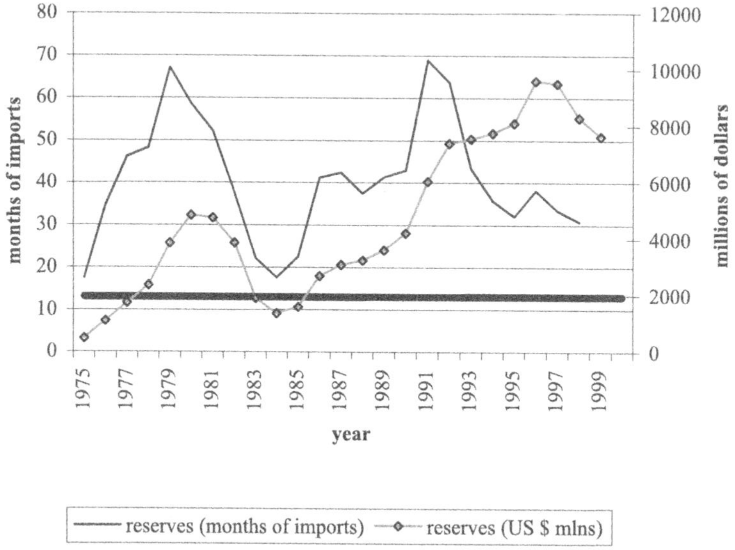

Figure A4.14
Colombia

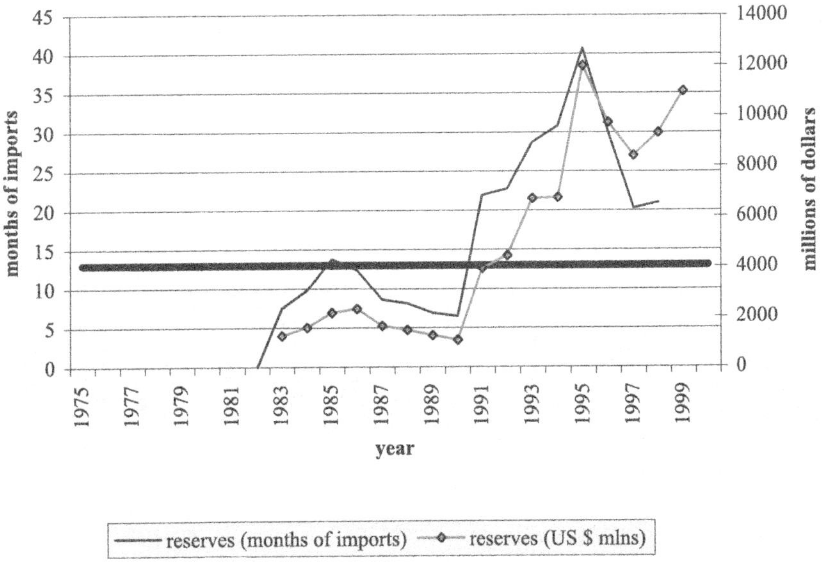

Figure A4.15
Hungary

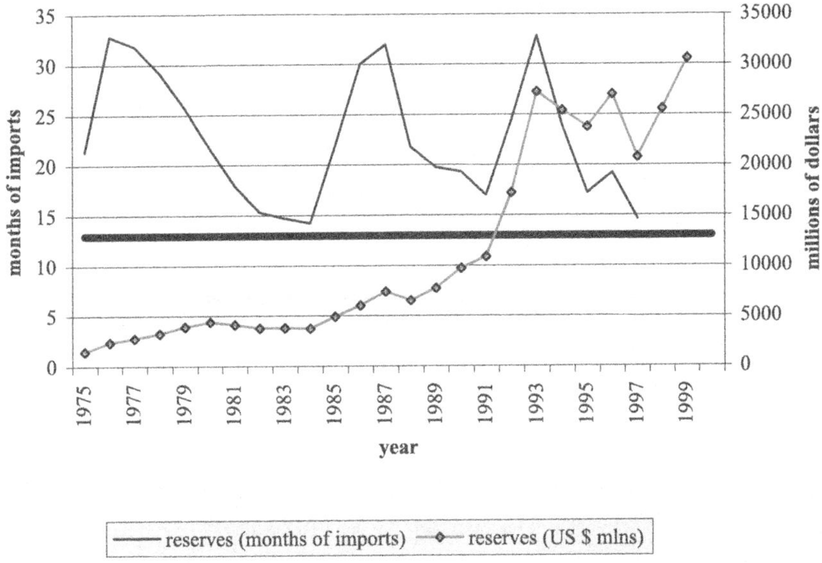

Figure A4.16
Malaysia

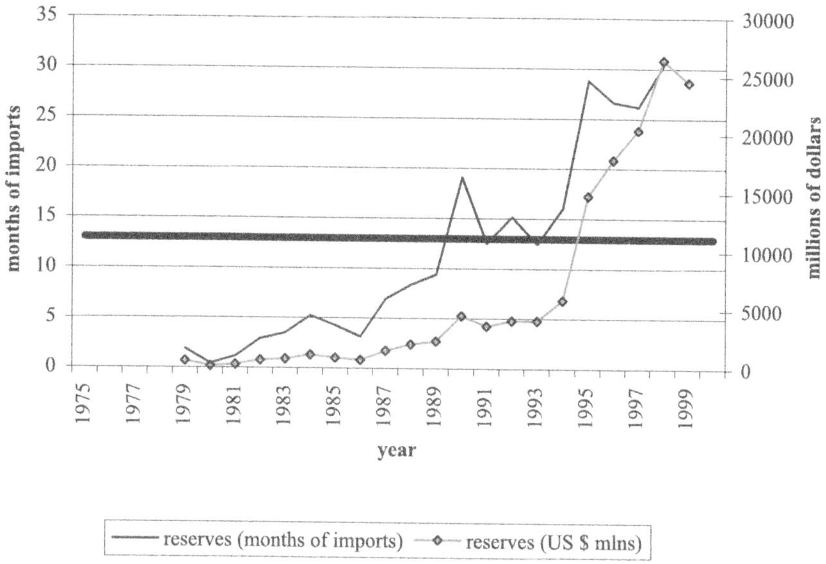

Figure A4.17
Poland

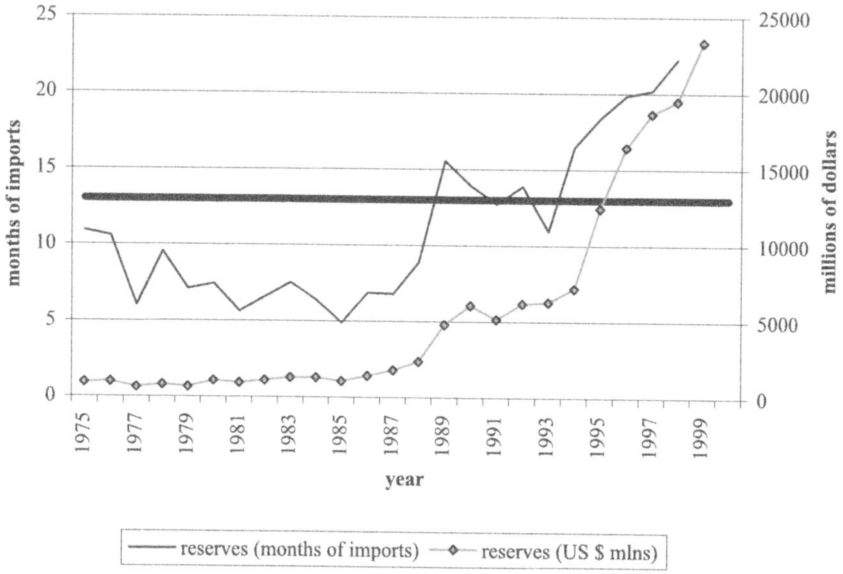

Figure A4.18
Turkey

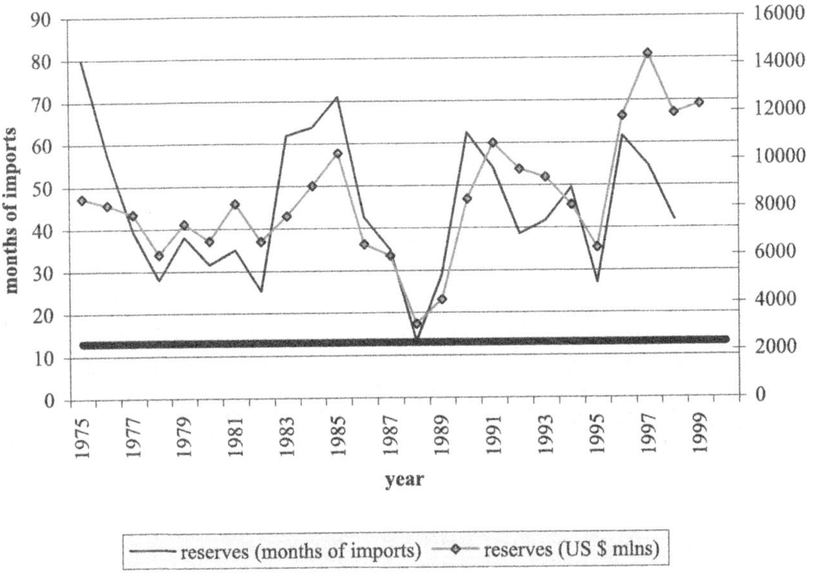

Figure A4.19
Venezuela

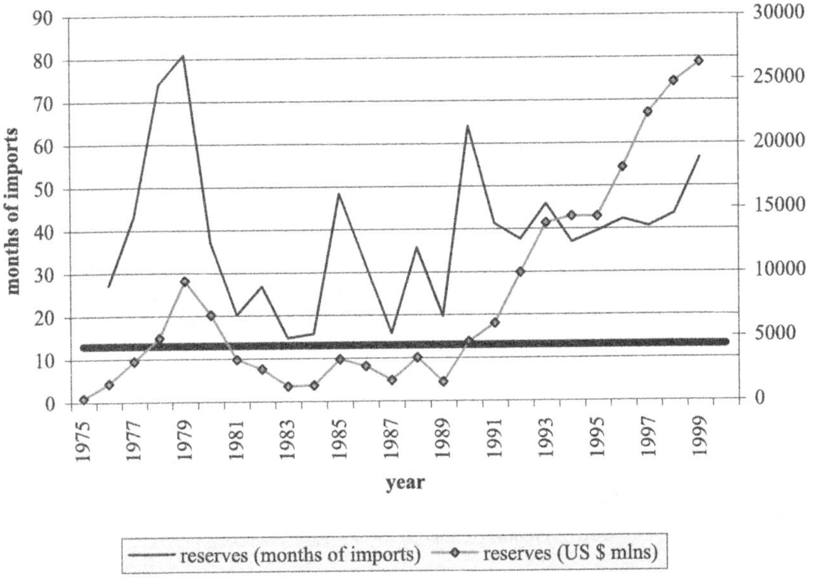

Figure A4.20
Argentina

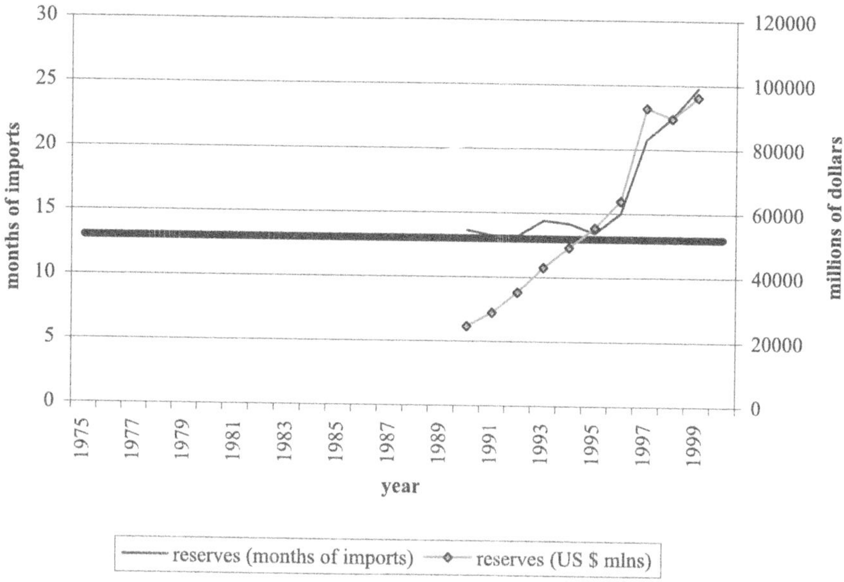

Figure A4.21
Hong Kong

Appendix 4.2 Reserves as a Percentage of Broad Money

Table A4.1
Reserves as a percentage of broad money

	1990	1991	1992	1993	1994	1995	1996	1997	1998	1999
Floating rates										
Brazil	5	5	6	4	11	25	29	24	20	24
Chile	34	30	31	27	31	26	24	25	22	20
Colombia	36	43	44	39	29	26	27	24	24	25
Czech Republic				16	21	36	30	26	31	29
India	1	3	4	7	12	10	11	12	12	12
Indonesia	18	19	18	17	15	14	15	14	40	32
Korea	15	12	14	14	15	16	15	10	28	22
Mexico	16	21	18	20	4	17	18	23	24	21
Peru	15	42	45	61	82	82	90	79	73	67
Philippines	7	26	29	26	26	22	30	20	33	37
Russia				19	10	30	20	20	17	29
South Africa	2	1	1	2	2	4	1	6	6	6
Thailand	18	20	20	20	21	21	20	17	23	21
Average	15	20	21	21	22	25	26	23	27	27
Pegged rates or bands										
China (mainland)	10	13	5	4	10	10	12	13	12	10
Hungary	7	21	20	31	31	55	44	39	44	40
Malaysia	23	21	26	33	27	21	19	15	25	27
Poland	22	15	14	13	17	34	35	38	42	37
Turkey	16	12	14	14	17	23	24	27	25	24
Venezuela	48	53	48	48	44	32	91	79	64	53
Average	21	22	21	24	24	29	38	35	35	32
Currency boards										
Argentina	31	30	32	28	26	27	28	27	28	25
Hong Kong		18	21	22	23	23	24	24	27	25
Average	31	24	26	25	24	25	26	26	27	25

Sources: IMF World Economic Outlook and International Financial Statistics.
Note: For the purpose of compiling the ratios, broad money was converted into U.S. dollars at the then-prevailing exchange rates.

Appendix 4.3 Reserves as a Percentage of Short-Term External Debt

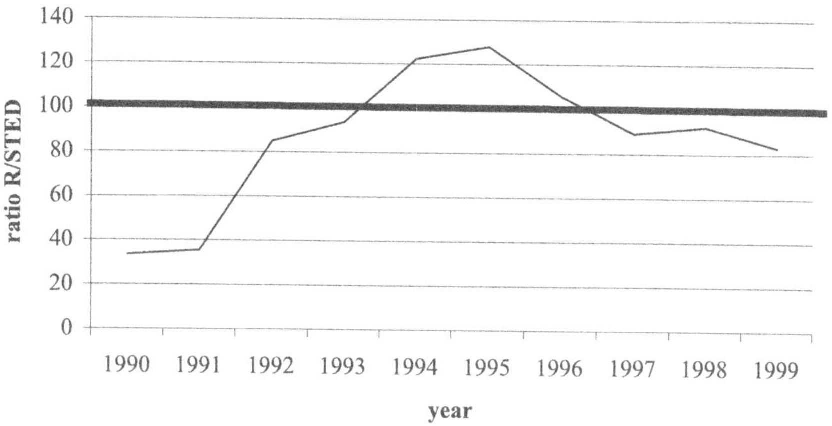

Figure A4.22
Brazil

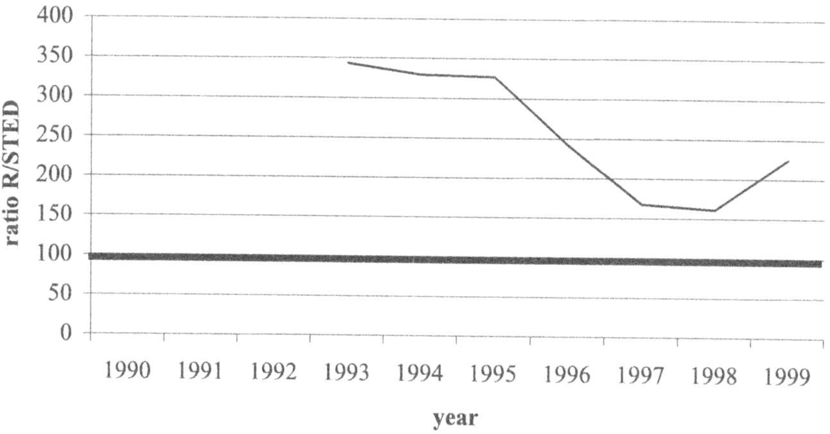

Figure A4.23
Czech Republic

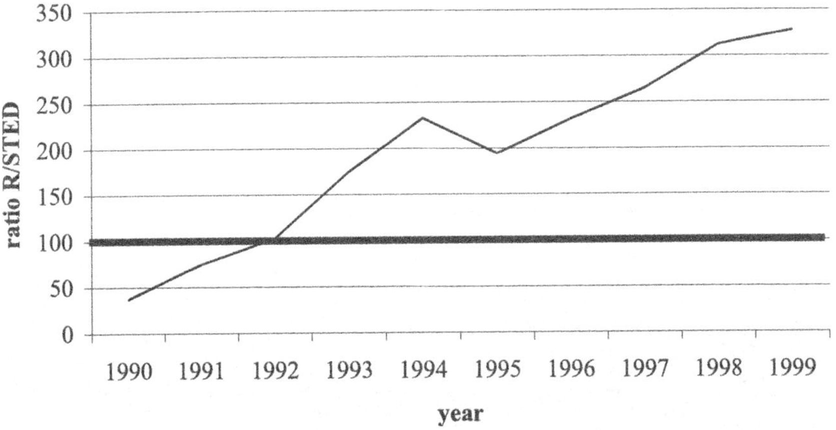

Figure A4.24
India

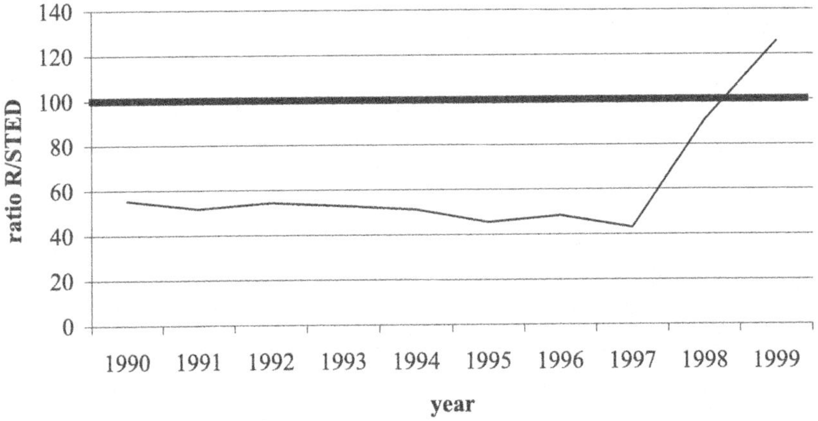

Figure A4.25
Indonesia

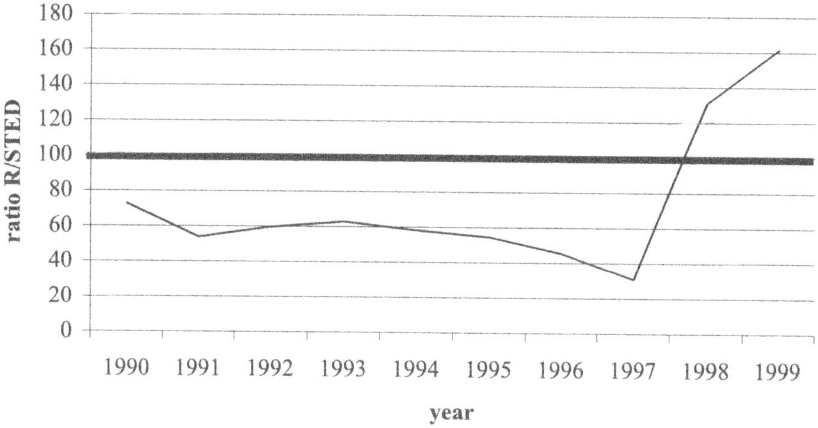

Figure A4.26
Korea

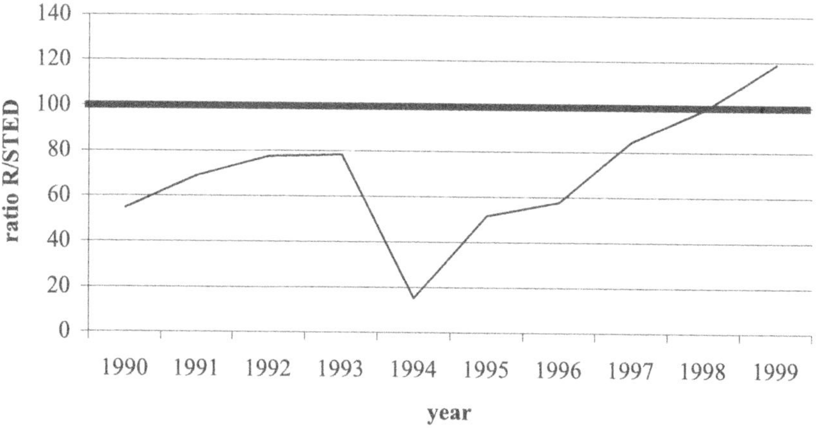

Figure A4.27
Mexico

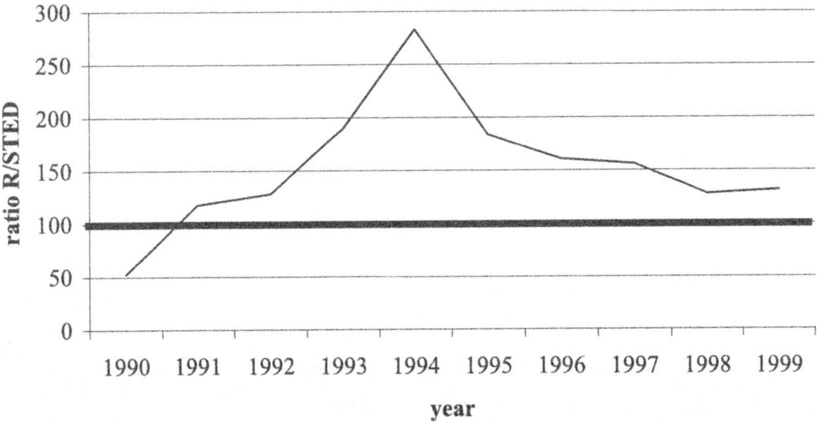

Figure A4.28
Peru

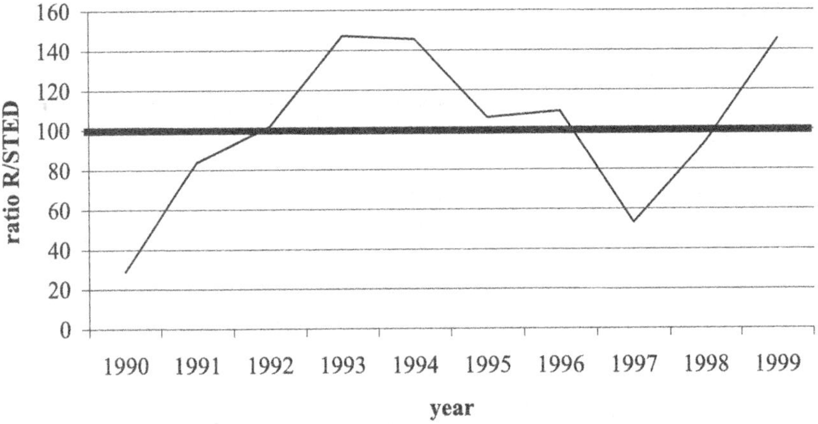

Figure A4.29
The Philippines

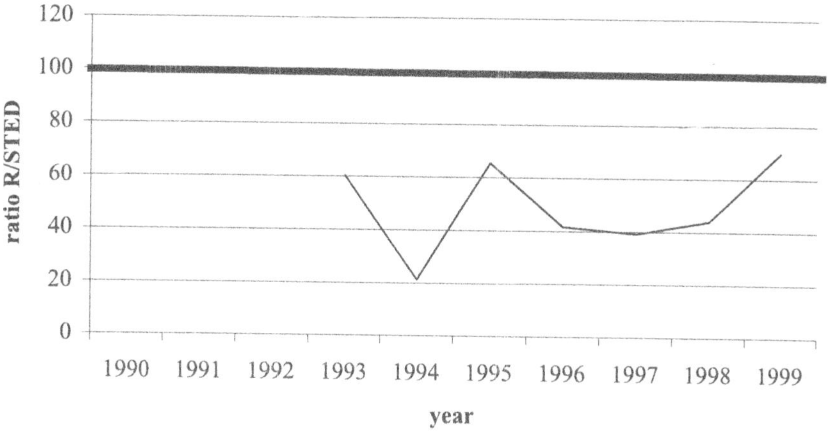

Figure A4.30
Russia

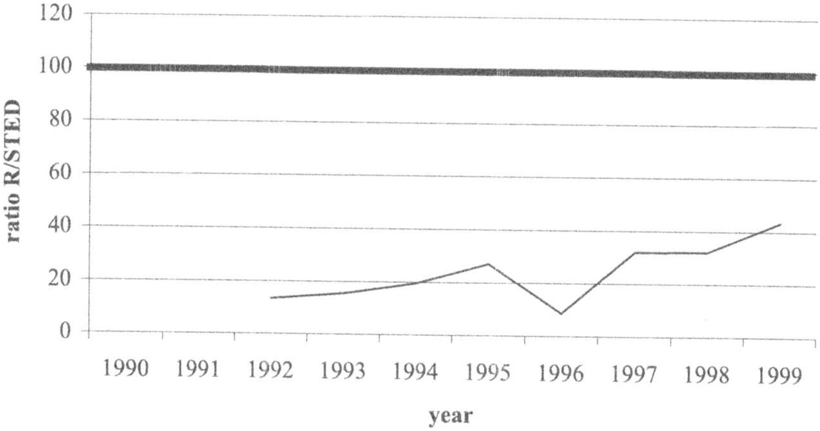

Figure A4.31
South Africa

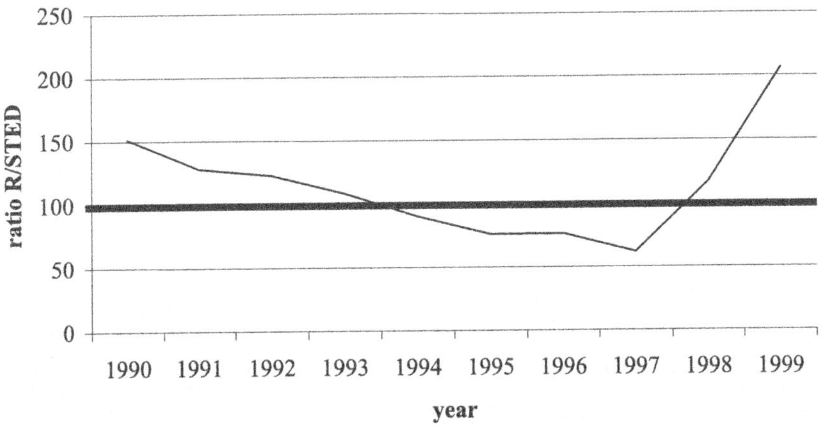

Figure A4.32
Thailand

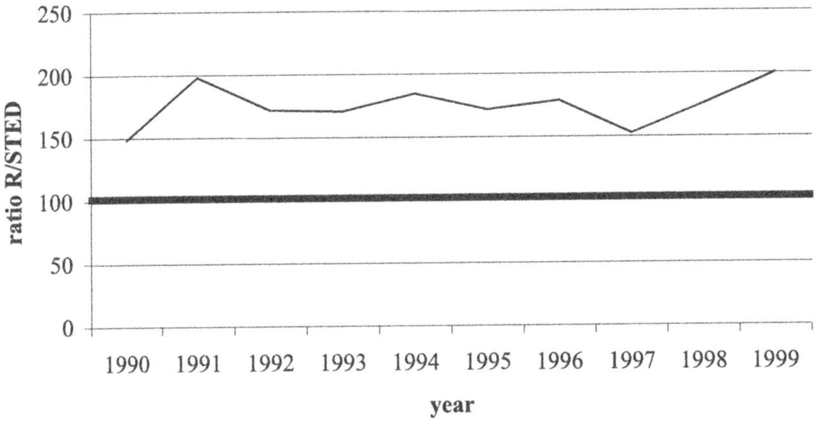

Figure A4.33
Chile

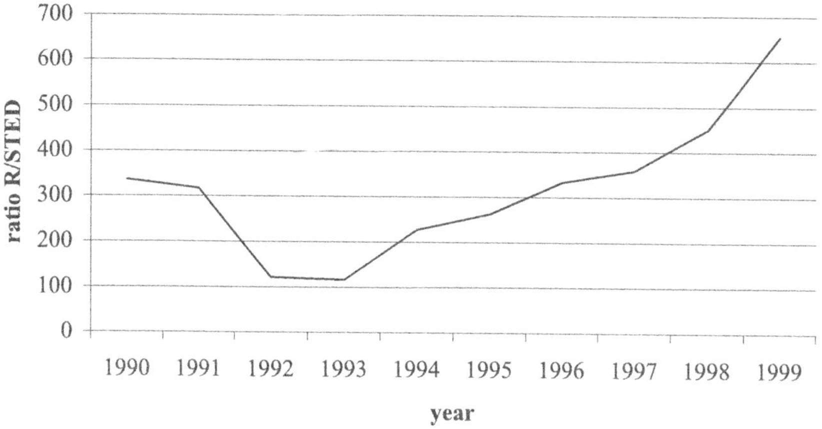

Figure A4.34
China (mainland)

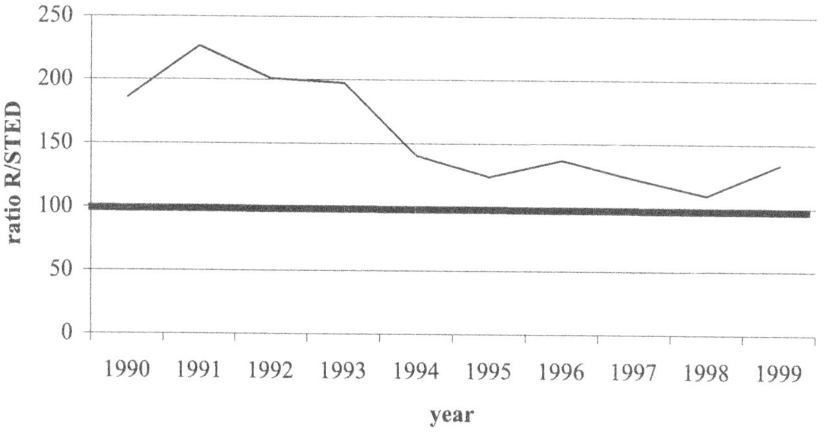

Figure A4.35
Colombia

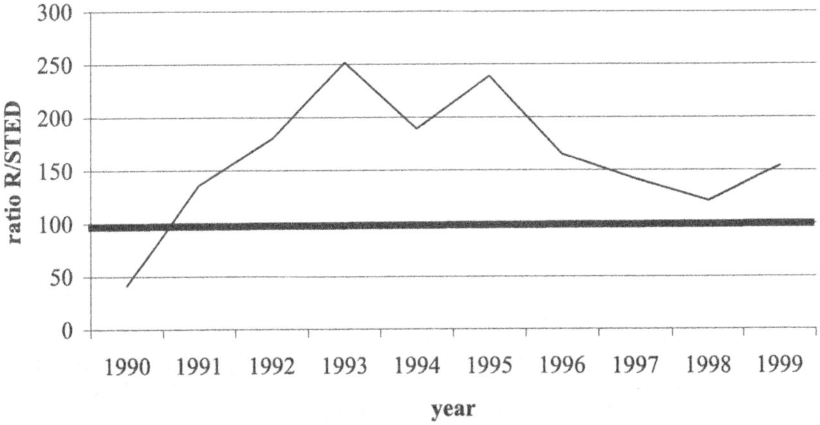

Figure A4.36
Hungary

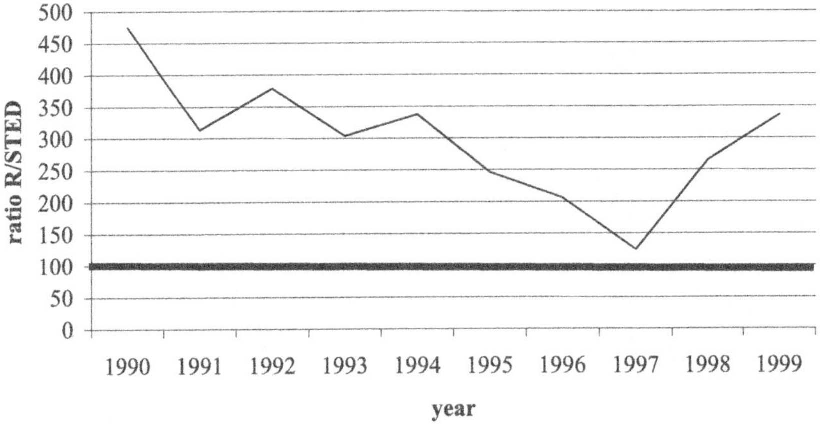

Figure A4.37
Malaysia

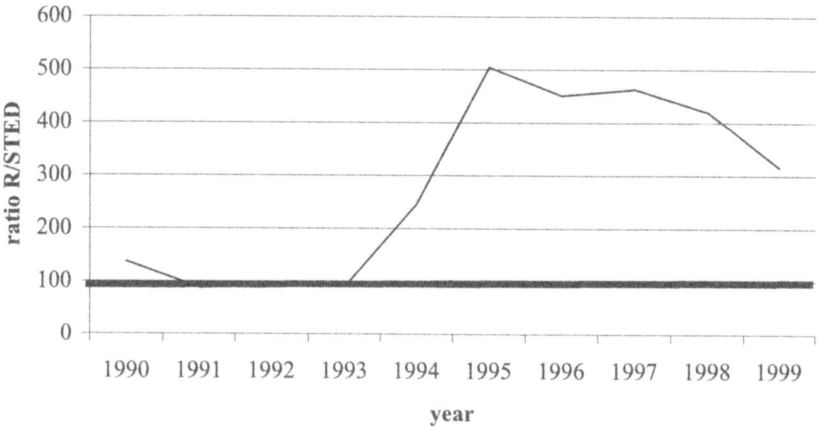

Figure A4.38
Poland

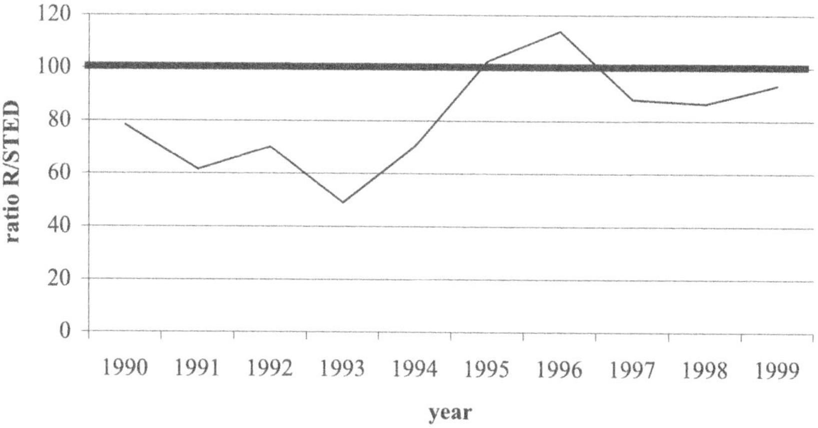

Figure A4.39
Turkey

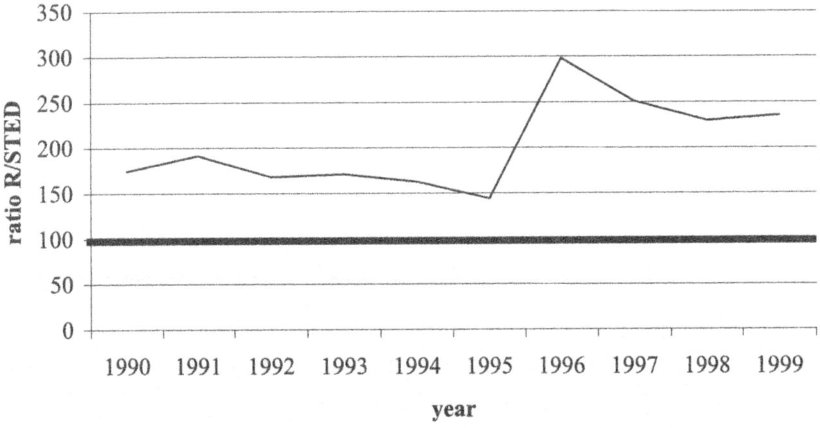

Figure A4.40
Venezuela

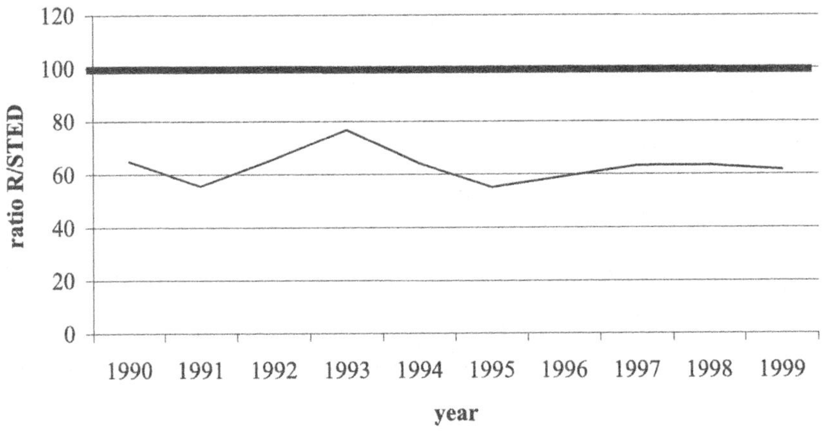

Figure A4.41
Argentina

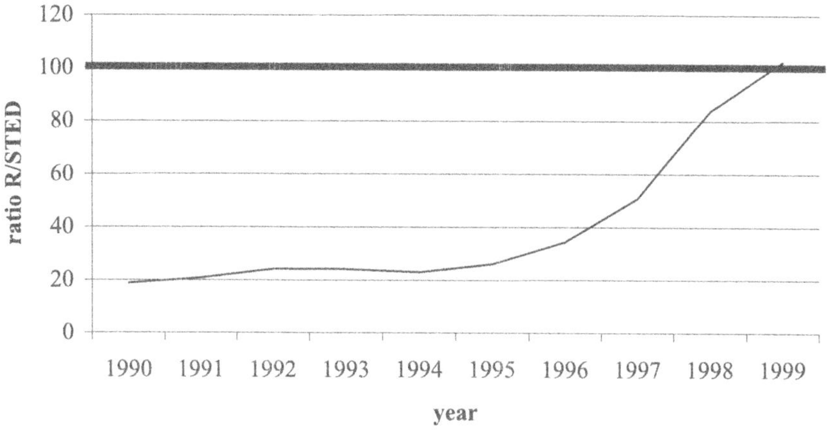

Figure A4.42
Hong Kong

Appendix 4.4 Capital Flight: What Proportion to Take of Broad Money?

Deciding which fraction of M2 to take as a buffer against domestic capital flight is fraught with difficulties. There are several reasons for this.

First, not all forms of capital flight constitute an internal drain in the sense that domestic currency is exchanged for foreign currency. That is, not all forms of capital flight affect M2 or official reserves. There are essentially three forms of capital flight: (1) the "internal drain," in which domestic currency assets are exchanged for foreign currency assets;[33] (2) the transfer abroad of foreign-currency assets that were foreign-currency assets to begin with; and (3) the nonrepatriation of profits earned abroad.[34] The latter two forms of capital flight do not involve an exchange of domestic currency and thus do not affect M2. Moreover, because the flight capital is already denominated in foreign currency, official reserves are also unaffected (other than that an increase in reserves is foregone because the flight capital stays abroad and is not transferred back to the home country).

Second, capital flight is not restricted to M2. Not all longer-term assets that are not part of M2 would be captured by taking a fraction of M2. Since such assets are less liquid, however, especially in nonindustrial countries, the probability that they will be utilized for capital flight is smaller than for broad money.

Third, there are significant problems in measuring capital flight. From a conceptual standpoint it is hard to distinguish "normal" capital outflows from those that are "abnormal" and thus constitute flight capital (see, for instance, Deppler and Williamson 1987, which defines capital flight as all outflows that are motivated by an attempt to avoid "large" losses; see also Eggerstedt, Brideau Hall, and Van Wijnbergen 1995). Dooley (1986), for instance, noted that capital flight need not even be embodied in a flow of capital but may occur when there is a shift in residents' motives for holding their stock of foreign assets. The difficulty involved in distinguishing capital flight from normal flows is reflected in the array of estimation techniques for capital flight. These range from a very narrow measure of net short-term outflows and "errors and omissions" in the balance of payments (Cuddington 1986) to a much broader measure of outflows of private financial assets, including direct and portfolio investments (World Bank 1985).[35]

Leaving aside these difficulties, it is nevertheless possible to establish a lower bound for a fraction of M2, which may be considered a minimum buffer against capital flight. For the lower bound, we elect simply to use the "errors and omissions" item in the balance of payments (following IMF 1998b and Abalkin and Whalley 1999). Note that this is an even narrower measure than that routinely used for "hot money" in the capital flight literature, to correct for the first two caveats raised in this appendix, namely, that not all capital flight affects M2, and that "errors and omissions" may of course also reflect true data shortcomings that are not necessarily indicative of capital flight. Table A4.2 shows the errors and omissions for our twenty-one emerging-market countries.[36] The table shows that in crisis years (e.g., Mexico in 1995, Asia in 1997–1998) the increase in errors and omissions was substantial and in the same direction as officially reported capital (out)flows, suggestive of unrecorded capital flows. In Korea, for instance, the errors and omissions jumped by roughly $5–6 billion in 1997–1998. China and Russia are unique in that they show consistently large and negative errors and omissions, in accordance with several studies of sustained capital flight in these countries (see Sicular 1998; Loukine 1998; and Abalkin and Whalley 1999).

Table A4.2
Errors and omissions in balance of payments (billions of dollars)

	1990	1991	1992	1993	1994	1995	1996	1997	1998	1999
Brazil	−0.30	0.85	−1.39	−0.81	−0.44	1.45	−1.99	−3.16	−2.91	
Chile	−0.05	0.39	0.37	−0.01	−0.56	0.13	−0.65	−0.44	−1.18	0.15
Colombia	0.07	0.19	0.19	−0.13	0.36	−0.07	−2.95	−3.13	−1.20	
Czech Republic				0.10	−0.21	0.60	−0.73	0.38	0.37	
India	−0.43	0.61	1.48	−0.99	1.49	0.97	−1.93	−1.35	1.39	1.08
Indonesia	0.74	0.09	−1.28	−2.93	−0.26	−2.25	1.32	−2.65	1.85	
Korea	−1.77	0.76	1.08	−0.72	−1.82	−1.24	1.09	−5.01	−6.36	
Mexico	1.23	−2.28	−0.85	−3.13	−3.32	−4.25	0.06	2.20	1.84	
Peru	−0.22	1.11	0.42	1.23	0.27	0.65	0.99	−0.31	0.42	
Philippines	0.59	−0.14	−0.52	0.09	0.16	−2.09	−2.99	−5.24	−0.97	
Russia					−0.27	−8.78	−5.74	−9.01	−8.97	−7.15
South Africa	−0.90	0.21	−1.18	−2.44	−0.45	−0.85	−2.36	−1.07	−1.98	0.36
Thailand	1.42	0.43	−0.14	−0.23	0.09	−1.20	−2.63	1.65	−2.82	−0.42
China (mainland)	−3.21	−6.77	−8.21	−10.10	−9.10	−17.82	−15.50	−16.82	−16.75	
Hungary	0.01	−0.08	0.00	0.72	0.21	1.30	1.86	0.30	0.25	
Malaysia	1.08	−0.15	0.08	3.62	0.15	−0.76	−2.12	−1.57		
Poland	0.16	−0.75	−0.18	0.22	−0.10	−0.56	0.32	1.31	−0.52	
Turkey	−0.47	0.95	−1.19	−2.22	1.77	2.36	−1.78	−2.59	−2.20	
Venezuela	−1.74	−1.52	−0.30	−0.54	−0.28	−0.49	−0.89	−1.46	−1.23	
Argentina	0.71	−0.34	0.05	−1.17	−0.87	−1.85	−1.32	−1.50	0.57	−1.05
Hong Kong	n.a.	n.a.	n.a.	n.a.	n.a.	n.a.	n.a.	n.a.	n.a.	n.a.

Source: IMF International Financial Statistics.
Note: n.a. = not available.

Table A4.3
Errors and omissions as a percentage of M2

	1990	1991	1992	1993	1994	1995	1996	1997	1998	1999
Brazil	−0.20	0.50	−0.39	−0.10	−0.14	0.74	−0.99	−1.48	−1.33	
Chile	−0.28	1.65	1.27	−0.04	−1.32	0.24	−1.06	−0.63	−1.68	0.20
Colombia	0.60	1.36	1.13	−0.70	1.34	−0.22	−8.30	−7.87	−3.43	
Czech Republic				0.39	−0.71	1.56	−1.79	1.00	0.91	
India	−0.30	0.46	1.09	−0.72	0.95	0.56	−1.03	−0.64	0.61	0.42
Indonesia	1.78	0.19	−2.21	−4.30	−0.33	−2.31	1.11	−2.16	3.25	
Korea	−1.82	0.66	0.88	−0.52	−1.10	−0.62	0.49	−2.34	−3.45	
Mexico	2.04	−2.64	−0.81	−2.53	−2.37	−4.26	0.06	1.76	1.42	
Peru	−3.12	19.28	6.54	22.01	3.13	6.52	8.43	−2.22	3.21	
Philippines	4.80	−1.09	−3.44	0.48	0.68	−7.07	−8.88	−14.49	−3.45	
Russia					−0.67	−18.14	−10.21	−13.94	−19.41	−25.14
South Africa	−1.44	0.31	−1.71	−3.78	−0.66	−1.10	−3.18	−1.32	−2.56	0.47
Thailand	1.89	0.49	−0.14	−0.19	0.06	−0.71	−1.41	1.07	−2.28	−0.30
China (mainland)	−1.04	−1.94	−1.86	−1.67	−1.67	−2.45	−1.69	−1.53	−1.33	
Hungary	0.06	−0.45	0.01	3.30	0.96	5.95	8.50	1.41	1.19	
Malaysia	2.54	−0.29	0.12	4.44	0.17	−0.66	−1.50	−1.10		
Poland	0.81	−3.02	−0.60	0.71	−0.29	−1.31	0.63	2.43	−0.82	
Turkey	−1.27	2.26	−2.64	−4.82	4.23	4.27	−2.64	−3.81	−2.84	
Venezuela	−10.05	−7.54	−1.51	−2.80	−1.53	−2.48	−6.90	−7.97	−6.60	
Argentina	4.85	−1.69	0.17	−2.40	−1.55	−3.45	−2.04	−1.83	0.64	−1.14
Hong Kong	n.a.	n.a.	n.a.	n.a.	n.a.	n.a.	n.a.	n.a.	n.a.	n.a.

Source: IMF International Financial Statistics.
Note: n.a. = not available.

Table A4.3 expresses errors and omissions as a fraction of M2. It shows that in Asian countries most affected by the recent financial crisis, for instance, the fraction of this narrow capital flight proxy ranged from roughly 1 percent of M2 for Malaysia (perhaps due to capital controls) to over 14 percent of M2 for the Philippines. Although our 5–20 percent fraction of M2 as a capital flight reserve buffer is an arbitrary one, it seems to be in the range of errors and omission outliers (i.e., the crisis/capital flight years) for most countries, taking into account that errors and omissions probably constitute an absolute minimum estimate of capital flight.

Finally, and alternatively, one could simply look at the degree of variation in the behavior of the R/M2 ratio (see table A4.4). It can be seen from table A4.5 that the 5–10 percent fraction of M2 for countries with floating exchange rates is roughly equal to the average standard deviation for this group of countries, with Peru being the outlier. That is, the average standard deviation (7) is equal to the midpoint in the range; eight out of thirteen floating-rate countries have a standard deviation that falls within that range. Brazil and South Africa show particularly high coefficients of variation. Interestingly, the average standard deviation for countries with a pegged exchange rate regime (10) is only marginally higher and lies at the lower end of the 10–20 percent fraction for countries with pegged exchange rates. The upper bound of that range is equal to twice the average standard deviation. Half of the countries with a fixed exchange rate have a standard deviation that falls within the range. Contrary to the group of floating exchange rate countries, however, where Peru by itself pulls up the average, there are three countries (Hungary, Poland, Venezuela) with a standard deviation (substantially) above the average. These are also the countries with the largest coefficient of variation, although that of China is also high.

Table A4.4
Reserves as a percentage of broad money: Summary statistics (1990–1999)

	Average 1990–1999	Standard deviation	Coefficient of variation
Floating rates			
Brazil	15	10	65
Chile	27	4	16
Colombia	32	8	25
Czech Republic	27	7	26
India	9	4	51
Indonesia	20	9	43
Korea	16	5	33
Mexico	18	6	30
Peru	64	23	37
Philippines	26	8	31
Russia	21	7	34
South Africa	3	2	67
Thailand	20	2	9
Average	23	7	36
Pegged rates or bands			
China (mainland)	10	3	32
Hungary	33	14	43
Malaysia	24	5	22
Poland	27	12	43
Turkey	20	6	29
Venezuela	56	18	31
Average	28	10	33
Currency boards			
Argentina	28	2	8
Hong Kong	23	3	11
Average	26	2	10

Source: Calculations with data from IMF International Financial Statistics.

Appendix 4.5 Current Account Deficit Minus FDI

Table A4.5
Current account deficit minus FDI

	1990	1991	1992	1993	1994	1995	1996	1997	1998	1999
Floating rates										
Brazil	2834	347	−8150	−1312	−1919	13277	12048	10841	1916	
Chile	−177	−723	23	1520	−998	−1607	−1124	−1491	−499	−9141
Colombia	−1042	−2806	−1629	1143	2151	3655	1716	315	2385	
Czech Republic				−1121	−58	−1194	2864	1984	−1346	
India	7037	4218	4209	1325	703	3420	3530	−612	4268	1609
Indonesia	1895	2778	1003	102	683	2085	1469	212	−3740	
Korea	1215	7138	3215	−1578	3057	6731	20680	5323	−45973	
Mexico	4902	10146	20049	19011	18690	−7950	−6858	−5377	5722	
Peru	1343	1565	1980	1657	−417	2314	417	1497	1870	
Philippines	2162	490	772	1778	1359	502	2436	3129	−3000	
Russia					−9486	−10042	−14928	−10180	−3798	−27885
South Africa	−1977	−2514	−1970	−1513	−488	956	1064	−1538	1385	−912
Thailand	4838	5557	4190	4559	6719	11486	12356	−723	−20989	−16768
Pegged rates or bands										
China (mainland)	−15484	−17638	−17557	−15906	−40695	−37468	−47423	−73954	−73076	
Hungary	−379	−1865	−1831	1913	2909	−1983	−294	−1097	368	
Malaysia	−1463	184	−3016	−2015	178	4291	−482	−314		
Poland	−3156	1855	2426	4073	−2829	−4513	−1234	836	536	
Turkey	1941	−1060	130	5797	−3239	1453	1715	1874	−2811	
Venezuela	−8730	−3652	3120	1621	−3354	−2999	−11097	−9003	−1873	
Currency boards										
Argentina	−6388	−1792	1137	5267	7502	−330	−1	3199	7748	−11000
Hong Kong	n.a.	n.a.	n.a.	n.a.	n.a.	n.a.	n.a.	n.a.	n.a.	n.a.

Source: IMF International Financial Statistics.
Note: A minus sign means that FDI more than covers the current account deficit or that the current account is in surplus. n.a. = not available.

Notes

This chapter was prepared as a paper for the Dubrovnik Economic Conference, June 29 and 30, 2000. The authors wish to thank Age Bakker, Augustin Carstens, Riccardo Faini, Stanley Fischer, Ron Keller, Christian Mulder, Jacques Polak, and Alexander Swoboda for their comments on an earlier draft. The usual disclaimer applies.

1. See the IMF Web site ⟨http://www.imf.org/external/⟩ for a comprehensive overview of the various reforms being undertaken. For two interesting non-IMF contributions to the debate see Independent Task Force 1999 and De Gregorio et al. 1999.

2. Total gross (residual) financing need under an IMF arrangement during the program period is defined as the sum of the current account deficit, amortization payments on medium- and long-term debt (including Fund repurchases), targeted reduction of arrears, and targeted accumulation of gross reserves. The financing need is of course not determined autonomously but depends, most importantly, on the strength of the adjustment effort (economic policy) and the external macroeconomic environment.

3. There is, to our knowledge, no clear theoretical or empirical basis for the rule of thumb.

4. Absent such rescheduling of spontaneous capital inflows, reserves would fall below the floor, and the country would be in violation of the performance criteria set under the program. The program would then be off track, and IMF financing would, in principle, be stopped.

5. See Williamson 1973, which provides an extensive survey of the postwar literature on international liquidity. See also de Beaufort Wijnholds 1977.

6. In 1953, Fund staff defined adequacy in terms of different degrees of exchange restrictions that a country would be required to introduce. It was also noted that the prevalent opinion of the international business community itself is a factor in determining the "real" adequacy of reserves. In other words, the reserves of a country are not adequate until the public thinks that they are adequate. This reasoning seems to have very much driven the size of the financial packages to some of the emerging-market countries in recent years.

7. This probability was estimated as the mean absolute first-difference of historical trend-adjusted annual reserves, and presumed independent of reserves. Later work by, among others, Frenkel and Jovanovich (1981) linked the probability of reserve depletion explicitly to the level of reserves.

8. Several methods have been used to estimate this variable, such as the mean absolute first-difference of the trend-adjusted par values of reserves, the standard deviation of these values, and the variance or standard deviation of the residuals obtained from estimating a first-order autoregressive process for the change in reserves.

9. The IMF in 1953 had noted that "in a world in which uncertainty is a major factor..., reserves must be considerably larger than would be indicated by any reasonable evaluation of the probabilities of actual use" (338).

10. See Eichengreen and Frankel 1996. Eichengreen and Frankel note that if dollar, yen, or deutsche mark liabilities ever become so great in relation to gold or other international reserves held by the issuing country (or the exports, GDP, or net inter-

national investment position) as to bring their value into question, central banks could simply switch to the currencies of new rising countries in which they have confidence. Moreover, capital mobility now increasingly allows central banks (of creditworthy countries) to obtain reserves from private markets, not just other central banks, and increased exchange rate flexibility, as an instrument of adjustment, supplements balance-of-payments financing. As such the Triffin dilemma no longer exists.

11. Guidotti made this suggestion at a seminar of the Group of 33 in Bonn in the spring of 1999. The notion of strengthening liquidity management, however, and specifically, of developing a best-practice standard for maintaining reserves plus credit lines in some proportion to short-term external debt, had already been discussed by policymakers well before that. To our knowledge, the first formal discussion on the topic was on December 7, 1997 (three days after the IMF Executive Board approved the standby arrangement for Korea), at a meeting of central bank governors at the Bank for International Settlements.

12. See de Beaufort Wijnholds 1974 for an early statement on this matter. The past twenty-five years have served only to strengthen this point. Recently, Mussa et al. (2000) have explained that a freely floating exchange rate can be especially problematic for developing countries given the lack of depth of their foreign exchange markets.

13. The IMF (1999b) has developed a capital control index illustrating the degree of restrictiveness for both developed and developing countries. Although capital restrictions are still prevalent in many countries, they are decreasing. Moreover, as a group, emerging markets are relatively homogenous (reflecting the correlation between the level of development and the degree of control).

14. At the margin, the IMF, as a mutual insurance fund consisting of the pooled reserves of its membership, of course generates some moral hazard, akin to any other form of insurance.

15. Canada has private contingent credit lines with both domestic banks ($1 billion) and foreign banks ($6 billion). See the Web site of the Canadian Ministry of Finance or the IMF's Web site (on the special data dissemination standard).

16. The IMF now categorizes two of the countries included as advanced economies (Korea, Hong Kong). In view of their large appetite for foreign capital and their vulnerability to crises, however, we consider them still to be emerging-market economies, though no longer developing economies, in which group the IMF categorizes all the other countries included in our exercise.

17. China's reserves ($158 billion) at the end of 1999 were the second largest in the world after those of Japan ($287 billion). It is striking to observe that Hong Kong ($96 billion) and Taiwan ($90 billion) also held very high reserves Singapore has also accumulated very high reserves ($77 billion), especially viewed against the size of its economy.

18. The largest holder of official gold among these countries at the end of 1999 was Russia (13.3 million ounces, or roughly $3.6 billion at current market price), followed by China (12.7 million ounces) and India (11.5 million ounces). South Africa held only 3.9 million ounces of gold in its official reserves.

19. For an overview of the EWS literature, see Kaminsky, Lizondo and Reinhart 1997 and Berg et al. 1999.

20. It should be noted that other studies, such as Bussière and Mulder 1999, did not find R/M2 to be significant (or to have the correct sign).

21. Similarly, a range of other adjustments could be made to the reserves and debt figures in assessing the liquidity of the national balance sheet. For instance, for oil-exporting countries, such as Mexico and Venezuela, one can be relatively certain about a minimum level of foreign exchange income, although such "near reserves" are still not as liquid as the foreign exchange reserves held by the central bank. Nevertheless, it is worth noting that a country's assets are broader than just its foreign exchange reserves. On the liability side, one could decide that trade-related credits need to be deducted from STED, as these have proven relatively stable in some recent crises. Conversely, however, it would also seem appropriate to add derivatives exposure and domestically issued debt held by nonresidents, as these are not covered by the BIS/IMF/OECD/World Bank debt statistics.

22. The extent to which its use of capital controls played a role is more difficult to assess.

23. It is sometimes suggested that the amount of the current account deficit be added to STED. This would seem necessary, however, only to the extent that the deficit exceeds net foreign direct investment. In quite a number of emerging-market countries, such investment covers a large part or all of the current account deficit. Appendix 4.5 shows the balance of these two items for emerging-market countries between 1990 and 1999.

24. The index also incorporates a short-term debt measure and the level of R/M2, leading to some endogeneity. Given the multitude of other variables, however, the effect of this endogeneity should be negligible.

25. Kletzer and Mody (2000) take a more negative view, stating that "short-term public borrowing to accumulate foreign reserves is at best costless and useless" (17).

26. For reserve accumulation resulting from attempts to sterilize capital inflows, the cost for Latin American countries for the post-1985 period have been estimated at between 0.25 and 0.5 percent of GDP (see Khan and Reinhart 1994). A similar result was obtained by Kletzer and Spiegel (1998) for Pacific Basin countries.

27. In several countries where governments have accumulated very large holdings of foreign exchange, these are usually not held as part of the official reserves but are instead placed in special government funds that invest in higher-yielding nonliquid assets. Well-known examples are the Kuwait Investment Authority and Norway's State Petroleum Fund.

28. The charges under the Fund's regular stand-by credits are presently a little over 5 percent. For countries using the Supplemental Reserve Facility, between 300 and 500 basis points are added.

29. The previous managing director of the IMF, Michel Camdessus (2000), advocated a similar approach at the end of his term at the Fund.

30. Opinions differ on whether the Tequila crisis of 1995, the Asian financial crisis of 1998, and the Russian collapse of 1998, along with the associated contagion, were truly systemic in nature.

31. The Task Force does make the point that while SDR allocations do not require authorization or appropriation from the US Congress, extensive consultations with the Congress would be needed.

32. As suggested by Jacques J. Polak in an internal memo. We have argued elsewhere (de Beaufort Wijnholds and Kapteyn 2000) that it is undesirable to have the IMF function as a full-fledged international lender of last resort.

33. This would include overinvoicing of imports in that one "pays" for the artificially higher reported imports (affecting both M2 and reserves). Conceptually it is useful to also categorize foreign-currency deposits as part of the internal drain, as they are part of domestic broad money and their withdrawal would affect reserves.

34. This would include underinvoicing of exports. The nonreported export revenues would presumably be denominated in foreign currency and thus not need to be exchanged (i.e., they would not constitute flight out of M2 into reserves).

35. Dooley (1986) has proposed a "derived" measure for measuring capital flight that avoids these conceptual and inherently normative problems. It measures capital flight as that part of a country's stock of foreign assets that does not yield a recorded inflow of investment of income credits, under the presumption that only the retention of investment income abroad is indicative of flight concerns. Deppler and Williamson (1987) have suggested that Dooley's derived measure could also be used to establish a lower bound for capital flight, as it likely excludes many "normal" flows. They note, however, that it is sensitive to the accuracy of balance-of-payments statistics on investment income credits, the choice of the interest rate used to capitalize the investment income credits, and the assumption that all assets yield a market rate of return. For this reason, we do not use the measure. (See Claessens and Naudé 1993 for a discussion of the main estimation methods of capital flight.)

36. It should be noted that there are large differences among regions in the proportion of wealth held abroad. Collier, Hoeffler, and Patillo (1999) note that East Asia holds only 6 percent of its wealth abroad, compared to 40 percent for Africa.

References

Abalkin, A., and J. Whalley. (1999). The Problem of Capital Flight from Russia. *World Economy* 22 (May): 421–44.

Berg, Andrew, Eduardo Borensztein, Gian Maria Milesi-Ferretti, and Catherine Patillo. (1999). Anticipating Balance of Payments Crises: The Role of Early Warning Systems. Occasional paper no. 186, International Monetary Fund, Washington, D.C.

Bussière, Matthíeu, and Christian Mulder. (1999). External Vulnerability in Emerging Market Economies: How High Liquidity Can Offset Weak Fundamentals and the Effects of Contagion. Working paper no. WP/99/88, International Monetary Fund, Washington, D.C.

Calvo, Guillermo. (1996). Capital Flows and Macroeconomic Management: Tequila Lessons. *International Journal of Finance and Economics* 3, no. 2 (July): 625–636.

Camdessus, Michel. (2000). The IMF We Need. Remarks by managing director of IMF at Institute for the Study of Diplomacy, School of Foreign Service, Georgetown University, Washington D.C., February 2.

Claessens, Stijn, and David Naudé. (1993). Recent Estimates of Capital Flight. Policy research working paper series no. 1186, World Bank, Washington, D.C.

Collier, Paul, Anke Hoeffler, and Catherine Patillo. (1999). Flight Capital as a Portfolio Choice. Working paper no. WP/99/171, International Monetary Fund, Washington, D.C.

Cooper, R. N. (1968). The Relevance of International Liquidity to Developed Countries. *American Economic Review* 58, no. 2 (May): 625–636.

Cuddington, John T. (1986). *Capital Flight: Estimates, Issues and Explanations*. Princeton Studies in International Finance, no. 58. Princeton: Princeton University Press.

De Beaufort Wijnholds, J. A. H. (1974). The Need for Reserves under Full and Limited Flexibility of Exchange Rates. *Economist* 122, no. 3: 225–243.

De Beaufort Wijnholds, J. A. H. (1977). *The Need for International Reserves and Credit Facilities*. Leiden, the Netherlands: Martinus Nijhoff.

De Beaufort Wijnholds, J. A. H., and A. Kapteyn. (2000). The IMF: Lender of Last Resort or Indispensable Lender. In Ian Vasquez (ed.), *Global Fortune; The Stumble and Rise of World Capitalism*, 225–239. Washington, D.C.: Cato Institute.

De Gregorio, Jose, Barry Eichengreen, Takatoshi Ito, and Charles Wyplosz. (1999). *An Independent and Accountable IMF*. Geneva Reports on the World Economy, no. 1. Geneva: International Center for Monetary and Banking Studies/Center for Economic Policy Research.

Deppler, Michael, and Martin Williamson. (1987). Capital Flight: Concepts, Measurement and Issues. In Research Department of the IMF, *Staff Studies for the World Economic Outlook*, 35–58. Washington D.C.: International Monetary Fund.

Dooley, Michael P. (1986). Country Specific Risk Premiums, Capital Flight and Net Investment Income Payments in Selected Developing Countries. Unpublished manuscript, International Monetary Fund, Washington, D.C. Mimeographed.

Economist Intelligence Unit. (1999). *Country Risk: Global Prospects for 2000*. Research report. London: Economist Intelligence Unit.

Eggerstedt, Harald, Rebecca Brideau Hall, and Sweder Van Wijnbergen. (1995). Measuring Capital Flight: A Case Study of Mexico. *World Development* 23, no. 2: 211–32.

Eichengreen, Barry, and Jeffrey A. Frankel. (1996). The SDR, Reserve Currencies, and the Future of the International Monetary System. In Michael Mussa, James Boughton, and Peter Isard (eds.), *The Future of the SDR, in Light of Changes in the International Financial System*. Proceedings of a seminar held in Washington D.C., March 18–19, 1996. Washington, D.C.: International Monetary Fund. p. 337–378.

Esquivel, Gerardo, and Felipe Larraín. (1998). Explaining Currency Crises. Development discussion paper No. 666, Harvard Institute for International Development, Cambridge, Mass.

Feldstein, Martin. (1999). A Self-Help Guide for Emerging Markets. *Foreign Affairs* 78, no. 2 (March/April): 93–109.

Fischer, Stanley. (1999). On the Need for an International Lender of Last Resort. *Journal of Economic Perspectives* 13, no. 4 (Fall): 85–104.

Frankel, Jeffrey A., and Andrew Rose. (1996). Currency crashes in emerging markets: An empirical treatment. *Journal of International Economics* 41 (November): 351–366.

Frenkel, Jacob. (1978). International Reserves: Pegged Exchange Rates and Managed Float. in K. Brunner and A. H. Meltzer (eds.), *Public Policies in Open Economies*, 111–40. Carnegie-Rochester Series on Public Policy, vol. 9. Amsterdam: North-Holland.

Frenkel, Jacob. (1983). International Liquidity and Monetary Control. In George von Furstenberg (ed.), *International Money and Credit: the Policy Roles*, 65–129. Washington D.C.: International Monetary Fund.

Frenkel, Jacob, and B. Jovanovich. (1981). Optimal International Reserves: A Stochastic Framework. *Economic Journal* 91: 507–14.

Greenspan, Alan. (1999). Currency Reserves and Debt. Remarks delivered at the World Bank Conference "Recent Trends in Reserves Management," Washington, D.C., April 29.

Grimes, A. (1993). International Reserves under Floating Exchange Rates: Two Paradoxes Explained. *Economic Record* 69, no. 207 (December): 411–15.

Heller, H. Robert. (1966). Optimal International Reserves. *Economic Journal* 76 (June): 296–311.

Heller, H. Robert, and M. S. Khan. (1978). The Demand for International Reserves under Fixed and Floating Exchange Rates. *IMF Staff Papers* 25 (December): 623–49.

Independent Task Force Sponsored by the Council on Foreign Relations. (1999). *Safeguarding Prosperity in a Global Financial System: The Future International Financial Architecture.* A Council on Foreign Relations-Sponsored Report. Institute for International Economics. Washington, D.C.

International Monetary Fund. (1953). The Adequacy of Monetary Reserves. *International Monetary Staff Papers* 3, no. 2 (October): 181–227.

International Monetary Fund. (1958). *International Reserves and Liquidity.* A Study by the Staff of the International Monetary Fund. Washington, D.C.: International Monetary Fund.

International Monetary Fund. (1998a). Early Warning Signals of Vulnerability to Currency Crisis. In *World Economic Outlook; A Survey by the Staff of the International Monetary Fund*, 94–97. Washington, D.C.: International Monetary Fund.

International Monetary Fund. (1998b). Unrecorded Capital Flight from Asia. In *International Capital Markets: Developments, Prospects and Key Policy Issues*, 17 (box 2.3.) Washington, D.C.: International Monetary Fund.

International Monetary Fund. (1999a). *International Capital Markets: Developments, Prospects and Key Policy Issues.* Washington, D.C.: International Monetary Fund.

International Monetary Fund. (1999b). *Exchange Rate Arrangements and Currency Convertibility: Developments and Issues.* Washington, D.C.: International Monetary Fund.

International Monetary Fund. (1999c). Balance of Payments Statistics. *IMF Newsletter* (year-end).

Iyoha, M. A. (1976). Demand for International Reserves in Less Developed Countries: A Distributed Lag Specification. *Review of Economics and Statistics* 60 (August): 351–55.

Kaminsky, Graciela, Saul Lizondo, and Carmen Reinhart. (1997). Leading Indicators of Currency Crises. Policy research working paper no. 1852, World Bank, Washington, D.C.

Khan, Mohsin S., and Carmen Reinhart. (1994). Macroeconomic Management in Maturing Economies: The Response to Capital Inflows. Issues paper, International Monetary Fund, Washington D.C.

Kletzer, Kenneth, and Ashoka Mody. (2000). Will Self-Protection Policies Safeguard Emerging Markets from Crises? Unpublished manuscript.

Kletzer, Kenneth, and Mark M. Spiegel. (1998). Speculative Capital Inflows and Exchange Rate Targeting. In R. Glich (ed.), *Managing Capital Flows and Exchange Rates*, 409–35. New York: Cambridge University Press.

Krugman, Paul. (1979). A Model of Balance-of-Payments Crises. *Journal of Money, Credit and Banking* 11 (August): 311–25.

Lipton, David. (2000). Refocusing the Role of the International Monetary Fund. In Peter Kenen and Alexander Swoboda (eds.), *Reforming the International Monetary and Financial System*, 345–365. Washington, D.C.: International Monetary Fund.

Lizondo, J. S., and D. J. Mathieson. (1987). The Stability of the Demand for International Reserves. *Journal of International Money and Finance* 6 (September): 251–82.

Loukine, Konstantin. (1998). Estimation of Capital Flight from Russia: Balance of Payments Approach. *World Economy* 21 (July): 613–28.

Mussa, Michael, Paul Masson, Alexander Swoboda, Esteban Jadresic, Paolo Mauro, and Andy Berg. (2000). Exchange Rate Regimes in an Increasingly Integrated World Economy. Occasional paper no. 193, International Monetary Fund, Washington, D.C.

Officer, Lawrence H. (1976). The Demand for International Liquidity. *Journal of Money, Credit and Banking* 8, no. 3 (August): 325–337.

Oliviera, Julio H. G. (1971). The Square-Root Law of Precautionary Reserves. *Journal of Political Economy* 79 (September/October): 1095–1104.

Polak, J. J. (1970). Money: National and International. In *International Reserves: Needs and Availability*, 510–520. Papers and proceedings of a Seminar at the International Monetary Fund, June 1–3. Washington, D.C.: International Monetary Fund.

Rodrik, Dani, and Andrés Velasco. Short-Term Capital Flows. Working paper no. 7364, National Bureau of Economic Research, Cambridge, Mass.

Rojas-Suárez, Lilana, and Steven Weisbrod. (1995). Financial Fragilities in Latin America: The 1980's and 1990's. Occasional paper no. 132, International Monetary Fund, Washington, D.C.

Sachs, Jeffrey, Aaron Tornell, and Andrés Velasco. (1996). Financial Crises in Emerging Markets: The Lessons from 1995. *Brookings Papers on Economic Activity* 1: 147–215.

Sicular, Terry. (1998). Capital Flight and Foreign Investment: Two Tales from China and Russia. *World Economy* 21 (July): 589–602.

Triffin, Robert. (1947). National Central Banking and the International Economy. *Review of Economic Studies* 14, no. 2 (February): 53–75.

Triffin, Robert. (1960). *Gold and the Dollar Crisis*. New Haven: Yale University Press.

Williamson, John. (1973). International Liquidity: A Survey. *Economic Journal* 83 (September): 685–746.

Williamson, John, and Molly Mahar. (1998). A Survey of Financial Liberalization. *Essays in international finance* no. 211, Princeton University, Princeton, N.J.

World Bank. (1985). *World Development Report*. Washington D.C.: World Bank.

II The Euro and Financial Policies in Central and Eastern Europe

5 The Eastern Enlargement of the EU and the Case for Unilateral Euroization

Jacek Rostowski

5.1 Introduction

As they approach accession to the EU and later to the EMU,[1] eastern applicant countries are likely to be faced with the simultaneous appearance of the following conditions:

1. rapid expected growth (far faster than in the EU itself)
2. real appreciation resulting from the well-known Harrod-Balassa-Samuelson effect
3. free capital movements
4. the need to satisfy the Maastricht criteria and join EMU within a few years of EU accession

These conditions are likely to lead to high current account deficits, which will be difficult for the authorities to limit to prudent levels. The best solution, for those countries with sufficient international reserves, is rapid unilateral adoption of the euro as their domestic currency, even before they join the EU.

At the core of my analysis in this chapter lies an attempt to combine what we know about the macroeconomics of rapidly growing poorer countries with the standard prescriptions of the Mundell-Flemming model under the free capital movements required in the pre-EU and pre-EMU accession periods. I describe these underlying pressures in section 5.2 and discuss standard macroeconomic policy responses and their drawbacks in sections 5.3 and 5.4. In section 5.5 I examine the implications for the fulfillment of the Maastricht criteria for EMU entry. In section 5.6 I describe how unilateral adoption of the euro would work and the benefits I believe it would bring.

5.2 Stylized Facts on Economic Trends in the Applicant Countries

Three principal factors that are likely to cause a "demand" for current account deficits by the applicant countries:

1. If people expect to be richer in the future than they are at present, they behave rationally if they smooth their consumption path by borrowing today and repaying their debt later. At the level of a whole country, this leads to foreign borrowing (capital inflow) and a current account deficit. If a number of countries expect their economies to grow, the faster-growing ones should borrow from the slower. Applicant countries are expected to be fast growing for a number of reasons:
• They have stopped pursuing the very bad economic policies that they had in the past under central planning.
• They will obtain considerable gains from learning by doing within the institutional framework of the market economy, which was initially nonexistent (e.g., bankruptcy courts, customs services, financial institutions).
• The new liberal economic structure allows them to benefit from the stock of innovations developed in the West during the forty years that the command economy held sway in the East, which they missed out on because of the rigidity and closed nature of the command system.
• New structural reforms are still coming on stream (e.g., pension reform, privatization of utilities).
• EU and EMU membership has certain expected benefits.

2. The well-known Harrod-Balassa-Samuelson effect (hereafter, the H-B-S effect) means that richer countries have higher price levels than poorer ones. A corollary of this is that faster-growing economies will experience real appreciation of their currencies, without loss of competitiveness, relative to countries with slower growth (as a result either of higher inflation or of nominal appreciation). The importance of this phenomenon in transition economies has been pointed out in Halpern and Wyplosz 1995.[2] Real appreciation means that national income measured in foreign currency rises faster than that measured in domestic currency. As a result the command of domestic residents over foreign resources increases faster than indicated by the growth of real GDP at domestic prices (in which the

inflation in the nontradables sector is discounted). This higher than conventionally measured real growth justifies more smoothing of consumption and a higher current account deficit than otherwise.

3. If a large part of the government's debt is denominated in foreign currency (as is the case in many transition countries), then real appreciation leads to a decline in the ratio of public debt to GDP and therefore of the ratio of public debt to the potential tax base. Even if Ricardian equivalence is only partial, residents can be supposed to expect that a lower share of taxes in national income will be needed to service the existing public debt. This raises future disposable income and the desire to smooth consumption (and raise the current account deficit) along with it.

To illustrate the above points, we start with an equation for the current account from Obstfeld and Rogoff 1996:

$$CA_t = B_t - B_{t-1} = Y_t - C_t - G_t - I_t, \tag{5.1}$$

where B is the net foreign assets owned by the residents of the country (including their government), Y is national income, C is consumption, G is government expenditure, I is investment, and t represents time. It is assumed, for the moment, that G is fully financed by taxation. In the long run the current account should be in balance, the economy should have zero net foreign assets, and therefore the net present value of consumption should equal the net present value of net income, $Z = Y - G - I$. The representative consumer, faced with uncertainty, maximizes the expected value of an intertemporal utility function of the form

$$U_t = E_t\left\{\sum_{s=t}^{\infty} \beta^{s-t} u(Cs)\right\}, \tag{5.2}$$

where t is the present and s is the date of every future period, subject to the constraint[3]

$$NPV(CA) = NPV(B) = NPV(Y - C - G - I) = 0, \tag{5.3}$$

which implies

$$NPV(C) = NPV(Y - G - I). \tag{5.4}$$

The operator $E_t\{\cdot\}$ is "a mathematical conditional expectation—a probability-weighted average of possible outcomes, in which probabilities are conditioned on all information available to the decision maker up to and including date t" (Obstfeld and Rogoff 1996, 79). C_t^* is what we call the level of consumption generated by the above procedure at time t. The current account is then given by

$$CA_t = Z_t - C_t^*, \tag{5.5}$$

so that the current account shows a surplus if $Z_t > C_t^*$ and a deficit if $Z_t < C_t^*$. Point 1 in the list above (rapid expected growth of the applicant countries) implies that first with consumption smoothing it will be usually the case that $Z_t < C_t^*$ and that $CA_t < 0$. Second, the H-B-S effect means that growth of national income in real foreign currency terms will be faster than in real domestic currency terms, justifying a higher time path of C_t^* and larger current account deficits than would otherwise be the case.[4] Third, real appreciation reduces the absolute value of B_t/Y_t, and since $B_t < 0$ is normal in fast-growing economies, this leaves scope for an increase in negative net foreign assets (net foreign liabilities or debt), which by equation (5.1) leads to a larger CA deficit. Perhaps most useful of all, equation (5.3) shows us that if the residents of an applicant country revise their expectations of $NPV(Y)$ upward, as it has been argued happens at various times during the transition process,[5] then they should also increase C_t^* for all t. If current Z_t does not increase by as much as C_t^*, and there is no reason why it should, then the current account deficit will also increase.

At the same time, a number of "supply" factors, inducing capital inflows, are likely to be present in the applicant countries:

1. Increased productivity in the tradable goods sector and increased relative prices in nontradables lead to an increased return on capital in both sectors in the fast-growing country.
2. The "Visegrad Three" all have full liberalization of inward FDI flows (including repatriation of profits and principal), and upon EU entry, truly fully free capital accounts will be mandatory.
3. Increased maturity of the institutional infrastructure will strengthen creditors' property rights and exit possibilities for shareholders.

Thus, from the perspective of foreign investors, high expected growth rates and real appreciation in applicant countries mean increasing asset values. This may induce further inflow of capital, causing further real appreciation, together with a desire for higher current account deficits and higher private-sector foreign debt on the part of applicant country residents. High current account deficits, even when financed largely by foreign direct investment, expose a country to the danger of a sudden "stop" in capital inflows (Calvo 1999), which may result in a currency crisis.[6]

This matters for two reasons. First, within the ERM-II mechanism (the second mechanism within the Exchange rate Mechanism), applicants will have to keep their exchange rates with the euro within a 30-percent band around their central rates in the two years before EMU accession. Second, and more important, many applicant countries have a high level of "liability euroization," with high public and private foreign debt (for the reasons described above) denominated in foreign currencies, and also often a high share of foreign currency–denominated bank deposits and domestic bank credit. As a result, a sharp depreciation causes a large increase in both the the gross and the net indebtedness of the economy, which may more than offset the positive effect of depreciation on the demand for exports and may even result in a severe depression, as happened recently in Indonesia. Greenwald and Stiglitz (1990) have shown that an increase in the debt/equity ratio can cause firms to reduce output. Common sense suggests that, in the presence of bankruptcy, an increase in gross leverage at the national level has an asymmetric effect on activity, with lenders increasing their demand less than borrowers reduce theirs, even if net foreign borrowing remains unchanged relative to GDP (which would not be the case). Calvo and Reinhardt (1999) have discussed the implications of "liability dollarization" for Latin America, and Hausmann, Panizza, and Stein suggest in chapter 2 of this volume that fear of such an outcome is important in limiting the willingness of governments to allow free floating in highly euroized or dollarized economies. Thus, setting a ceiling on the current account deficit at some prudent level may be a justified aim of public policy for the applicant countries. The dilemmas of conducting macroeconomic policy with such an aim, under the conditions likely to hold in the run-up to EU and EMU membership, is the subject of the next section.

5.3 The Effect of Fiscal Policy on the Current Account in the Medium and Long Run

What policies will allow applicant countries to keep their current account deficits at "prudent levels"? We first look at an adaptation of the consumption-smoothing model discussed in the previous section to help us analyze the policy implications in the medium and long term.

We adapt the consumption-smoothing model by adding tax revenue as a determinant of the current account and by specifying the medium-term determinants of the right-hand side of the current account equation. Including tax revenue is justified by the weakness of the empirical evidence for Ricardian equivalence (e.g., Wilcox 1989). G and I can be spent on imports just like C and therefore subtract from any positive CA_t, whereas taxes subtract from disposable income that could be spent on imports. Since $Y - C = S$ (savings), we rewrite equation (5.1) as follows (including the behavioral determinants of the variables on the right-hand side):

$$CA_t = B_t - B_{t-1} = S_t(Y, \varepsilon) - (G_t - T_t) - I_t(r^*, \eta). \tag{5.6}$$

We make the Keynesian assumption that savings depend on national income and the neoclassical assumption that investment I depends on the world interest rate r^*, and we add the shift variables ε and η, which represent the effects of (upward) changes in expectations regarding growth. Increases in the variable ε cause S to decline, whereas increases in η cause I to increase.[7] Changes in both variables are assumed to be random but are restricted to being nonnegative (i.e., if $\varepsilon_t < \varepsilon_{t-1}$ when random values of ε are drawn, then we set $\varepsilon_t = \varepsilon_{t-1}$, and we do the same for η). Finally, consumers are assumed to be unable to anticipate future values of ε or to calculate their expected value $E(\varepsilon_t) > 0$ (the same goes for η). We seek justification for these highly irrational expectations in the completely unprecedented nature of the transition from communism to capitalism.[8] Thus over time, but in a highly unpredictable way, the gap between I and S increases, in turn increasing the current account deficit. The only way the authorities can offset this trend is to reduce the budget deficit $G - T$, possibly to the extent of turning it into a large surplus.

As in the earlier version of the consumption-smoothing model, an unanticipated reduction in the absolute value of B_t/Y_t (due to an increase in Y_t or to real appreciation) implies a reduction in net foreign liabilities/GDP, since normally $B_t < 0$ in fast-growing economies and therefore brings about a desire by consumers to increase the net foreign liabilities/GDP ratio. As before, this implies a reduction in B_t below B_{t-1} and therefore a current account deficit. We encounter an ambiguity, however, regarding the policy implications of the model at this point: although the direct effects of a reduction in the budget deficit should reduce a current account deficit (the traditional two-gap model result), if a significant part of public debt is owed to foreign residents, as is the case in the applicant countries, an unanticipated tightening in fiscal policy reduces government net foreign liabilities and therefore induces the private sector to increase its own net foreign liabilities. The result might be that total net foreign liabilities remain unchanged. In such a case (which we can call the "crowding in of private-sector foreign debt"), the current account deficit is unaffected by reductions in the fiscal deficit in the medium term.

This is the equivalent of so-called Ricardian equivalence but relates to the impact of fiscal policy on the current account rather than on aggregate demand. Although empirical evidence for standard Ricardian equivalence is weak, I believe the effect may be stronger in relation to the current account, because of constraints originating from the international suppliers of credit. We know that these suppliers often look at the total indebtedness of a country's residents, both public and private, when assessing an individual resident's credit risk.[9]

5.4 The Implications of the Mundell-Flemming Model for the Short Term and an Extension

Similar doubts as to the efficacy of fiscal (and also monetary) policy for current account deficit reduction resurface in the context of the Mundell-Flemming model and its application to policymaking in the short term. We look now at the Mundell-Flemming model with perfect capital mobility, risk-neutral investors, and fully flexible exchange rates. We assume that in the short term the exchange rate is not expected to change; that is,

$$\rho_t + u_t = \rho_t^e = \rho_{t-1}, \tag{5.7}$$

where the last period's expectations of the current period's exchange rate (ρ_t^e), which are simply the last period's actual exchange rate (ρ_{t-1}), efficiently predict the current period's actual exchange rate (ρ_t, where u_t is a normally distributed error term). In such a case, if there were a difference between the rate of return on domestic and foreign assets, investors would put all of their money into the asset with the higher return. Since both kinds of assets are held, it follows that their returns must be equal. Since exchange rate expectations are static, it follows that rates of return (i.e., interest rates) must be the same in the two countries:

$$i = i^*, \tag{5.8}$$

where i is the domestic rate of interest, and i^* is the world rate (given exogenously). This means that the Liquidity, Money (LM) curve (representing equilibria in the "money" market) becomes

$$M/P = L(i^*, Y), \qquad L_1 < 0, \quad L_2 > 0, \tag{5.9}$$

and the "goods market equilibrium" Investment, Savings (IS) curve becomes

$$Y = C(Y - T) + I(i^* - \pi^e) + NX(Y, \rho P^*/P) + G,$$
$$C_1 > 0, \quad I_1 < 0, \quad NX_1 < 0, \quad NX_2 > 0, \tag{5.10}$$

where π^e is expected domestic inflation, P^* is the foreign price level, P is the domestic price level and NX is net exports (the remaining variables are as conventionally or previously defined).[10]

The result in (ρ, Y) space is a vertical LM curve and an upward-sloping IS curve, as shown in figure 5.1. Any tightening of monetary policy by the authorities is immediately offset "one for one" by capital inflows, because i cannot rise above i^*. Such capital inflow must be offset by a deterioration of the current account, so that the policy is in fact counterproductive as far as reducing the current account

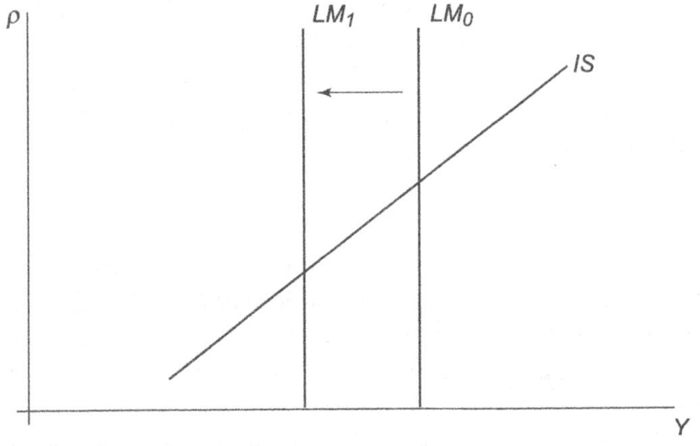

Figure 5.1
Monetary policy response to capital inflow in an IS-LM framework

deficit is concerned.[11] Intuitively we can understand this if we remember that, given that the domestic interest rate is fixed at the level of the world rate, a reduction in M can affect only the exchange rate, which appreciates, reducing net exports.[12] If capital movements were not perfectly free in the very short term, so that the authorities could succeed in reducing M (in spite of their difficulty in raising i) this would have two offsetting effects. On the one hand it would reduce Y, increasing net exports (NX) and improving the current account balance. On the other hand, it would lead to a nominal appreciation of the domestic currency—a reduction in ρ—and if P (the domestic price level) is sticky downward, we would also have real appreciation, so that net exports would decline and the current account balance would deteriorate (see figure 5.1, in which ρ is defined as units of domestic currency/unit of foreign currency, so that a decline indicates an appreciation). Which of the two effects will be stronger depends on the various elasticities, but in neither case is the policy likely to be very powerful.

Returning to the case of perfect capital mobility in the short term, expanding rather than contracting M will lead to capital outflow (to obtain the infinitesimally higher interest rate abroad) and therefore to nominal depreciation. In the short run there will also be real depreciation if prices are sticky upward, so that the current account deficit will be successfully reduced.[13] In the medium term, however, increased M would lead to higher prices (not allowed for in the fixed price level Mundell-Flemming model), which would likely mean breaching the Maastricht criterion on inflation and also to an erosion of the real depreciation and a reversal of the improvement in the current account. Thus, in the medium term, sustaining a "prudent" level of the current account through expansionary monetary policy would require accelerating inflation, which would clearly be inconsistent with the Maastricht inflation criterion.

If the exchange rate is credibly fixed, then the domestic authorities have no influence over M. They have to respond to sales (purchases) of foreign (domestic) currency with a supply of central bank domestic (international) reserves, so that M becomes entirely endogenous and cannot affect the current account in any way. Monetary policy is thus unlikely to be effective in reducing a current account deficit no matter which of the two exchange rate regimes, floating or fixed, is in force. This result is confirmed by empirical studies that find that in the Mundell-Flemming model and its Dornbusch (1976) extension,

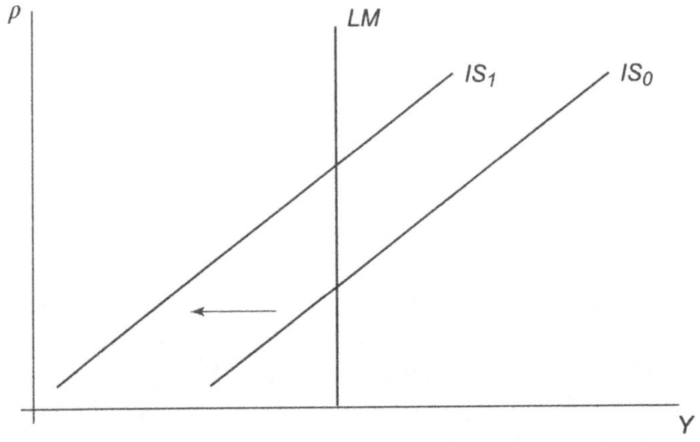

Figure 5.2
Fiscal contraction and the equilibrium exchange rate and output

changes in monetary policy are unable to predict either nominal or real exchange rate changes (Obstfeld and Rogoff 1996, 622–666).

On the other hand, with fully free capital movements, the Mundell-Flemming model suggests that fiscal policy becomes highly effective in determining the current account balance, under both free and fixed exchange rate regimes. If the exchange rate floats and the fiscal deficit is reduced so that $G - T$ in equation (5.10) falls, then the *IS* curve in figure 5.2 shifts up, leading to depreciation of the exchange rate without any effect on output: aggregate demand falls as a result of the direct effect of the fall in $G - T$ (together with any multiplier effects it may have), and the depreciation of the currency increases net exports (*NX*) by an exactly offsetting amount. National income remains constant, because it is determined by real money balances (M/P) in the money market equation (5.9), but the accompanying nominal depreciation leads to an improvement in the current account. The depreciation may have some inflationary effects over time, which may partly offset the current account improvement; with no increase in domestic *M*, however, such effects need not be very powerful, as shown in the figure. With a fixed exchange rate the model consists in equation (5.10) and

$$\rho = \text{cons.} \tag{5.11}$$

In (Y, ρ) space this gives equilibria as shown in figure 5.3. A reduction in the budget deficit causes a fall in Y and thus an increase

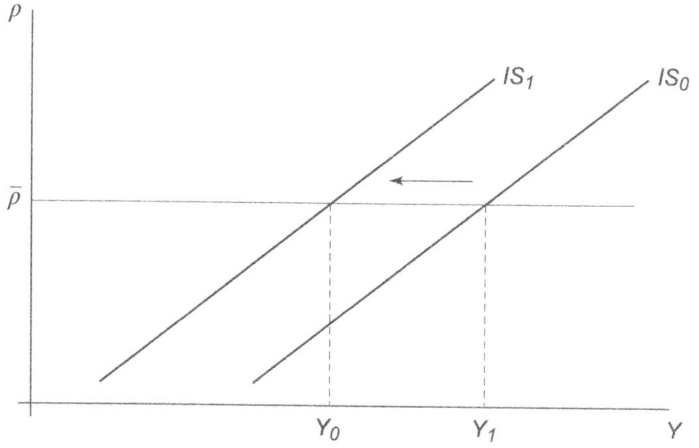

Figure 5.3
Output effects of fiscal contraction under fixed exchange rates

in *NX*, helping to achieve the aim of a "prudent" level for the current account deficit. As previously stated, under a fixed exchange rate, a reduction (increase) in the domestic credit counterpart of *M* merely leads to an increase (reduction) in the international reserves of the central bank. Thus, the overall conclusion is that keeping the economy on course for EMU membership, in the face of the medium-term effects (described in section 5.3), which are pushing the applicant countries towards larger current account deficits, *implies ever-tightening fiscal positions for these countries*. Since the Czech Republic and Poland already have fiscal deficits well within the Maastricht fiscal balance criterion, achieving a prudent current account position may require them to run significant budget surpluses in their last pre-EMU entry years.

This conclusion, though, is brought into question by the medium-term consumption-smoothing model we looked at in the previous section. There we saw that even the effect of fiscal policy on the current account might be ambiguous. That result inspires one to ask whether there are other indirect effects of a tightening of fiscal policy that might cast doubt on the conclusions we arrived at within the Mundell-Flemming framework, even in the short term. For instance, a tightening of fiscal policy could lead to a positive reevaluation of the expected future worth of a country's productive assets, leading to an increase in investment demand and therefore to an *increase*, rather than a reduction, in the current account deficit.[14] This problem can be highlighted by examining a simple extension of the Mundell-Flemming model we have used above. We rewrite equation (5.10) as

$$Y = C(Y - T, \theta) + I(i^* - \pi^e, \eta) + NX(Y, \rho P^*/P) + G,$$

$$C_1 > 0, \quad C_2 > 0, \quad I_1 < 0, \quad I_2 > 0, \quad NX_1 < 0, \quad NX_2 > 0, \qquad (5.12)$$

where θ and η are shift variables that represent the effects of upward changes in expectations regarding growth. As in equation (5.6) the shift variables are assumed to always be nonnegative and completely unanticipated by consumers and investors. Under a floating exchange rate, positive θ and/or η will result in a downward shift in the *IS* curve in figure 5.2 (from IS_1 to IS_0) and thus in nominal appreciation, a fall in net exports, and an increase in the current account deficit. If the exchange rate is fixed, the *IS* curve shifts out as in figure 5.3 (from IS_1 to IS_0), directly increasing the current account deficit. In either case, policymakers will need to offset these effects by increasing T and/or reducing G. The problem is that it may also be true that

$$\eta = \eta(G - T), \qquad \eta_1 < 0, \qquad (5.13)$$

so that when growth expectations are revised, the size of the revision is positively related to the fiscal position. In that case, an improved fiscal position *increases* investment demand and may increase the current account deficit overall.[15] Indeed, evidence from OECD countries shows that, although sharp reversals of fiscal policy may affect the current account deficit in the expected direction, the link between levels of fiscal and current account deficits is usually insignificant (Obstfeld and Rogoff 1996, 144–145).

5.5 Implications for Conformity with the Maastricht Criteria

Because of their expected rapid growth rate, the H-B-S effect may be very strong in the applicant transition countries. Thus, in the 1990s, real appreciation has occurred at a rate of 2 percent per annum in Portugal in 1990–1997 and only 0.4 percent per annum in Spain over the same period, whereas in Poland it averaged 7.5 percent during 1993–1997. This difference is related to the difference in growth rates, with the Portuguese and Spanish economies growing at under 2 percent per annum, whereas Poland's economy grew at about 6 percent. As growth rates accelerate in the other applicant countries, we can expect rates of real appreciation to reach high levels as well. The implications for the fulfillment of the Maastricht criteria for stage 3 of EMU by the applicant countries are profound.

To be clear about the H-B-S effect, let us assume that economies produce two kinds of goods: tradables (e.g., manufactures), for which productivity differs among countries, grows relatively fast and can grow at different rates in different countries; and nontradables (e.g., services and construction), for which productivity is uniform throughout the world and grows slowly. We also assume that all goods are sold on perfectly competitive markets, that labor is homogeneous, and that labor markets are perfectly competitive. In such a world, differences in income between any two countries are due to the productivity of their tradable goods sectors. Furthermore, in the faster-growing economy productivity in the tradable goods sector rises faster than in the slower-growing one, with the result that real wages rise faster. Because of the homogeneity of labor and the competitiveness of labor markets, however, real wages must increase by the same amount in both sectors in the faster-growing economy. Since productivity in nontradables grows slowly, this means that prices have to increase in this sector. As a result, if the share of the two sectors is similar in the two countries, average prices will rise faster in the faster-growing country even if the nominal exchange rate is constant, implying real appreciation. Since unit labor costs denominated in foreign currency remain unchanged in the tradables sector (the same number of domestic workers can produce more tradable goods and get paid proportionally more), the nominal exchange rate need not be affected in any way.

This is why it may be unwise for the applicant countries to fulfill the Maastricht inflation criterion, which at present requires that inflation not exceed the average of the three best performers within EMU + 1.5 percent. If the H-B-S effect required a real appreciation of 7.5 percent per annum relative to the euro zone (as Polish experience suggests it might), then this criterion would imply an equal nominal appreciation of almost the same amount. Thus, satisfying the Maastricht inflation criterion may entail two kinds of risks:

1. The current Maastricht inflation criterion is unsuitable for countries with a strong H-B-S effect, since it seeks to limit what is better thought of, in their case, as a *relative price change* (between traded and nontraded goods) rather than as an increase in the overall price

level. In fact, for average prices across both sectors to be constant in a rapidly growing economy, its currency needs to appreciate nominally to such an extent that the ensuing fall in the domestic price of tradables compensates for inflation in nontradables, so that

$$-\alpha P_T(\partial\rho/\partial t)/\rho = (1-\alpha)\pi_{NT} \tag{5.14}$$

is required for $\pi = 0$ (where α is the share of tradables in national income, P_T is the price of tradables, ρ is the exchange rate, defined as units of domestic currency per unit of foreign currency, π_{NT} is the rate of inflation on nontradable goods, and π is the average inflation rate). If we assume some downward price rigidity for domestically produced tradable goods, such a nominal appreciation implies a deterioration in the trade and current accounts of the rapidly growing country, so that the Maastricht inflation criterion would export instability and recession to the applicant countries.[16]

2. If nominal appreciation is sufficient for equation (5.14) to hold, then the interest parity condition,

$$-[(\partial\rho/\partial t)/\rho]^e + i = i^*, \tag{5.15}$$

may imply negative short-term nominal interest rates in the applicant country.[17] For example, if we take the rate of nominal appreciation implicit in (1) meeting the Maastricht inflation criterion (of inflation not exceeding the average of the three best-performing members of the euro zone + 1.5 percent) and (2) having the same real appreciation vis-à-vis the euro zone as Poland did during 1993–1997,[18] then with $i^* = 4$ percent, i needs to be negative 3 percent! In the spirit of Dornbusch 1976, we suggest that this anomaly may be avoided through an initial upward jump in the value of the domestic currency, so that subsequent expected appreciation is low enough for $i > 0$. Subsequent expectations of a delay in EU entry, however, may then cause a currency crisis.

Moreover, there are a number of difficulties in devising a suitable exchange rate regime for the Central and Eastern European (CEE) applicants for the period immediately prior to EMU entry. There are two main possible exchange rate arrangements in the pre-EMU period (Kopits 1999):

1. Pegged rate. Such a system is very likely to be incompatible with the Maastricht inflation criterion, because of the operation of the

H-B-S effect. Expected rapid growth will lead to high levels of capital inflows, which may result in the need to choose between (1) dangerously high current account deficits as a result of periodic revaluations or (2) inflation well above that due solely to the H-B-S effect.[19]

2. Wide fluctuation bands (± 15 percent) around the central rate, as in the current ERM-II. This is the case at present in the Czech Republic and Poland and is likely to lead to nominal appreciation and high current account deficits but may preserve the possibility of fulfilling the inflation criterion. One danger is an "appreciation bubble," which leads to an exchange rate that is unsustainable. This could lead to a collapse of the exchange rate before accession to EMU, which would be against the Maastricht requirements, or to an overvalued exchange rate at the time of joining, which could mean a lengthy period of low growth within EMU.

We can summarize the discussion so far as follows:

- The H-B-S effect means that there will be powerful pressures for real appreciation in the applicant countries in the medium term.
- Rapid expected growth, the H-B-S effect (via its effect on the ratio of foreign debt/GDP) and various factors increasing the supply of foreign capital mean that applicant countries are likely to run large and growing current account deficits.
- Monetary policy will be either counterproductive, likely to risk the return of high inflation, or ineffective.
- Only fiscal policy may have the potential to limit current account deficits to what the authorities may consider prudent levels (and this is so under both fixed and flexible exchange rate regimes). As a result of their need to tighten fiscal policy each year while they are EMU pre-ins, countries with relatively low fiscal deficits at present, such as the Czech Republic and Poland, may need to run substantial surpluses (possibly on the order of several percentage points of GDP) by the time they join EMU. We should consider the extent to which this is likely to be politically feasible.
- Even tight fiscal policy may, however, prove ineffective in limiting current account deficits, as a result of its effect on the private sector's willingness to increase its foreign indebtedness and foreigners' willingness to lend. In that case, there is a serious danger that a large current account deficit will lead to a currency crisis and blow applicant countries off their course to EMU membership.

- Because of the H-B-S effect, only nominal appreciation is likely to make the fulfillment of the Maastricht inflation criterion possible. This might, however, be at a high cost in terms of foregone output and increased risk of currency crisis. Therefore the Maastricht inflation criterion for EMU membership should not be applied to the CEE applicant countries, although the exchange rate criterion should be maintained.
- Neither a pegged nor a wide-band exchange rate policy allows an applicant country to avoid these fundamental problems.

5.6 Benefits and Costs of Unilateral Euroization

A number of CEE applicants have sufficient international reserves not only to exchange all existing domestic currency–denominated central bank monetary liabilities for euros (coins, notes, and commercial bank reserves at the central bank), but also to create an emergency fund to provide lender-of-last-resort liquidity to the banking system (since the central bank would no longer be able to create high-powered money—in euros—for this purpose).[20] In what follows I shall use the example of Poland, which I know best.

One way to implement unilateral euroization is simply to pass, as soon as is technically feasible, the very law establishing the euro as legal tender that would have to be passed in the country concerned upon its entry into EMU by the traditional route. Only those parts of the law that relate to the role of the national central bank (NCB) would have to be different than adopting the euro by becoming an EU member first. Instead of providing for the NCB's membership in the European System of Central Banks (ESCB), they would provide for the NCB to run the lender-of-last-resort facility for the banking system, using owned (or borrowed) international reserves. In the case of Poland, whose international reserves are very high (about $26 billion),[21] about half of this sum would be used to exchange all the NCB's zloty-denominated monetary liabilities into euros. The remaining $13 billion would be paid into a "banking sector liquidity fund" (BSLF) to be used in cases of runs on solvent but illiquid banks (see Caprio et al. 1996). This amount is equivalent to some 90 percent of sight deposits and 25 percent of all deposits in the Polish banking system and should therefore be quite sufficient. If there was reason to suppose that $13 billion might prove inadequate for this purpose, then the Polish government could arrange a euro-denominated credit line to supplement the BSLF, as the Argentine government has done.[22] It is worth remembering that a number of euro zone central banks do not have true lender-of-last-resort facilities. This includes the Bundesbank, which can lend to banks for liquidity purposes only against the security of government paper, and indeed also the European Central Bank (ECB) itself, which is similarly restricted.

The main advantages of rapid unilateral euroization are as follows:

1. Capital inflows would accelerate rapidly, boosting investment and economic growth.

2. Interest rates would be reduced rapidly, through the elimination of currency risk, to levels that exceed those in the euro zone only by the amount of pure country risk. Since dollar-denominated Polish government paper currently trades at about 120 basis points above U.S. Treasury paper of the same maturity, rates on previously zloty-denominated Polish government paper could be expected to fall to about 7.5 percent compared to 15 percent at present, and rates on bank loans could be 9–12 percent compared to some 20 percent at present.

3. Lower interest rates on previously zloty-denominated government and central bank paper should save the public sector the equivalent of about 1.5 percent of GDP per annum. This significantly outweighs the loss of central bank seigniorage revenue, which would amount to less than 0.4 percent of GDP.[23] This would enable Poland to satisfy the Maastricht fiscal deficit criterion.[24]

4. Perhaps most important, all these benefits could be reaped within two years (rather than the five I would expect Poland to need to enter EMU by the traditional route), and moreover, without the need to meet the Maastricht inflation criterion, with its ensuing nominal appreciation and the (possibly devastating) effects on the competitiveness of the tradable goods sector.

What of the disadvantages of unilateral euroization? The following are those most frequently mentioned:

1. There would be a loss of seigniorage. As regards current seigniorage, we have already discussed and dismissed this. It has been suggested, however, that a country that euroizes unilaterally will forego the benefit of receiving euros from the ECB when it joins the

EMU by the orthodox route. This is a misunderstanding of how EMU accession works and is dealt with in appendix 5.1.

2. A contractionary shock may result from unilateral euroization (Lutkowski 1999). The benefits described above suggest that the effect is more likely to be expansionary than contractionary: falling interest rates will increase demand rather than reduce it, capital inflows will improve the supply side, and the avoidance of nominal appreciation should help the tradable goods sector when compared to the traditional approach.

3. Inertial inflation in the tradable goods sector inherited from the zloty regime could continue after euroization, causing the tradable goods sector to become uncompetitive (Buiter 1995), which might require a long recession to cure. A variant is the claim that CEE applicants need to make their economies more flexible before they can expose them to the discipline of the euro (Orlowski and Rybinski 1999). My first response to such assertions is that this problem can only be worse when a country follows the traditional approach to EMU, with its need for nominal *appreciation* to offset the H-B-S effect on the prices of nontradable goods. Second, under unilateral euroization, any inertial inflation in the tradable goods sector anticipated by the authorities can be allowed for by an up-front devaluation of the domestic currency at the moment of conversion. This is something that may not be allowed when countries follow the traditional route, as the exchange rate at which a country joins EMU has to be negotiated with existing members. Finally, rapid productivity growth as compared to the EU should quickly absorb both inertial inflation in tradable goods prices and any initial error in setting the "conversion rate" of the applicant's currency to the euro.

4. "Real convergence" is required before the euro can be adopted safely: applicant countries need to develop industrial structures that are similar to the average of the existing eurozone members (Orlowski and Rybinski 1999; Rosati 1999). Otherwise, ECB policy in response to an asymmetric supply or demand shock, which affects existing members differently from applicants, will be unsuitable for the needs of the latter. However, since Poland (the largest applicant economy by far) accounts for about 2 percent of euro zone GDP, its needs will hardly be taken into account when the ECB sets monetary policy, even when it becomes a fully fledged EMU member. The argument is therefore one against *early* EMU entry in any form and

not against *unilateral* euroization in particular. Second, we should note that the structures of the CEE applicant countries do not, in fact, differ all that much from those of existing EMU members. Thus, the structure of Poland's economy differs from the EU average more than do those of France or Germany, but less than those of Finland, Greece, Ireland, or Sweden, two of which are not only members of the EU but also of EMU (table 5.1). As regards the structure of industry, Poland's differs from the EU average less than do those of Ireland and Portugal, both of which are EMU members (table 5.2).

One danger to which I have drawn attention myself in a joint article with a collegue (Bratkowski and Rostowski 1999) is that the large influx of capital that we expect to follow upon euroization may lead to a credit boom, which could result in loose lending practices, the accumulation of bad debt, and ultimately a banking crisis. But CEE countries must in any case expect very large capital inflows over the next decade (a large part of which will be mediated by their banking systems), so they must ensure a major improvement in the quality of their banking skills and bank supervision in any case. Unilateral euroization will merely increase the magnitude of the phenomenon.

Finally, I need to mention the differences between the unilateral euroization that I propose and the establishment of a currency board based on the euro, as suggested by others (Dornbusch and Giavazzi 1998). The precise differences between the effects of these proposals will depend on the legal framework of the monetary system in each CEE country. As described above, and as applied to Poland, my proposal consists in unilaterally declaring the euro the only legal tender in the state. This makes the regime one that is likely to be more credible than a simple currency board, because under a currency board, the domestic currency continues to exist, and the rules that bind it to the euro can be repealed. With euroization, exit is a harder process: a *new* domestic currency would have to be created and declared legal tender. But speculation against the continuation of the euro regime—that is, against the as yet nonexistent new domestic currency—would still be possible. It could be undertaken by borrowing in Poland and investing abroad, on the assumption that the authorities would create, then devalue, a "new zloty," in which existing liabilities would be denominated.[25] To describe this "exit path" should be sufficient to show how unlikely it would be,

Table 5.1
Structure of gross value added

	Agriculture, fisheries, and forestry		Fuels and energy		Manufacturing		Construction		Market services		Nonmarket services		Distance from EU average	
	1986	1995	1986	1995	1986	1995	1986	1995	1986	1995	1986	1995	1986	1995
Finland	7.5%	3.1%	3.0%	2.7%	24.6%	26.6%	7.8%	5.7%	38.1%	40.3%	18.9%	20.7%	9.7%	13.9%
France	3.9%	2.5%	4.8%	4.0%	21.4%	18.9%	5.4%	4.7%	47.1%	51.9%	17.4%	18.0%	4.1%	4.1%
Greece	16.2%	14.2%	4.2%	3.7%	18.9%	13.8%	6.9%	6.2%	38.3%	47.3%	15.5%	14.7%	15.8%	14.7%
Germany	1.8%	1.0%	4.7%	4.0%	30.7%	24.1%	5.5%	5.4%	43.3%	52.1%	14.0%	13.4%	7.0%	3.6%
Holland	4.4%	3.3%	8.7%	6.3%	18.1%	16.9%	5.1%	5.2%	51.7%	57.6%	12.0%	10.7%	10.1%	8.7%
Italy	4.3%	2.9%	4.9%	5.9%	24.1%	21.1%	6.1%	5.1%	47.7%	52.2%	12.9%	13.0%	3.4%	2.4%
Ireland	8.4%	6.0%	3.1%	2.7%	29.1%	30.8%	5.6%	4.8%	37.2%	40.8%	16.6%	14.9%	11.1%	15.0%
Portugal	7.2%	3.7%	5.3%	4.2%	27.5%	23.7%	5.1%	5.3%	41.6%	46.2%	13.2%	16.9%	6.6%	6.4%
Spain	5.6%	3.1%	5.9%	5.8%	23.1%	19.8%	6.5%	8.7%	46.8%	48.0%	12.1%	14.6%	4.3%	5.2%
Sweden	3.3%	2.2%	3.8%	3.2%	22.4%	21.7%	6.0%	4.6%	38.3%	43.6%	26.2%	24.7%	13.4%	12.8%
United Kingdom	1.6%	1.6%	8.2%	6.0%	23.7%	20.9%	5.8%	5.0%	45.2%	53.7%	15.5%	12.7%	3.5%	3.4%
Europe 15	3.5%	2.3%	5.4%	4.7%	24.5%	21.2%	5.8%	5.4%	45.6%	51.5%	15.3%	14.8%	8.1%	8.2%
Poland		5.5%		7.0%		22.6%		8.0%		43.8%		13.1%		9.3%

Source: Eurostat 1997, *GUS Yearbook*, Poland.

Table 5.2
Shares in gross value added in manufacturing industry

	Textiles		Food Processing		Transport equipment		Chemicals and petrochemicals		Electrical and optical		Iron and steel		Distance from the EU10 average	
	1990	1995	1990	1995	1990	1995	1990	1995	1990	1995	1990	1995	1990	1995
Finland	3.5%	2.3%	12.2%	11.0%	4.7%	4.2%	6.5%	6.5%	9.2%	15.5%	4.4%	6.5%	7.05%	7.65%
France	4.4%	3.6%	8.3%	8.4%	9.8%	7.9%	8.7%	9.1%	10.6%	10.5%	5.1%	4.5%	0.99%	1.98%
Germany	3.4%	2.3%	6.3%	6.3%	12.4%	10.8%	9.5%	9.5%	14.0%	11.7%	7.4%	6.7%	5.31%	4.66%
Holland	2.5%	1.7%	15.8%	13.1%	4.9%	3.4%	14.2%	12.5%	10.5%	9.4%	3.6%	3.7%	10.69%	8.12%
Ireland	4.0%	2.8%	31.2%	28.7%	1.9%	1.5%	16.0%	26.5%	16.3%	18.5%	—	—	25.49%	27.81%
Italy	8.0%	11.4%	5.7%	9.6%	6.3%	6.0%	6.4%	8.6%	8.9%	11.3%	4.2%	5.4%	6.38%	7.32%
Portugal	19.4%	13.8%	9.3%	10.7%	4.8%	3.4%	4.8%	3.6%	5.0%	5.5%	2.9%	1.4%	16.98%	14.00%
Spain	8.1%	7.0%	14.4%	15.5%	9.6%	11.4%	8.4%	10.0%	8.3%	8.7%	4.5%	4.4%	7.10%	7.53%
Sweden	1.4%	1.2%	7.5%	8.0%	8.2%	12.8%	5.7%	8.0%	10.1%	12.8%	4.6%	5.8%	5.21%	6.00%
United Kingdom	4.8%	4.5%	11.5%	11.4%	11.4%	9.3%	9.1%	10.0%	10.7%	11.1%	4.3%	3.8%	3.50%	2.58%
EU 10	5.1%	4.7%	8.7%	9.4%	9.7%	8.8%	8.6%	9.5%	11.1%	11.1%	5.3%	5.2%	8.87%	8.74%
Poland 1990 and 1995	9.3%	10.8%	22.1%	18.7%	8.8%	6.3%	10.7%	13.6%	7.7%	3.7%	14.3%	6.5%	17.17%	14.27%
Poland 1997		9.5%		19.2%		6.5%		12.7%		4.3%		5.6%		13.51%

Source: Eurostat Yearbook 1997, OECD STAN database 1978–1997, GUS Poland.

especially during the few years between unilateral euroization and full EMU membership. Furthermore, such an exit would also be possible after fully fledged accession to EMU.

5.7 Conclusion

The traditional route to EMU membership seems to be fraught with difficulties, the most important of which is the absence of macroeconomic policy instruments that would allow CEE applicant countries to satisfy the exchange rate and inflation criteria of the Maastricht treaty together with the maintenance of prudent levels of the current account deficit in the context of rapid economic growth and free capital movements. Nor are the difficulties removed if the Maastricht inflation criterion were to be suspended for the CEE applicants as I have suggested. The problem of achieving the exchange rate criterion together with a prudent level of the current account deficit would remain. Unilateral euroization seems the best solution to this conundrum, and none of the objections that have been put forward against it are fully convincing when they are tested against the conditions obtaining in most of the first-wave CEE applicant countries.

Appendix 5.1

Unilateral euroization entails the exchange of euro notes and coins for a country's existing currency. Under unilateral euroization the euros for this purpose must be bought using an applicant's own or borrowed international reserves. In the case of Poland, own international reserves are fully adequate, being equivalent to about two and a half times zloty notes and coins in circulation. Some critics claim, however, that in joining EMU in the normal way, Poland would get its notes and coins exchanged for euros *free*. This means that the roughly ten billion euro that would be used for unilateral euroization would be wasted and could probably never be recovered. To answer this point I have analyzed what happens when a country joins the EMU in the normal orthodox way and becomes a shareholder in the ECB. The analysis is based on the statute of the ECB and the annual reports (including balance sheets) of the ECB for 1998 and 1999, which are available at ⟨www.ecb.int⟩.

Critics might be right if by joining the ESCB, the National Bank of Poland received the right to exchange its outstanding zloty notes for euro ones issued by itself, while *at the same time* its right to dispose freely of its assets remained unaffected. It is indeed the case that both the ECB and the NCBs can issue euro banknotes (Article 16 of the ECB statute), so that the euro notes initially exchanged for notes in a country's currency will presumably be those issued by the NCB of the country concerned and not by the ECB. As a result there is no need for an NCB to issue a claim on itself to the ECB for the euro notes that the latter would exchange for domestic currency notes.

What the statute calls the "monetary income" of the NCB, however, (i.e., its income derived from those assets it holds to back notes in circulation and deposit liabilities to credit institutions; article 32.2), will *not* remain in the hands of the NCB (to be transferred to its shareholder, the state budget, as profit). Rather, "the sum of the national central banks' monetary income shall be allocated to the national central banks in proportion to their paid up shares in the capital of the ECB" (article 32.5). This is the crucial point, since it means that *the link between the size of the monetary base issued by an NCB (or the assets held against it) and the NCB's profits is broken.* Instead, an NCB's contribution to ECB income will depend on its "own monetary income," whereas its profits will depend, like its share in ECB capital, equally on its country's share in the euro zone's GDP and population. Thus, Germany's share is 24.49 percent of present capital, whereas Poland's would be about 6.5 percent (depending on which other countries were members).

If a country euroizes unilaterally, it reduces its monetary liabilities by the amount of outstanding notes and coins in its own currency (which it buys for euro), and therefore it follows that it reduces its "own monetary income" and the obligatory contribution to ECB revenue that it will have to pay upon EMU entry very substantially. Indeed, only income derived from assets held against the deposit liabilities of credit institutions would remain as the NCB's contribution to the total monetary income of the ESCB.[26] Its share of seigniorage upon EMU entry, however, will be unaffected by the fact of its previous unilateral euroization. Upon accession it begins to receive seigniorage, in proportion to its share in ECB capital, on all euro notes in circulation, including those that it had bought earlier with part of its international reserves (IR) so as to carry out the unilateral euroization exercise. Thus, the "*net* own monetary income" of the NCB (i.e., its share in ECB profits less its contribution to ECB revenues)[27] is *completely unaffected by previous unilateral euroization.* Unilateral euroization means shortening the balance sheet of the NCB, reducing both assets (IR) and liabilities (own-currency notes and coins), but leaves its net worth unchanged. The reduction in assets is compensated for immediately by the reduction in own-currency liabilities and translates into a reduction in the forced contribution to ECB revenues (own monetary income) upon EMU entry.

The only way for an NCB to reduce its own monetary income without also reducing its international reserves is for it to reduce the euro value of its monetary liabilities through an up-front devaluation on the eve of EMU entry. This might help explain existing EMU members' strong opposition to such a policy (e.g., in the case of Sweden).

Notes

1. We follow the common usage in referring to the "third stage" of EMU as simply EMU.

2. For a formal treatment of how differential productivity growth in the tradable and nontradable sectors of two countries affects the real exchange rate between their currencies, see Obstfeld and Rogoff 1996, (204–212).

3. Where $NPV(CA) = NPV(CA_t + CA_{t+1} + CA_{t+2} + \cdots + CA_{t+\infty})$. The same holds for $NPV(B)$, $NPV(Y - C - G - I)$, and so on.

4. The model does not take into account the direct relative price effects, by which foreign goods become cheaper to domestic residents as a result of real appreciation.

5. This point has been made forcefully to me by Stanislaw Gomulka in personal communications.

6. There is also the risk that real appreciation means further capital gains for foreign investors, so that a "capital inflow–real appreciation" bubble develops, with the real exchange rate and the current account deficit rising ever more above their medium-term equilibrium levels until, finally, the bubble bursts.

7. I am grateful to Stanislaw Gomulka for suggesting this approach to me.

8. A more acceptable way of putting this might be that $E(\varepsilon_t) = 0$ and that the effects we are discussing will occur if the actual values of ε_t exceed this over a sustained period (the same goes for η).

9. Of course, the extent to which this actually happens depends on the proportion of the reduction in the fiscal deficit that goes toward reducing foreign public debt below its previously expected level. The lower this proportion, the stronger the standard effect of public-sector deficit reduction on the current account deficit will be.

10. A more general formulation is

$$Y = E(i^* - \pi^e, G - T, \rho P^*/P, Y), \qquad E_1 < 0, \quad E_2 > 0, \quad E_3 > 0, \quad 0 < E_4 < 1.$$

11. If the international reserves of the central bank increase, then the the exchange rate is not, in fact, fully floating.

12. This reduces Y. Hence in a small open economy with a floating exchange rate, contractionary monetary policy affects Y via ρ rather than via i.

13. Alternatively we can think of the expansionary monetary policy as causing a one-to-one offsetting capital outflow, which by definition improves the current account. For the extent to which the final outcome necessarily does or does not involve a depreciation of the domestic currency, see Kouri 1978.

14. That this might not be mere theorizing is indicated by the view of some Hungarian economists that their currency's avoidance of rapid real appreciation over recent years has been due to the government's large fiscal deficit, something that cannot be explained in the Mundell-Flemming framework.

15. An alternative mechanism could generate the same result if a tightening of the fiscal position resulted in a positive reevaluation of the expected future worth of a country's currency, leading to increased demand for money and an inward shift in the *LM* curve in figures 5.1 and 5.2. The effect on the exchange rate and the current account would depend on whether this inward shift in the *LM* curve outweighed the simultaneous inward shift in the *IS* curve due to the direct effect of the fiscal deficit reduction.

16. Since the growth in the productivity of labor in the tradables sector does not require real appreciation, this is likely to be a move *away* from the equilibrium exchange rate. Much depends on the nature of what is produced by the nontradable goods sector. If it is exclusively nonstorable services, then the result we described above indeed follows. If nontradables include assets (e.g., land or buildings, the returns to which are expected to increase with increased productivity in the tradables sector and real appreciation in the nontradables sector), then the anticipation of these processes can be expected to induce a capital inflow, which will cause an appreciation of both the equilibrium and the actual nominal exchange rate. The latter effect will help to stifle average inflation without a move away from the equilibrium exchange rate.

17. Because ρ is defined as units of domestic currency/unit of foreign currency, appreciation involves a reduction in it (i.e., a negative growth rate of ρ), which therefore has to be subtracted from the domestic interest rate (giving a positive effect to the left-hand side of equation (5.15)) to arrive at the foreign interest rate.

18. Together these two conditions imply a nominal appreciation of 7 percent per annum, if average euro zone inflation exceeds that of the best three performers by 1 percent.

19. Due to the effect of capital inflow on the domestic money base. The ensuing inflation will ultimately lead to a high current account deficit as well.

20. Estonia, the Czech Republic, Slovenia, and Poland certainly qualify, with Slovakia and Hungary as possibles.

21. As a result of the sterilization policy pursued over the last five years in a vain attempt to avoid real appreciation of the domestic currency.

22. This possibility means that even countries that have international reserves that are adequate to cover only the euroization of coins and notes and other monetary liabilities of the NCB to the banking sector can still establish a BSLF by setting up credit lines with euro zone commercial banks, if their governments have a sufficiently good credit rating.

23. The National Bank of Poland earns seigniorage by emitting non-interest-bearing currency and investing the international reserves it obtains in this way in interest-bearing foreign assets (U.S. and German government bills and bonds, current accounts with OECD commercial banks, etc.). These reserves amount to some $26 billion. About $10 billion of this, or two fifths, would need to be converted into euro notes and coins for circulation within the country. The remainder, which would back the bank's non-cash liabilities to the banking sector (obligatory and voluntary reserves and repos) as well as the institution's net worth (which would fund the BSLF already described), could largely remain invested as at present. The *gross* loss of seigniorage would thus amount to about $600 million per annum (at an interest rate of 6 percent) or merely some 0.38 percent of GDP.

24. For the last four years the consolidated general government deficit, measured according to EU statistical conventions, has remained stubbornly at about 3.3 percent of GDP (0.3 percent of GDP above the "reference value").

25. I am grateful to Boguslaw Grabowski for this point.

26. In the case of Poland (using the 1999 balance sheet of the National Bank of Poland) such deposits were the equivalent of about 2.2 billion euros, compared to a value for zloty notes and coins of 9.5 billion euros.

27. This can, of course, be negative as well as positive.

References

Buiter, Willem. (1995). Macroeconomic Policy during Transition to a Monetary Union. Discussion paper no. 261, Centre for Economic Performance, London School of Economics.

Bratkowski, Andrzej, and Jacek Rostowski. (1999). Wierzymy w Euro (we believe in Euro). *Rzeczpospolita*, April 26.

Calvo, Guillermo, and Carmen Reinhardt. (1999). Capital Flow Reversals, the Exchange Rate Debate and Dollarization. *Finance and Development* 36, no. 3: 13–15.

Caprio, Gerald, Michael Dooley, Danny Leipziger, and Carl Walsh. (1996). The Lender of Last Resort Function under a Currency Board: The Case of Argentina. Policy research working paper no. 1648, World Bank, Washington, D.C.

Dornbusch, Rudiger. (1976). Expectations and Exchange Rate Dynamics. *Journal of Political Economy* 84 (December): 1161–76.

Dornbusch, Rudiger, and Francesco Giavazzi. (1998). Hard Currency and Sound Credit: A Financial Agenda for Central Europe. Unpublished manuscript, MIT. Mimeographed.

Greenwald, Bruce, and Joseph Stiglitz. (1990). Macroeconomic Models with Equity and Credit Rationing. In Glenn Hubbard (ed.), *Asymmetric Information, Capital Markets and Investment*, 15–41. Chicago: University of Chicago Press.

Halpern, Laszlo, and Charles Wyplosz. (1995). Equilibrium Real Exchange Rates in Transition. Discussion paper no. 1145, Centre for Economic Policy Research, London.

Kopits, George. (1999). Implications of EMU for Exchange Rate Policy in Central and Eastern Europe. Working paper no. WP/99/9, International Monetary Fund, Washington, D.C.

Kouri, Pentti. (1978). International Investment and Interest Rate Linkages under Flexible Exchange Rates. In R. Aliber (ed.), *The Polital Economy of Monetary Reform*, 132–148. London: MacMillan.

Lutkowski, Karol. (1999). Memorandum. April. Ministry of Finance, Warsaw, Poland. Mimeographed.

Obstfeld, Maurice, and Kenneth Rogoff. (1996). *Foundations of International Macroeconomics*. Cambridge: MIT Press.

Orlowski, Witold, and Krzysztof Rybinski. (1999). Recepta na kryzys walutowy. (A recipe for currency crisis). *Rzeczpospolita*, May 12, 8.

Rosati, Dariusz. (1999). Jeszcze nie czas na likwidacje zlotego (Not yet the right time to liquidate the zloty). *Rzeczpospolita*, May 19, 9.

Wilcox, David. (1989). Social Security Benefits, Consumption Expenditure, and the Life-Cycle Hypothesis. *Journal of Political Economy* 97 (April): 288–304.

6 The Costs and Benefits of Euroization in Central and Eastern Europe before or instead of EMU Membership

D. Mario Nuti

6.1 Introduction

The current simultaneous EU enlargement and monetary unification are about to create an unprecedented economic segmentation in Europe. Previous instances of enlargement and deepening treated equally old members among themselves and, subject to short-lived transition arrangements, old and new members. Countries were either in or out of the European Community (as it then was); any other diversification existed previously and was not actually generated by the progress and pattern of European integration.

Membership in the EMU is an integral part of the *acquis communautaire*, which new and old members alike are committed to implement, subject to three qualifications (see Temprano Arroyo and Feldman 1999):

1. possible "derogations," such as those negotiated by the United Kingdom and Denmark, which no new member is allowed;
2. before joining EMU, at least two-year successful participation in the exchange rate mechanism (ERM),[1] which Sweden deliberately has failed to implement to date but new members are expected to join soon after accession;
3. before examination of a country's application to join the EMU, achievement of the other Maastricht Treaty standards for monetary and financial convergence, in terms of public debt and deficit, inflation, and interest rates;[2] failure to achieve these standards delayed Greece's membership in the EMU until the Lisbon summit of June 2000.

Even if all new members opted to join the EMU at the earliest possible date (and a fortiori if they did not), therefore, in the European Union's transition to a fully integrated and enlarged Monetary Union, Europe is going to be segmented into at least four groups:

- members of both the EU and the EMU (at present twelve, including Greece)
- members of the EU that are either excluded (Greece until recently) or self-excluded (United Kingdom, Denmark, Sweden) from the EMU, soon to be joined by the next batch of new members for at least their first two years of ERM participation after accession (unless a record of exchange rate stability is treated as equivalent to ERM; see below)
- ten applicant countries from central Europe already engaged in detailed accession negotiations: Bulgaria, the Czech Republic, Estonia, Hungary, Latvia, Lithuania, Poland, Romania, the Slovak Republic and Slovenia; plus Cyprus and Malta. These may be followed by Turkey and other countries from southeastern Europe, some of whom may overtake some of the first group, for instance in the possible case of Croatia. The admission of all these countries to the EU is subject to economic and political conditions and will be staggered over time beginning not earlier than 2003–2004
- the rest of Europe and of the former Soviet Union (FSU), excluded from the EU and the EMU at least for the foreseeable future.

Union and Euroland enlargement is going to have, in the words of ECB President Wim Duisemberg, "deep and wide-ranging consequences" for the ECB (quoted in "ECB Heads for Turbulence" 2000; see also Bekx 1998). *Before* EMU membership or, for the excluded or self-excluded, *instead of* EMU membership, there are two possible and, most important, *unilateral* ways for countries to secure a closer monetary integration with the EMU area if they wish. The first is the adoption of a currency board managing a domestic currency linked to the euro or (until 2002, when euro coins and banknotes appeared) to any of the EMU member currencies; for the sake of convenience and of psychological impact the currency, whatever it is called, could also be scaled so as to make its unit equivalent to one euro, at no extra cost. The second, more drastic alternative is the *official* adoption of the euro or, until it has a bodily existence, of any of the EMU member currencies—plausibly the deutsche mark (DM)—as the exclusive or primary domestic means of payment, which in many countries is facilitated by already existent *unofficial* DM-ization or dollarization.

This chapter seeks to identify the theoretical and empirical issues involved in these two options and to evaluate euroization costs and benefits for both accession candidates and the EU and its member states, drawing policy conclusions that should also be relevant for EU outsiders.

6.2 Euroization to Date

Both a currency board and domestic currency replacement can be regarded as forms of *euroization* (by analogy with the more euphonic *dollarization*, on which see Calvo 1999; IMF 1999; U.S. Senate 1999; Berg and Borensztein 2000). The currency board is euroization in a broad sense, whereas the use of the actual euro is euroization in a strict sense, though both fall short of the full-fledged euroization obtained through full EMU membership.

Currency boards with links to the DM or the euro already exist in Estonia (8 kroons = 1 DM, i.e., EEK 15.6466 = 1 euro), Bulgaria (with the lev in 1997 originally tied to the DM, then in 1999 repegged to the euro, which is the same thing, BGL 1.95583 = 1 euro), and Bosnia, with the "convertible mark" equivalent to the DM. Lithuania had a currency board linked to the U.S. dollar (from 1994, 4 litas = 1 US$; see Korhonen 1999, 2000). Any currency whose exchange rate was irrevocably tied to a currency, the DM, which in turn was irrevocably fixed to the euro obviously was already indirectly pegged to the euro; thus they switched from a link to the DM to a link to the euro at a stroke. This could be followed by a redenomination of their domestic currency so as to equal one euro.

The euro is also the reference currency for the exchange rate pegs in the Czech Republic, Slovakia, and Slovenia (on the extremely diversified exchange rate regimes in the transition, see Nuti 1996a; Backé 1999; Lavra 1997). Poland, Hungary, and Romania are only partly linked to the euro (the first two respectively at 55 percent and 70 percent only), with the residual still being represented by the U.S. dollar (see Nuti 2000a).

The Lithuanian Currency Board initial link to the U.S. dollar indicated a lower degree of euro-optimism there (see Korhonen 1996); the same considerations apply to any other country that has succeeded in maintaining a fixed exchange rate in relation to a reference hard currency other than the euro or an EMU member currency, such as Latvia's lat (since 1994, an informal peg to the Special Drawing Rights (SDR) has been maintained, at 0.8 lats = 1 SDR, ±1 percent).

It can be argued that an EMU candidate that has experienced a period of preaccession euroization in either form, currency board or currency replacement by an EMU currency, should have the two-year ERM-II membership requirement shortened or even waived. Indeed the same treatment may be plausibly requested by any other country that has maintained an exchange rate stability comparable to that of ERM-II in the run-up to accession. The Latvian lat, for instance, having maintained its peg to the SDR in spite of the August 1998 Russian crisis and its significant impact on all Baltic economies, also deserves to have its two years' waiting time significantly shortened; Latvia's foreign minister, Indulis Berzins, has announced that his country hopes to join the euro zone as early as 2003. Neither enlargement nor successful unilateral euroization were being contemplated when the Maastricht Treaty was being negotiated; hence the case for relaxing the two-year ERM-II membership, though not automatic, is exceptionally strong.

Informal DM-ization (now euroization) already exists on a large scale in eastern Europe and the FSU, though it is often dominated by (informal) dollarization. In 1995 the German Bundesbank estimated that 30–40 percent of all DM notes and coins in circulation were held abroad (Seitz 1995), which compares with a Federal Reserve estimate of 40–60 percent for the U.S. dollar (corresponding to $192–288 billion; Feige et al. 2000). Montenegro has formally adopted the DM as a dual legal tender next to the Yugoslav dinar; the DM is de facto the domestic currency in Kosovo. Any DM-ized country eventually (in 2002) became strictly euroized.

Proposals for an extension of the currency board regime have been put forward for other EU accession candidates (e.g., by Mundell 1999, Gros 1999; CEPS 1999; Bratkowski and Rostowski (2000) recommend an early official replacement of the Polish zloty by the euro.

6.3 Advantages of Euroization

By and large the prevailing view, both in economic literature and in policy circles, is that euroization has immediate and dominant positive net advantages, especially in transition countries where government institutions lack the credibility and track record needed to successfully adopt alternative exchange rate regimes and the monetary policies necessary to back them. One argument for dollarization or euroization is the national governments' ability to overcome their inability otherwise to borrow internationally in their domestic currency (Hausmann 1999, Hausmann, Panizza, and Stein 2000). Euroization or dollarization also avoids both the volatility and inflationary bias of floating rates and the vulnerability to speculative crises of fixed rates that are not irrevocably fixed (see Mundell forthcoming). Even successful regimes of fixed exchange rate can be made vulnerable by their own success, as they attract capital inflows that lead to real revaluation undermining competitiveness; at some point those flows can be easily, suddenly, and massively reversed. Irrevocably fixed rates, unlike pegs subject to intermittent adjustments, do not encourage speculation, as demonstrated by the experience of EMU members since May 1998 as opposed to the September 1992 ERM crisis and the abandonment of the ERM by the United Kingdom and Italy (a difference between irrevocably fixed rates and pegs neglected by Larrain and Sachs [2000] in their feeble rehearsal of arguments against dollarization).

In addition, the benefits of euroization, as in the case of monetary unification, are as follows:

- lower transaction costs, precisely as for the EMU members
- greater economic integration, through both greater trade and greater foreign direct investment, especially if euroization is accompanied by mutual trade liberalization or possibly a free trade area without the considerable restrictions still impeding trade with present European Associates candidates for accession (see section 6.8 below)
- basic interest rates that are probably lower in comparable units than otherwise (though interest rates are invariably higher than in the reference country, for they are subject to risk premiums for any individual country or borrower), in the case of a currency board; perhaps even lower interest rates for domestic currency replacement by actual euros

Finally, euroization would involve automatic, self-regulating adjustments in money supply, which in both cases (currency board and currency replacement) would be determined by trends in domestically held foreign assets, expanding for a balance-of-payments surplus and contracting at times of deficits, as is supposed to happen under a gold standard.

Unlike partial, unofficial euroization or dollarization, total and official currency replacement would not complicate the choice of intermediate targets of monetary policy by introducing a dual-currency component in the money supply and would not impose the shocks of exchange rate adjustments on producers and financial institutions.

Initially, euroization might be accompanied by a degree of undervaluation of the old currency with respect to the euro; this weakness might be compounded by an initial weakness of the euro with respect to other hard currencies (as in 1999–2000). Undervaluation might be a blessing in disguise from the viewpoint of competitiveness and employment (though not with respect to inflation; see below).

6.4 Possible Disadvantages of Euroization: Differences from EMU Membership

Although it is perfectly possible that euroization forms will yield the expected net advantages, this is not by any means a foregone conclusion. It is not just a question of a possible rejection of euroization on grounds of national pride, with countries temporarily or permanently excluded from EMU hanging on to a domestic currency as a symbol of national sovereignty. *Whether forms of euroization can be successful is an empirical question, depending on the relative strength of accompanying disadvantages.* In fact the local adoption of the euro as domestic currency, whether as a banknote or as a backing for domestic banknotes, is not quite the same thing as being a member of EMU.

There are distinct disadvantages associated with the operation of a currency board with respect to EMU membership (see Nuti et al. 1995, 1997):

1. A currency board regime needs initial endowment with sufficient foreign exchange reserves to back the entire currency in circulation (whether new or unchanged) at the permanently fixed exchange rate preselected by the government. Estonia benefited from the return of eleven tons of gold that had been sent to the West before 1940;

Lithuania also benefited from the return of six tons of gold as well as purchases from the IMF (OECD 2000). Other countries might be less fortunate: Bratkowski and Rostowski (2000) claim that Poland (with US$26 billion, i.e., twice the reserves necessary to back or replace the domestic currency), the Czech Republic, and Slovenia certainly could afford euroization, whereas Slovakia and Hungary are classed as "possible." Gros (1999) suggests that the resources necessary to introduce a currency board (which he estimates at $269 million for the former Yugoslav republics, probably an underestimate) could be borrowed, but this would undermine credibility and lead to expectations that the exchange rate would not be permanent but would last only as long as the loan would last and be renewed. The arrangement would be indistinguishable from an ordinary fixed exchange rate regime subject to occasional adjustments. Instead, reserves must be instantly and permanently available against possible requests for conversion; a currency board therefore cannot be run on borrowed money, unless, as in Bulgaria, finance is being provided only partly by Bretton Woods institutions and on a long-term basis, in which case foreign lending amounts to assistance and really might as well take the form not of a loan but of a gift.

2. Seigniorage, the revenue obtained from issuing domestic currency, would be lost. Such loss is sometimes underestimated (for instance, Bratkowski and Rostowski [2000] neglect the loss of likely *increases* in seigniorage after the domestic currency is shed) but it can also be overplayed (e.g., by Larraín and Sachs [2000]). In the case of a currency board, this loss could be offset at least partly by interest earned on reserves. Also, a seigniorage-sharing arrangement could be made with the ECB (Calvo 1999; Daviddi 1999); such an arrangement is contemplated, for dollarized countries, by the International Monetary Stability Act of 2000, introduced in the U.S. Senate by the Chairman of the Joint Economic Committee Senator Connie Mack, though later abandoned. According to Larry Summers then U.S. Treasury Secretary, "In the long term, finding ways of bribing people to dollarize, or at least give back the extra currency that is earned when dollarization takes place, ought to be an international priority" (quoted in U.S. Senate 1999); the same argument would apply to euroization.

3. The lack of a lender of last resort would involve a considerable degree of financial fragility, particularly serious in the early stages

of transition. The U.S. International Monetary Stability Act cited above specifically stated that "the Federal Reserve System has no obligation to act as a lender of last resort to the financial systems of dollarized countries" (section 2.b). The mythical advantage of a currency board is that the domestic currency is "fully backed" by foreign exchange (see, e.g., "ECB Heads for Turbulence" 2000). Thus the board could lend as a last resort only any excess reserves it might have over and above what is required to back the domestic currency; such reserves would be substantial in Poland but nowhere else in the area. Unfortunately all that is backed up by foreign exchange is primary money (i.e., M0), whereas in a currency crisis, there is absolutely nothing to prevent the public from wishing to convert into foreign exchange more than M0, up to their entire liquid assets (i.e., anything up to M2). In this case limits would have to be introduced, whether de facto or de jure, on the convertibility of bank money into cash, thus reinstating a monetary segmentation that was one of the typical features of the old-style centrally planned economy. In a "normal" monetary economy this occurrence is prevented, short of a total meltdown, by the national central bank's acting as a lender of last resort, in principle standing by to provide unlimited liquidity at a penal interest rate against good-quality securities. The limits of a currency board regime have been spectacularly confirmed by the Argentinian financial crisis of December 2001.

It follows that *either* the country has an arrangement for the ECB *to act as* lender of last resort, which would expose the ECB and ultimately the euro to an intolerable level of risk for countries not constrained to Maastricht Treaty parameters of fiscal and monetary convergence, *or* the ECB *does not act* as lender of last resort in the euroized country, in which case its financial system will be particularly fragile, and a financial crisis would take the form of a premium for euro cash over euro bank money. Standby arrangements by private banks taking on a lender-of-last-resort function (Calvo 1999) may have limited effect. Banks could be bankrupted as a result, not for straight insolvency, which might be regarded as a necessary and even desirable development, but for sheer illiquidity artificially created by the currency board's rules of monetary issue. The problem would be aggravated by the fact that the ECB could not take on any responsibility for the supervision of financial institutions in euroized countries (a provision to that effect was included in the

U.S. International Monetary Stability Act for the Federal Reserve System).

4. It would be impossible to eliminate entirely the risk of a parity change, whether under a currency board regime or even currency replacement (Larraín and Sachs [2000] regard this as irreversible, whereas Bratkowski and Rostowski [2000] contemplate a possible reversal). By linking its domestic currency to a more credible currency, a government, contrary to what is widely believed, cannot acquire the other currency's credibility; government policy credibility will be the product of its own and the other currency's credibility (in other words, the strength of a chain cannot be greater than that of its weakest link). Replacement of a country's currency, say, with euros might give rise to a euro scarcity unless interest rates were raised (or aggregate demand otherwise lowered) enough to match demand for and supply of cash.

5. Current account deficits arising in a domestic currency at risk for currency crises would be transformed into regional underdevelopment risks in a single currency area, especially without provisions for transfers from the EU budgets, which would benefit only EU members. Bratkowski and Rostowski (2000) see the rise of current account deficits as the inevitable consequence of consumption smoothing in countries experiencing or expecting growth acceleration and regard the elimination of currency crises risk as a major benefit of euroization. Even if this benefit was so obtained, it would be matched by the risk of regional underdevelopment instead, which may be potentially more difficult to deal with, and span over a longer run, than a temporary currency crisis.

6.5 Possible Disadvantages of Euroization: Unsuitability of Any Peg to the Euro

In addition to the disadvantages posed by euroization that falls short of full EMU membership, the euro may prove unsuitable as a pegging currency *in any form*:

1. The euro may not be the preferred currency in a particular country's invoicing practices in foreign trade. Settlement practices are often regarded as relevant, to the choice of a monetary anchor, but they are immaterial. For instance, according to Helmut Aancans,

head of monetary policy at the Latvian central bank, "Our structure of settlement currencies reflects the SDR basket.... When the euro goes down the dollar goes up and there is no net instability" (quoted in "Baltic States" 2000). But such stability obtains only if the SDR is the currency in which contracts are denominated. The Lithuanian lita, while it was pegged to the U.S. dollar, appreciated instead in real terms with respect to other currencies used in its pricing and invoicing, thus incurring a large-scale current account deficit. As Arvidas Krejzde, deputy governor of the Lithuanian central bank, has noted, "Trade in Euros is not as big as trade in dollars" (quoted in "Baltic States" 2000), but 40 percent of Lithuania's foreign trade was with the EU, and appreciation was therefore a nonnegligible problem.

2. Moreover, a number of countries have raised a very large part of their external debt in U.S. dollars: in 1997 the share of dollar-denominated external debt was 77.9 percent in the Czech Republic, 75.1 percent in Bulgaria, 61.6 percent in Lithuania, and 46 percent in Poland, against DM shares respectively of 4.7 percent, 4.7 percent, 6.2 percent, and 9.9 percent (Deutsche Bank Research 2000). For such countries any euro devaluation with respect to the dollar, such as that which occurred in the first eighteen months of the euro's life in 1999–2000, would raise the domestic burden of foreign debt service; a significant redenomination of external debt would have to accompany their euroization.

3. *Any* fixed peg to the euro (i.e., even short of a currency board) has inflationary implications for the long-term real exchange rate revaluation that has been observed and can be expected in all transition economies. Real revaluation is usually associated with the so-called Harrod-Balassa-Samuelson effect of faster productivity in tradables driving up wages and prices in nontradables, but this effect can easily be overplayed: after all, tradables are both inputs in nontradable goods and substitutes for nontradables; moreover, faster productivity in tradables is a worldwide phenomenon that will be reflected in world price trends. Regardless of this effect, or in addition to it, *any* exchange rate (whether fixed or floating) at which convertibility is introduced in inflationary and troubled times is bound to be undervalued in real terms. For a fixed nominal exchange rate, real revaluation can be achieved only through a positive inflationary differential with respect to the peg currency. Far from aiding

the control of inflation, in such circumstances a fixed exchange rate regime can turn into an inexorable inflationary machine. The necessary real revaluation could be be achieved without inflation only through a nominal revaluation.

Of course a real revaluation can be inconsistent with the parallel commitments to price stability and nominal exchange rate stability within the bounds of the Maastricht criteria, and unilateral euroization can be seen as a way to evade those bounds (Bratkowski and Rostowski 2000). The very broad fluctuation margins envisaged by ERM-II (±15 percent), however, and the applicability of the Maastricht inflation limits only in the run-up to EMU membership (for just one year before examination) should still leave large enough scope to accommodate the necessary real revaluation without violating the Maastricht criteria for price and nominal exchange rate stability.

4. More generally, the monetary policy pursued by the ECB may be unsuitable to the fundamentals of the countries undertaking euroization. Apart from providing liquidity to euroized countries against foreign exchange, the ECB would have no obligation to consider their particular needs, just as the U.S. International Monetary Stability Act states that "the Federal Reserve System has no obligation to consider the economic conditions of dollarized countries when formulating or implementing monetary policy" (Section 2.b). De Grawe and Aksoy (1997; see also De Grawe and Lavra 1997) investigate whether central European countries are part of an optimum currency area (as theorized by Mundell's classic article of 1961) and conclude that they are not.

Of course the stabilization needs of transition economies may not leave much margin for an independent monetary policy, which is totally lost for any fixed exchange rate regime, but the instant abatement of inflation may not necessarily be the best policy, as confirmed by the dominant success of the Polish economy, which for all the talk of shock therapy has been disinflated at an excruciatingly gradual rate. Moreover, all central and eastern European transition economies are facing extremely challenging issues of social welfare reform, on a greater scale than the rest of Europe (see Nuti et al. 2000). Before worrying about convergence, many transition regions such as Serbia or Kosovo would have to worry about reconstruction (IMF and World Bank 1999). Also, the experience of Bosnia, where the DM euro continued to circulate as a parallel currency (though to a rapidly diminishing extent), shows that even the adoption of a currency board can be ineffective unless it is preceded by extensive economic and political reforms.

All the arguments in this section make a case not against unilateral euroization per se, but more generally, against early membership in the EMU. Seeing, however, that the main—indeed the only—point of unilateral euroization is that of replicating the effects of joining the EMU earlier than otherwise possible, they are also arguments against unilateral euroization.

6.6 Costs and Benefits of Euroization for the ECB and the EMU Members

Euroization of countries outside the EMU would also involve advantages and disadvantages for the ECB and for EMU members. (On the mutual impact of EU and transition economies, see Nuti 1994, 1996b.) The main advantage would be seigniorage, net of the possible net cost of ECB sterilization of the currency board country's euro bonds and deposits if their effects on euro monetary expansion are judged to be excessive. An additional advantage would be avoiding the complications generated by the growth in the ECB governing council's membership following EMU enlargement (which otherwise would require complex solutions such as the drawing of constituencies, rotation, or outright exclusions). The main disadvantage would be the risk of a monetary expansion in the currency board country generated by its accumulation of noneuro assets, if it was sufficiently threatening to induce some loss of ECB control over the monetary mass of euros and euro substitutes.

Euroization in the strict sense of currency replacement would have similar implications for the euroized country, except that its introduction would probably be partial and spontaneous at the end of a hyperinflation process and its legalization the only form of necessary administrative sanction; loss of seigniorage (unless it was shared out by the ECB) would be unmitigated; and all the other drawbacks of a currency board would apply. For the ECB and the EMU area, the risk of monetary expansion originating outside would be much smaller for outright currency replacement than in the case of a currency board, because the ECB would retain control over primary euro supply.

6.7 Convergence?

A great deal of attention has been given to both financial and monetary convergence as represented by the Maastricht criteria (table 6.1) and to the progress of systemic transition as exemplified by the EBRD scoreboard in the *Transition Reports* of 1994–1999 (table 6.2). On both counts the picture is encouraging, at least for the front-runners lined up for accession, but also very misleading. The share of government deficit and debt in GDP are below or near the Maastricht parameters; inflation and interest rates are much higher but still within striking distance in most cases; and the transition progress recorded by the EBRD, especially in privatization and foreign trade, is impressive. But Maastricht criteria ignore essential and worrisome features of transition economies such as quasi-fiscal deficits and debt due to public contingent and delayed commitments, extrabudgetary funds, and hidden subsidies; they also ignore non-performing loans in the balance sheets of state banks and the low share of credit to the private sector and the low capitalization and/or low liquidity of financial markets throughout transition economies, as well as the extraordinary volatility of their rates of return (see EBRD 2000). Once quasi-fiscal items are taken into account, even exemplary candidates such as the Czech Republic lose much of their attraction (see Drabek 2000). The share of credit to the private sector appears to be inversely related to the share of bad loans (EBRD 1997). Transition economies seem to have either low market capitalization or low ratio of value traded to market capitalization (i.e., illiquidity) of their stock markets (e.g., respectively 2.6 and 36.3 percent of GDP in Romania, 39.7 and 3.9 percent in Russia) or both (e.g., 5.8 and 7.6 percent in Bulgaria and 6.2 and 11.6 percent in Latvia) (EBRD 2000).

The EBRD indicators suffer from an overoptimistic bias, not least because of the adoption of scores ranging from 1 to 4+ instead of starting from 0, which therefore credit even transition nonstarters with achievement of more than 20 percent of the road to a full-fledged market economy (see Nuti 2000b). They also neglect any notion of minimum requisites for a country to operate as a market economy, or of possible weights to be attached to their different indicators, or of the relative difficulty of making progress at different scores and in different fields. *Real* convergence of transition economies—apart from their almost instant convergence to EU

Table 6.1
EMU convergence criteria: Central and East European accession candidates in comparison (January 2000)

	Inflation rate (% per year)			Government balance (% of GDP)			Government debt (% of GDP)			Long-term interest rates on government bonds	Exchange rate regime, January 1, 2000
	1997	1998[a]	1999[b]	1997	1998[a]	1999[b]	1996	1997	1998[a]		
Reference value	2.7	2.1	2.0	−3.0	−3.0	−3.0	60.0	60.0	60.0	6.77 (10-year)	ERM-II
Bulgaria	1,082	22.3	2.0	−3.0	1.0	n.a.	n.a.	n.a.	n.a.	n.a.	Currency board (EUR)
Czech Republic only	8.5	10.7	2.5	−1.2	−1.5	−3.8	9.9	10.3	10.7	7.01 (5-year)	Flexible
EE	11.2	8.2	3.3	2.2	−0.3	−3.0	6.9	5.6	4.6	n.a.	Currency board (EUR)
Estovia	18.3	14.3	9.0	−4.5	−4.8	−4.3	71.5	62.9	59.8	9.17 (10-year)	Peg (EUR)
Lithuania	8.9	5.1	1.6	−1.8	−5.8	−7.0	n.a.	n.a.	n.a.	n.a.	Currency board (EUR)
Latvia	8.4	4.7	2.2	0.1	−0.8	−3.8	n.a.	n.a.	n.a.	n.a.	Peg (SDR)
Poland	14.9	11.8	7.0	−1.3	−1.2	−3.0	51.1	46.3	41.0	10.15 (10-year)	Peg (EUR/USD basket)
Romania	154.8	59.2	45.0	−3.6	−3.1	−5.0	24.3	26.1	26.4	n.a.	Flexible
Slovenia	8.4	8.0	7.5	−1.7	−1.4	−1.0	23.2	23.5	24.0	n.a.	Flexible
Slovakia	6.1	6.7	10.6	−4.4	−5.8	−3.2	n.a.	n.a.	n.a.	n.a.	Flexible

Sources: Deutsche Bank Research; EBRD, *Euro Watch* no. 82, February 2000.
Note: n.a. = not available. EUR = Euro. USD = U.S. dollar.
[a] Expected. [b] Forecast.

unemployment average and variance, not requested by any treaty but promptly achieved in the early 1990s—appears to be a much slower and more protracted process than anticipated (see Kolodko 2000; see also Salvatore 2000).

These considerations invite greater caution in assessing the progress of new members' convergence to a single European Union standard and therefore in evaluating the net advantages to be obtained both from their membership in the EMU and from possible EMU membership surrogates.

6.8 Improved Trade Access versus Monetary Integration

The primary purpose of monetary integration, and of euroization as its earlier substitute, is promoting the economic integration of central and eastern European countries with the EU. This purpose could be achieved, to a much greater extent than under current arrangements, simply by the EU's unilaterally removing or at any rate reducing residual trade barriers with those countries, such as those of Common Agricultural Policy (CAP), quotas for lower-duty trade as in textiles, impositions of "voluntary" (as in the case of steel) antidumping provisions, and other measures of contingent protection in case of "injury" or "likely injury" to national producers. The European Association Agreements signed with all accession candidates envisaged the creation of a free trade area in ten years, in two stages, with the immediate removal of quantitative restrictions and the gradual abatement of import tariffs at a faster rate (but from a higher level) in the EU, but the process—speeded up by only six months after the momentous Copenhagen summit that paved the way to eastern enlargement—is still incomplete, and residual barriers, though falling, are still a significant impediment to trade. Meanwhile European Union members have turned their trade balance with the ten accession candidates from a deficit of ECU 2 billion in 1989 to a steadily increasing surplus up to over 18 billion euro in 2000.

The EU surplus exists with every single one of the ten countries; it originates primarily in manufacturing products, especially for investment and intermediate goods, but it arises even for food and beverages (with the exception of Hungary) and for labor-intensive products (with the exception of the Czech Republic, Romania and to a smaller extent Bulgaria) (see Smith 2000).

In these circumstances there is no justification for the European Union to resist, by means of artificial barriers, a higher volume of

Table 6.2
Progress in transition in Central and Eastern Europe, the Baltic States and the CIS

	Private-sector share (%) of GDP, mid-1999 (EBRD estimate)[a]	Enterprises			Markets and trade			Financial institutions	
		Large-scale privatization	Small-scale privatization	Governance and enterprise restructuring	Price liberalization	Trade and foreign exchange system	Competition policy	Banking reform and interest rate liberalization	Securities markets and nonbank financial institutions
Albania	75	2	4	2	3	4	2	2	2–
Armenia	60	3	3+	2	3	4	2	2+	2
Azerbaijan	45	2–	3	2	3	3+	1	2	2–
Belarus	20	1	2	1	2–	1	2	1	2
Bosnia and Herzegovina	35	2	2	2–	3	3–	1	2+	1
Bulgaria	60	3	3+	2+	3	4+	2	3–	2
Croatia	60	3	4+	3–	3	4	2	3	2+
Czech Republic	80	4	4+	3	3	4+	3	3+	3
Estonia	75	4	4+	3	3	4	3–	4–	3
FYR Macedonia	55	3	4	2	3	4	1	3	2–
Georgia	60	3+	4	2	3	4	2	2+	1
Hungary	80	4	4+	3+	3+	4+	3	4	3+
Kazakhstan	55	3	4	2	3	3	2	2+	2
Kyrgyzstan	60	3	4	2	3	4	2	2+	2
Latvia	65	3	4	3–	3	4+	3–	3	2+
Lithuania	70	3	4+	3–	3	4	2+	3	3–
Moldova	45	3	3+	2	3	4	2	2+	2
Poland	65	3+	4+	3	3+	4+	3	3+	3+

Romania	60	3−	4−	2	3	4	2	3−	2
Russian Federation	70	3+	4	2−	3−	2+	2+	2−	2−
Slovak Republic	75	4	4+	3	3	4+	3	3−	2+
Slovenia	55	3+	4+	3−	3	4+	2	3+	3
Tajikistan	30	2+	3	2−	3	3−	1	1	1
Turkmenistan	25	2−	2	2−	2	1	1	1	1
Ukraine	55	2+	3+	2	3	3	2	2	2
Uzbekistan	45	3−	3	2	2	1	2	2−	2

Source: From EBRD *Transition Report 1999*, November.

[a] The "private-sector shares" of GDP represent rough EBRD estimates, based on available statistics from both official (government) sources and unofficial sources. The underlying concept of private-sector value added includes income generated by the activity of private registered companies as well as that generated by private entities engaged in informal activity in those cases in which reliable information on informal activity is available. Here the term "private companies" refers to all enterprises in which a majority of the shares are owned by private individuals or entities. The roughness of the EBRD estimates reflects data limitations, particularly with respect to the scale of informal activity. The EBRD estimates may in some cases differ markedly from available data from official sources on the contribution to GDP made by the "private sector" or by the "nonstate sector." This is in most cases because the definition of the EBRD concept differs from that of the official estimates. Specifically for the CIS countries, official data in most cases refer to value added in the "nonstate sector," a broad concept that incorporates collective farms as well as companies in which only a minority stake has been privatized.

Large-scale privatization

1 Little private ownership.
2 Comprehensive scheme almost ready for implementation; some sales completed.
3 More than 25 percent of large-scale enterprise assets in private hands or in the process of being privatized (with the process having reached a stage at which the state has effectively ceded its ownership rights), but possibly with major unresolved issues regarding corporate governance.
4 More than 50 percent of state-owned enterprise and farm assets in private ownership and significant progress on corporate governance of these enterprises.

Table 6.2 (continued)

Small-scale privatization	
2	Substantial share privatized.
3	Nearly comprehensive program implemented.
4	Complete privatization of small companies with tradable ownership rights.
4+	Standards and performance typical of advanced industrial economies: no state ownership of small enterprises, effective tradability of land.
Governance and enterprise restructuring	
1	Soft budget constraints (lax credit and subsidy policies weakening financial discipline at the enterprise level); few other reforms to promote corporate governance.
2	Moderately tight credit and subsidy policy but weak enforcement of bankruptcy legislation and little action taken to strengthen competition and corporate governance.
3	Significant and sustained actions to harden budget constraints and to promote corporate governance effectively (e.g., through privatization combined with tight credit and subsidy policies and/or enforcement of bankruptcy legislation).
Price liberalization	
2	Price controls for several important product categories; state procurement at nonmarket prices remains substantial.
3	Substantial progress on price liberalization: state procurement at nonmarket prices largely phased out.
Trade and foreign exchange system	
1	Widespread import and/or export controls or very limited legitimate access to foreign exchange.
2	Some liberalization of import and/or export controls; almost full current account convertibility in principle but with a foreign exchange regime that is not fully transparent (possibly with multiple exchange rates).
3	Removal of almost all quantitative and administrative import and export restrictions; almost full current account convertibility.
4	Removal of all quantitative and administrative import and export restrictions (apart from agriculture) and all significant export tariffs; insignificant direct involvement in exports and imports by ministries and state-owned trading companies; no major nonuniformity of custom duties for nonagricultural goods and services; full current account convertibility.
4+	Standards and performance norms of advanced industrial economies: removal of most tariff barriers, WTO membership.

Competition policy

1 No competition legislation or institutions.
2 Competition policy legislation and institutions set up; some reduction of entry restrictions or enforcement action on dominant firms.
3 Some enforcement actions to reduce abuse of market power and to promote a competitive environment, including breakups of dominant conglomerates; substantial reduction of entry restrictions.

Banking reform and interest rate liberalization

1 Little progress beyond establishment of a two-tier system.
2 Significant liberalization of interest rates and credit allocation; limited use of direct credit or interest rate liberalization ceilings.
3 Substantial progress in establishment of bank solvency and of a framework for prudential supervision and regulation; full interest rate liberalization, with little preferential access to cheap refinancing; significant lending to private enterprises and significant presence of private banks.
4 Significant movement of banking laws and regulation towards BIS standards; well-functioning banking competition and effective prudential supervision; significant term lending to private enterprises; substantial financial deepening.

Securities markets and nonbank financial institutions

1 Little progress.
2 Formation of securities exchanges, market makers and brokers; some trading in government paper and/or securities; rudimentary legal and regulatory framework for the issuance and trading of securities.
3 Substantial issuance of securities by private enterprises; establishment of independent share registries, secure clearance and settlement procedures, and some protection of minority shareholders; emergence of nonbank financial institutions (e.g., investment funds, private insurance and pension funds, leasing companies) and associated regulatory framework.

imports from central and eastern European countries, whether or not they are accession candidates. The relative impact of EU trade's opening on these countries can be gauged by reference to the well-known asymmetry in the importance of mutual trade turnover, amounting to 3–4 percent of total trade for the EU and around 60 percent for central and eastern Europe. Greater trade access granted by the EU could be matched by parallel, automatic, or conditional reduction of remaining barriers to EU exports in central and eastern European countries, such as import surcharges and other, mostly retaliatory restrictions. Greater central and eastern European net exports would not only speed up real convergence but also alleviate social problems and, last but not least, presumably reduce the pressures for migration of labor to the EU.

The two ways to intensify economic integration, monetary unification or euroization and the removal of residual trade barriers, are not at all in conflict with each other and could be pursued simultaneously, mutually enhancing their effectiveness. Indeed, they could be pursued and implemented *even before accession.* It is simply inappropriate—for the EU and accession candidates alike—to place almost exclusive emphasis on enlargement and monetary unification, neglecting at the same time the existing, immediate opportunities for deeper and faster trade integration.

6.9 Conclusions

To a visitor from outer space the arrangements of the present EMU area and those of the wider Euro area enlarged to include strict euroization and/or euro-backed local currency would be absolutely indistinguishable. But there would be an immensely important difference in the different role of the ECB, which in a strictly euroized country would not act as a central bank. Namely, in such a country, the ECB would not be regulator and supervisor of the banking system; most importantly, it would not be a lender of last resort. Instead it would act, by definition, as an institute of issue but would have no responsibility toward a euroized non-EMU-member country in deciding its monetary or exchange rate policy.

Ultimately the net balance of costs and benefits, both for the euroized country and for Euroland and its members, is an empirical question depending on the degree of monetary, real, and institutional convergence already achieved before euroization and its subsequent progress; the initial endowment of currency reserves; the initial currency of choice for invoicing and payment practices in foreign trade; the size and denomination of foreign debt; the existing degree of utilization of foreign exchange in the domestic economy; the international credibility of domestic monetary institutions; and the degree of cooperation between domestic and European institutions, both political and monetary.

Current trends in financial and monetary convergence, and even more so in institutional and real convergence, are probably overoptimistically evaluated by observers and officials. Positive net advantages may well derive from euroization but should not be taken for granted. Meanwhile, the unexploited potential for greater economic integration through greater trade access to EU markets should not be neglected.

Notes

Earlier drafts of this chapter were presented as papers at the Sixth Dubrovnik Economic Conference, "Exchange Rate and Financial Vulnerability in Emerging Markets," June 29–30, 2000; and at the Twelfth Annual Meeting of the Society for the Advancement of Socio-Economics, London School of Economics, July 7–10, 2000, in a panel discussion, "The Economic Impact of Exclusion from EU and EMU." Acknowledgements are due to Jacek Rostowski and Milica Uvalic, as well as other participants in both conferences, for useful comments and suggestions. Financial support from the ESRC program "One Europe or Several?" project no. L213 25 2003, is gratefully acknowledged.

1. The ERM to which the Maastricht Treaty referred was replaced as of January 1, 1999, by ERM-II, including criteria such as the development of market integration, current account balance, monitoring of unit labor costs, and other price indices.

2. More precisely, in addition to two-year ERM-II membership: (1) an average rate of inflation over a period of one year before the examination that does not exceed the average of that of the three best-performing member states by more than 1.5 percent; (2) an average nominal long-term interest rate on government bonds, also over a period of one year before the examination, that does not exceed by more than two percentage points the average of that of the three best performing member states in terms of price stability; (3) a government deficit of at most 3 percent of GDP and (4) a government debt of at most 60 percent of GDP, unless the ratios for both deficit and debt are close to the reference values and either have already declined substantially or exceed the reference value only temporarily.

References

Backé, Peter. (1999). Exchange Rate Regimes in Central and Eastern Europe. In *Focus on Transition*, vol. 2. Österreichische Nationalbank, Vienna.

Baltic States Knock on Gates of Euro-Zone. *Financial Times*, February 16.

Bekx, Peter. (1998). The Implications of the Introduction of the Euro for non-EU Countries. Euro papers no. 26, Directorate General II (DGII), European Commission, Brussels.

Berg, Andrew, and Eduardo Borensztein. (2000). The Pros and Cons of Full Dollarization. Working paper no. WP/00/50, International Monetary Fund, Washington, D.C.

Bratkowski, Andrzej, and Jacek Rostowski. (2000). Unilateral Adoption of the Euro by EU Applicant Countries: The Macroeconomic Aspects. Paper presented at the Sixth Dubrovnik Conference, June 29–30, Dubrovnik, Croatia.

Calvo, Guillermo. (1999). On dollarization. Unpublished manuscript, University of Maryland. College Park. Available online at ⟨www.bsos.umd.edu/econ/ciecalvo.htm⟩.

Centre for European Policy Studies (CEPS). (1999). A System for Post-war South-East Europe. Working document no. 131, CEPS, Brussels.

Daviddi, Renzo. (1999). "Hyper-fix" Exchange Rate Regimes and Transition. Background paper, Directorate General II (DG-II), European Commission, Brussels.

De Grawe, Paul, and Y. Aksoy. (1997). Are Central European Countries Part of the European Optimum Currency Area? Conference paper, Ljubljana, Slovenia.

De Grawe, Paul, and V. Lavra (eds.). (1997). *Inclusion of Central European Countries in the European Monetary Union*. Leuven University.

Deutsche Bank. (2000). Deutsche Bank Research, December.

Drabek, Zdenek. (2000). Are Even Balanced Budgets Sustainable? Paper presented at American Social Sciences Association (ASSA) Conference Boston, January.

ECB Heads for Turbulence. *Economist*, January 29, pp. 106–7.

European Bank for Reconstruction and Development (EBRD). (1994–1999). *Transition Report*. London: EBRD.

European Bank for Reconstruction and Development (EBRD). (2000). *Transition Report Update*. London: EBRD.

Feige, Edgar L., Michael Faulend, Velimir Šonje, and Vedran Šošić. (2000). Unofficial Dollarization and Currency Substitution Revisited. Paper presented at Sixth Dubrovnik Conference, June 29–30, Dubrovnik, Croatia.

Gros, Daniel. (1999). An Economic System for Post-War South East Europe. Companion paper to working document no. 131, CEPS, Brussels.

Hausmann, Ricardo. (1999). Should There be Five Currencies or One Hundred and Five? *Foreign Policy* (Fall).

Hausmann Ricardo, Ugo Panizza, and Ernesto Stein. (2000). Why Do Countries Float the Way They Float? Working paper no. 418, Inter-American Development Bank–BID Washington, D.C.

International Monetary Fund (IMF). (1999). Monetary Policy in Dollarized Economies. Occasional paper no. 171, IMF, Washington, D.C.

International Monetary Fund (IMF) and World Bank. (1999). *The Economic Consequences of the Kosovo crisis*. Washington, D.C.: IMF and World Bank.

Kolodko, Grzegorz W. (2000). Globalization and Catching-Up: From Recession to Growth in Transition Economies. Working paper no. 100, International Monetary Fund, Washington, D.C.

Korhonen, Iikka. (1996). Dollarization in Lithuania. *Review of Economies in Transition* (Bank of Finland) (May).

Korhonen, Iikka. (1999). Some Implications of EU Membership on Baltic Monetary and Exchange Rate Policies. *Bank of Finland Institute for Transition*. Online working paper no. 6, Robert Schuman Centre, European University Institute, Florence.

Korhonen, Iikka. (2000). Currency Boards in the Baltic Countries: What Have We Learned? *Post-Communist Economies* 12, no. 1 (March).

Larraín, Felipe, and Jeffrey Sachs. (2000). "Why Dollarization Is More Straightjacket than Salvation. *Foreign Policy* (Fall).

Lavrač, V. (1997). Exchange Rate Policies of Central European Countries in the Context of European Monetary Integration. Conference paper Ljubliana, Slovenia.

Mundell, Robert A. (1961). A Theory of Optimum Currency Areas. *American Economic Review* 51, no. 4 (November): 509–17.

Mundell, Robert A. (1999). Exchange Rate Arrangements in Transition Economies. In Mario I. Blejer and Marko Škreb (eds.), *Balance of Payments, Exchange Rates, and Competitiveness in Transition Economies*, 95–130. Boston/Dordrecht/London: Kluwer Academic.

Mundell, Robert A. (forthcoming). Currency Areas, Volatility and Intervention. *Journal of Economic Modeling*.

Nuti, D. Mario. (1994). The Impact of Systemic Transition on the European Community. In Steve Martin (ed.), *The Construction of Europe*, 143–181. Dordrecht: Kluwer Academic.

Nuti, D. Mario. (1996a). Inflation, Interest and Exchange Rates in the Transition. *Economics of Transition* 4, no. 1: 137–158.

Nuti, D. Mario. (1996b). European Community Response to the Transition: Aid, Trade Access, Enlargement. *Economics of Transition* 4, no. 2: 503–511.

Nuti, D. Mario. (2000a). The Polish Zloty 1990–1999: Success and Underperformance. *American Economic Review, Papers and Proceedings* 90, no. 2 (May): 53–58.

Nuti, D. Mario. (2000b). On the Over-optimistic Bias of EBRD Indicators of Transition Progress. Paper presented at Economic and Sound Research Council (ESRC) seminar, June 7, London Business School.

Nuti, D. Mario, John Eatwell, Michael Ellman, Mats Karlsson, and Judith Shapiro. (1995). *Transformation and Integration: Shaping the Future of Central and Eastern Europe*. London: Institute for Public Policy Research (IPPR).

Nuti, D. Mario, John Eatwell, Michael Ellman, Mats Karlsson, and Judith Shapiro. (1997). *Not "Just Another Accession"—Political Economy of EU Enlargement to the East*. London: Institute for Public Policy Research (IPPR).

Nuti, D. Mario, John Eatwell, Michael Ellman, Mats Karlsson, and Judith Shapiro. (2000). *Hard Choices, Soft States: Social Welfare Policy in the Transition*. London: Institute for Public Policy Research.

Organisation for Economic Cooperation and Development (OECD). (2000). *Baltic States: A Regional Economic Assessment*. Economic surveys. Paris: OECD.

Roussenova, Lena. (1997). *The Bulgarian Currency Board*. Sofia, Bulgaria: World Bank.

Salvatore, Dominick. (2000). Narrowing the Structural Gap in Transition Economies. Paper presented at conference of the Austrian Ministry of the Economy, Vienna, June.

Seitz, Franz. (1995). The Circulation of Deutsche Mark Abroad. Discussion paper no. 1/95, Economic Research Group, Deutsche Bundesbank, Frankfurt am Main, Germany.

Smith, Alan. (2000). *Return to Europe*. Cambridge: Cambridge University Press.

Temprano-Arroyo, Heliodoro, and Robert A. Feldman. (1999). Selected Transition and Mediterranean Countries: An Institutional Primer on EMU and EU Accession. *Economics of Transition* 7, no. 3: 741–806.

U.S. Senate Joint Economic Committee. (1999). *Encouraging Official Dollarization in Emerging Markets*. Washington, D.C.: U.S. Government Printing Office.

7 Currency Substitution, Unofficial Dollarization, and Estimates of Foreign Currency Held Abroad: The Case of Croatia

Edgar L. Feige, Michael Faulend, Velimir Šonje, and Vedran Šošić

7.1 Introduction

Monetary and fiscal policies, the choice of exchange rate regime, and interventions in foreign exchange markets are often undertaken in economies that experience "unofficial dollarization," that is, those in which individuals and firms choose to use a foreign currency as a substitute for some of the monetary services of the domestic currency. The existence of a typically unknown amount of foreign currency in circulation (FCC) makes the outcome of domestic monetary policy uncertain. The effective money supply may be much larger than the domestic money supply and is subject to endogenous behavioral responses reflecting currency substitution on the part of the public. Hausmann et al. (1999) suggest that under such circumstances, expansionary monetary policy can have procyclical instead of countercyclical consequences, and Eichengreen and Hausmann (1999) note that the market for domestic government debt may be completely missing in dollarized countries, with adverse consequences for economic growth (Fry 1997). On the other hand, unofficial dollarization tends to dampen government efforts to employ inflationary finance to impose implicit taxes on domestic monetary assets.

Cocirculating foreign currency holdings reflect both currency substitution and asset substitution, and the two may have different economic consequences, making the implications of unofficial dollarization for macroeconomic decisions more difficult to predict. The greater the extent and variability of dollarization, the weaker is the central bank's knowledge and control over the effective money supply. Growing unofficial dollarization reduces the ability of the monetary authority to earn seigniorage from its own currency issue.

Unofficial dollarization reflects citizens' perceptions of the stability of the domestic monetary regime, the credibility of monetary policies, and the perceived stability of the domestic banking system.

Unofficial dollarization not only makes the outcomes of monetary policy less certain, it also has fiscal consequences. Foreign cash transactions rarely leave a paper trail. They therefore reduce the costs of tax evasion and increase the size of the unreported (unofficial) economy. This weakens the government's fiscal ability to command real resources from the private sector and deepens fiscal deficits. The shifting of economic activity toward the underground economy distorts macroeconomic information systems (Feige 1990, 1997), thereby adding to the difficulty of formulating macroeconomic policy. By obscuring financial transactions, unofficial dollarization also reduces the cost of enterprise theft and may facilitate greater corruption and rent seeking. Given these extensive ramifications, informed policy decision making requires better knowledge of the nature, extent, causes, and consequences of unofficial dollarization as well as the specific effects of its components, currency substitution and asset substitution.

Despite the substantive importance of the issues cited, there is virtually no reliable empirical information concerning the actual extent of unofficial dollarization. In their review of the key issues concerning currency substitution, Calvo and Végh (1992) observed, "In the final analysis, the relevance of currency substitution is an empirical issue.... At the empirical level, the study of currency substitution faces a fundamental problem: there is usually no data available on foreign currency circulating in an economy. Therefore the importance of currency substitution is basically unobservable."

This chapter employs newly collected data (Feige 1996, 1997) on the amount of foreign currency in circulation, in the form of U.S. dollars, in various countries in the world. These new data enable us finally to circumvent the fundamental problem of "unobservability" that has plagued the currency substitution literature since its inception. These new data permit a refinement of definitions and measures of the extent of currency substitution, asset substitution, unofficial dollarization, and the credibility of domestic banking institutions.

Once the nature and extent of unofficial dollarization is empirically measurable, it becomes possible to examine the causes of dollarization and the circumstances under which unofficial dollarization is likely to become irreversible.[1] Irreversibility will depend upon network externalities associated with the use of foreign currency.

Much of the dollarization literature has focused on the experience of Latin America and those transition countries whose hyperinflationary episodes have induced a flight to dollars. With new estimates of the extent of dollar currency holdings in these countries, we set out to model the dollarization process. The models we developed are then used to investigate a more complex issue, namely, the use of other nondollar foreign currencies as substitutes for domestic monetary assets. In particular, the citizens of a number of CEE transition countries have chosen the deutsche mark rather than the dollar as a substitute currency. In addition to the aforementioned issues concerning the consequences of currency substitution, "unofficial DM-ization" presents a special logistical problem of considerable urgency. On January 1, 2002, the euro was introduced as the common paper currency of the EU and the DM will cease to be legal tender. At the end of 1999, there were 2.8 billion DM banknotes in circulation with an estimated value of DM $274 billion. Indirect estimates (Seitz 1995; Doyle 2000) suggest that 30–69 percent of the total DMs outstanding may be held outside of Germany. Anecdotal evidence suggests that unofficial DM-ization has occurred in many of the central and eastern European countries, including Croatia. Unfortunately, no current estimates exist concerning the exact location of the estimated 82–189 billion DMs held abroad. If there is to be a smooth transition from DMs to the euro in non-EU countries, it is important for the European Central Bank to have estimates of the amount of euros that will be required to replace DMs overseas. We therefore develop methodologies designed to obtain estimates of the use of nondollar substitute currencies in foreign countries and present preliminary estimates of the extent of DM-ization in Croatia.

Section 7.2 briefly reviews earlier efforts to measure dollarization by indirect means and defines several measures of unofficial dollarization that attempt to distinguish between currency and asset substitution. Currency substitution occurs when a foreign currency substitutes as a medium of exchange for the domestic currency, whereas asset substitution refers to the substitution of foreign-denominated monetary assets for domestically denominated monetary assets. Section 7.3.1 presents new empirical estimates of the extent of dollarization and compares these estimates to earlier proxy measures employed by the IMF. We find that earlier estimates of dollarization are highly correlated with our estimates of asset substitution but appear to be imprecise measures of currency substitution.

Section 7.3.2 introduces two methods for determining the unknown amount of a nondollar foreign currency like the DM that may be in circulation in some of the CEE transition countries. The "denomination displacement method," discussed in section 7.3.3, is based on the hypothesis that foreign currency substitution often involves high-denomination foreign notes that tend to replace the highest-denomination notes of the domestic currency. By examining the observed denomination structure of the domestic currency, we hope to infer the extent of foreign currency usage. The second method, discussed in section 7.3.4, employs estimates of the demand function for FCC in countries known to be highly dollarized. The model's parameter estimates are then used to simulate the demand for nondollar FCC holdings in countries that are believed to employ DMs as a substitute for the domestic currency. Empirical estimates for Croatia are used to illustrate the use of the two methods proposed for obtaining estimates of nondollar holdings of foreign currency in circulation in transition countries.

7.2 Definitions

In an economy with unofficial dollarization, the effective broad money supply (EBM) consists of local currency (cash) in circulation outside the banking system (LCC), foreign currency (cash) in circulation outside the banking system (FCC), local checkable deposits (LCD), foreign currency deposits (FCD) held with domestic banks, and local currency time and savings deposits (LTD). Quasi money (QM) consists of FCD and LTD. Thus, the typical definition of broad money (BM) falls short of EBM by the unknown amount of FCC. The narrow money supply (NM) is typically defined to include only LCC and LCD. In a dollarized economy, however, the effective narrow money supply (ENM) also includes FCC.[2] Thus,

$$\text{EBM} \equiv \text{LCC} + \text{FCC} + \text{LCD} + \text{QM} \equiv \text{BM} + \text{FCC}, \tag{7.1}$$

where

$$\text{QM} \equiv \text{FCD} + \text{LTD}, \tag{7.2}$$

$$\text{BM} \equiv \text{LCC} + \text{LCD} + \text{QM}, \tag{7.3}$$

$$NM \equiv LCC + LCD, \tag{7.4}$$

$$ENM \equiv NM + FCC. \tag{7.5}$$

In a regime with unofficial dollarization, the recorded money supply falls short of EBM largely because of the omission of FCC, which is typically unknown and is not directly controllable by the local central bank.

Due to the data limitation on measuring the amount of FCC cited by Calvo and Végh (1992), the entire literature on currency substitution has been forced to accept, as a proxy for dollarization, the observable amount of FCD. Studies of currency substitution often associated with the IMF (Sahay and Végh 1995; Ize and Levy-Yeyati 1998; Baliño, Bennett, and Borensztein 1999) employ the ratio of FCD to BM as the means of establishing the extent to which countries are dollarized.[3] We denote this common dollarization index as DIIMF:

$$DIIMF \equiv FCD/BM. \tag{7.6}$$

Unofficial dollarization, as studied in the context of Latin America, has often been a response to hyperinflation. Calvo and Végh (1992) point out that under such circumstances, a foreign currency may first serve as a unit of account and store of value and only later as a circulating medium of exchange. "Currency substitution" suggests that the foreign currency largely displaces the domestic currency as the medium of exchange. If one is primarily concerned with the extent to which a foreign nation's currency has substituted for local currency primarily as the medium of exchange, it is useful to define an explicit currency substitution index. When the main impact of dollarization takes the form of asset substitution, it is useful to define an asset substitution index. Finally, when both asset substitution and currency substitution take place, we define a broader unofficial dollarization index that reflects the fraction of EBM that is composed of foreign currency and foreign deposits. We use a number of definitions throughout the chapter.

DEFINITION 7.1. Currency substitution occurs when foreign currency is partly or entirely used as a unit of account and medium of exchange. Currency substitution can be official or unofficial. Although official cases are rare,[4] unofficial dollarization is widespread. Indeed, recent studies (Feige 1996, 1997; Porter and Judson 1996) suggest that between 40 and 60 percent of the U.S. currency supply ($192–288 billion) may be held overseas. The most sensitive measure of currency substitution is represented by the *currency substitution index* (CSI), which shows the fraction of a nation's total currency supply made up of foreign currency.[5] Thus,

$$\mathrm{CSI} \equiv \mathrm{FCC}/(\mathrm{FCC} + \mathrm{LCC}). \tag{7.7}$$

Since domestic transactions are typically settled by debiting and crediting local demand deposit (LDD) accounts, when institutional circumstances warrant, it may also be useful to modify the CSI and use instead CSIn, defined as the fraction of the effective narrow money supply made up of foreign currency:

$$\mathrm{CSIn} \equiv \mathrm{FCC}/\mathrm{ENM}. \tag{7.8}$$

DEFINITION 7.2. Asset substitution involves the use of foreign denominated monetary assets as substitutes for domestic ones, in their capacity as a store of value. It is measured by the *asset substitution index* (ASI), defined as the ratio of foreign-denominated monetary assets to domestic-denominated monetary assets excluding cash outside banks:[6]

$$\mathrm{ASI} \equiv \mathrm{FCD}/(\mathrm{LCD} + \mathrm{QM}). \tag{7.9}$$

DEFINITION 7.3. Dollarization is a summary measure of the use of foreign currency in its capacity to produce all types of money services in the domestic economy. It is measured by the *unofficial dollarization index* (UDI), which represents the fraction of a nation's EBM composed of foreign monetary assets. Thus:

$$\mathrm{UDI} \equiv (\mathrm{FCC} + \mathrm{FCD})/\mathrm{EBM}. \tag{7.10}$$

DEFINITION 7.4. Bank Credibility represents perceptions of credibility of the domestic banking system by individuals. The choices individuals make concerning the disposition of their monetary assets reflects their perceptions of the bank credibility. Since this perceived credibility might be an important factor affecting the ability of the monetary authority to pursue its macroeconomic objectives, it is useful to define a *bank credibility index* (BCI) reflecting the ratio of monetary assets held in the domestic banking system to assets held in the form of currency outside the banking system. Thus,

$$\mathrm{BCI} \equiv (\mathrm{LDC} + \mathrm{FCD} + \mathrm{LTD})/(\mathrm{LCC} + \mathrm{FCC}), \tag{7.11}$$

where LTD represents time and savings deposits in domestic banks.

Each of the indices developed in the preceding definitions depends upon a number of economic variables that reflect the relative incentives to hold the different assets described in both the denominator and numerator of each index. These incentives include relative rates of return as reflected by interest rate differentials, inflation differentials, and exchange rate depreciation as well as the relative costs associated with network externalities and risks of banking institutions.

With the notable exception of Kamin and Ericsson (1993) on Argentina, no other studies have employed direct estimates of foreign currency holdings to estimate the currency substitution process. Balino et al. (1999) distinguish between currency and asset substitution and report some FCC data based on cross-border U.S. dollar flows, but they end up relying on DIIMF to characterize the extent to which different countries are dollarized.

The IMF dollarization index is an adequate proxy of overall dollarization when foreign currency holdings are of marginal importance or when FCC and FCD are highly complementary. If significant amounts of foreign currency circulate for transaction purposes, however, and if FCC and FCD are in fact substitutes for one another, then DIIMF is likely to perform poorly as an indicator of unofficial dollarization. Typically, DIIMF will understate the true extent of dollarization because it omits FCC holdings. Moreover, DIIMF does not permit one to distinguish between the currency substitution and asset substitution processes that our more refined indicators attempt to capture. To examine the adequacy of DIIMF, we now turn to a discussion of our efforts to obtain direct estimates of U.S. currency holdings in different countries around the world.

7.3 Measurement

7.3.1 *Direct Measurement of FCC*

There is a growing body of evidence (Feige 1994, 1996, 1997; Porter and Judson 1996) that U.S. currency is widely used outside of the United States. Although the exact percentage of U.S. currency held abroad is difficult to determine and still subject to debate, various estimates suggest that 40–60 percent of all U.S. currency in circulation is held overseas.[7]

U.S. currency (cash) has many desirable properties. It has a reputation as is a stable currency and is therefore a reliable store of value.

It is available in many countries, is widely accepted as a medium of exchange, and protects foreign users against the threat of bank failures, devaluation, and inflation. U.S. dollar usage preserves anonymity because it leaves no paper trail of the transaction for which it serves as the means of payment.

Indeed, the very characteristics that make the U.S. dollar a popular medium of exchange also make it difficult to determine the exact amount and location of U.S. notes circulating abroad. Nevertheless, there is a direct source of information that can be used to determine the approximate amounts of U.S. cash in circulation in different countries. Over the past two decades, the U.S. Customs Service has been required to collect systematic information on cross-border flows of U.S. currency. As of October 1970, the Currency and Foreign Transactions Reporting Act (also known as the Bank Secrecy Act) required persons or institutions importing or exporting currency or other monetary instruments in amounts exceeding $5,000 to file with the Customs Service a Report of International Transportation of Currency or Monetary Instruments. The Customs Service has collected these reports, commonly known as Currency and Monetary Instrument Reports (CMIRs) since 1977. In 1980, the limit for requiring a report was raised to $10,000.

Although the CMIR data system was established with the aim of recording individual instances of cross-border inflows and outflows of currency and monetary instruments, its micro records can be usefully aggregated to study the size, origin, and destination of cross-border currency flows. The CMIR data system consists of more than 2.5 million inbound filings and more than 300,000 outbound filings. With the cooperation of the Customs Service and the U.S. Treasury Department's Financial Crimes Enforcement Network, the information contained in the millions of accumulated confidential individual CMIR forms has been aggregated to permit the use of the data while preserving the confidentiality of individual filers. The aggregated data yield time series observations on the gross inflows and outflows of U.S. currency to different destinations. We employ these aggregated data to analyze the approximate extent of informal dollarization throughout the world.

Cross-border currency flows are known to consist of several components, only some of which are recorded in a systematic manner. The largest component of cross-border currency flows is wholesale bulk shipments of U.S. currency by large financial institutions that specialize in the international transport of currency. U.S. dollars can be obtained in most countries through the local commercial banking system. To satisfy the overseas demand for U.S. dollars, overseas banks typically order U.S. currency from one of the large wholesale shippers that transport the bulk currency directly to commercial banks. The shipper is required to file an outgoing CMIR form that contains information on the size, origin, and destination of the shipment. Conversely, when an overseas financial institution finds itself with excess U.S. currency, a wholesale bulk shipper is enlisted to transport the excess currency back to the United States and must legally file an incoming CMIR form.

The second component of cross-border flows consists of retail currency shipments that exceed the $10,000 filing threshold. This currency is physically transported by currency retailers, firms, and individuals. These flows also require the filing of a CMIR form, except when the transporting agent is a Federal Reserve Bank. The New York Federal Reserve Bank maintains records of its own direct cross-border currency shipments, and all currency flows reported in this study have been adjusted to include direct dollar shipments to and from Federal Reserve Banks.

The third component of cross-border currency flows consists of currency transfers by individual travelers and remittance grantors that fall below the $10,000 filing threshold. These transactions represent smaller amounts of currency legitimately imported to or exported from the United States, but these shipments do not require the filing of a CMIR report and are therefore not included in our data. Feige (1996, 1997) has estimated that the cumulative net outflows of currency arising from these sources in 1977–1994 was between $2.9 billion and $24.7 billion, a relatively small fraction of total estimated net outflows.[8] Moreover, most of these cross-border flows involve Mexico and Canada, which have common borders with United States.

A final component of cross-border flows involves illegal currency transfers that evade or circumvent legal reporting requirements. These unrecorded international currency flows represent currency smuggled out of the United States for the purpose of laundering cash proceeds from illegal activities, most notably the traffic in narcotics. Data are available on drug-related monetary seizures, however, the extent of currency smuggling is subject to a great deal of conjecture. The economics of criminal activity provides strong incentives to launder cash proceeds from illegal activities so that they cannot be traced. This often requires that large amounts of cash, in small and mid-sized denominations, be smuggled out of the country, laundered, and then returned through legitimate and reported channels. The logistical problems of exporting the cash proceeds from drug-related activities might be as great as the problem of importing the narcotics themselves.[9]

This observation suggests that compliance rates for reported currency outflows from the United States are likely to be lower than the compliance rates for currency inflows. CMIR measures of net currency outflows by currency retailers, firms, and individuals are therefore likely to understate the actual amounts of currency transferred abroad. The omitted flows are most likely to effect destination countries in Central and South America, however, rather than flows to and from transition countries.

Given the adjusted CMIR data on gross inflows and outflows of U.S. currency to different nations, it is possible to obtain an estimate of the stock of FCC in various countries and more precisely, an indication of how that stock has changed over time. In particular, the difference between gross outflows of U.S. currency from the United States to a particular nation and gross inflows of U.S. dollars from that nation is taken as a first-order approximation of the growth of FCC in that country. Temporal aggregation of these net outflows of dollars yields an estimate of the stock of FCC in each country over time. The stock estimate is of course understated to the extent that local residents held stocks of U.S. dollars prior to the beginning of the observation period in 1977. It is also understated to the extent that additional dollars have flowed into the country from other countries, both from illegal sources and from legitimate sources such as tourist expenditures and remittances that fall below the reporting requirement. The estimate is overstated to the extent that unrecorded dollars have flowed out of each country via unreported cross-border flows to pay for imports from third countries, including tourist expenditures in other countries.

On the basis of available data, it is impossible to determine whether the adjusted CMIR-based estimates of FCC are overestimates or underestimates of the true amount of dollars in circulation with the overseas public. Despite these limitations, however, CMIR currency flow data are the best available information source for determining the stocks of U.S. dollars in particular countries abroad.

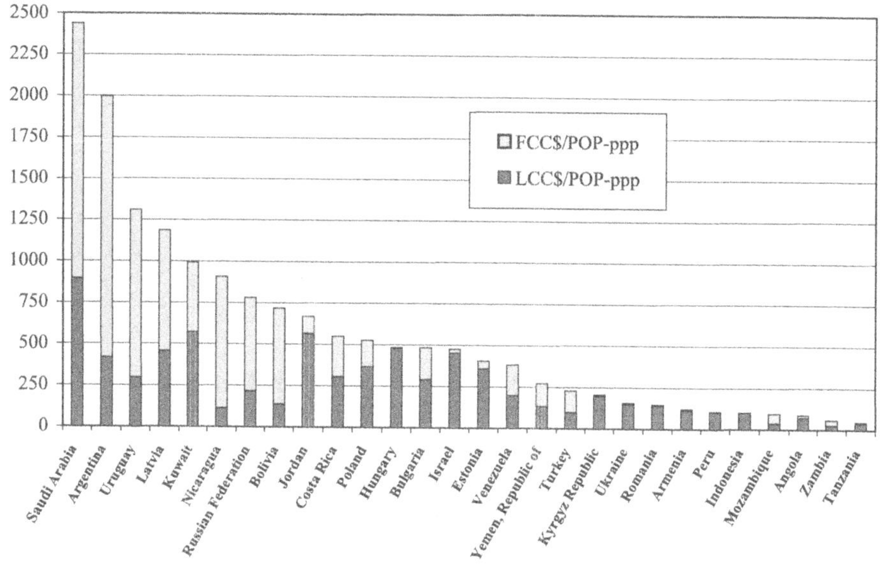

Figure 7.1
FCC and LCC per capita (in U.S. dollars, PPP adjusted)

Figure 7.1 presents 1997 estimates of per capita holdings of domestic and foreign currency in circulation for various countries. Among the most dollarized countries, as measured by per capita holdings of U.S. dollars (PPP adjusted), are Argentina, Saudi Arabia, Kuwait, Russia, Latvia, Uruguay, Bolivia, and Nicaragua.

Estimates of dollar FCC holdings are then used to calculate the asset substitution, bank credibility, currency substitution, and dollarization indices described in section 7.2. Table 7.1 displays the correlation matrix of these various indices of unofficial dollarization and DIIMF. The widely used IMF index is highly correlated with ASI but appears to be an imprecise measure of currency substitution.

Table 7.2 displays a country-by-country comparison of DIIMF and our broader dollarization index (DI), which takes explicit account of the estimated amount of FCC in circulation in each nation. The first column of table 7.2 displays the value of DI for different countries, and column 2 displays the corresponding ranking of each country according to the value of DI for that country. The third and fourth columns, respectively, display the same information based on our recalculation of the value of DIIMF, employed in most previous studies. Column 5 displays the percentage difference between the

Table 7.1
Correlation matrix between selected dollarization measures

	ASI	BCI	CSI	CSIn	DI	DIIMF
ASI	1.00	−0.27	0.73	0.65	0.83	0.87
BCI	−0.27	1.00	−0.48	−0.42	−0.35	−0.16
CSI	0.73	−0.48	1.00	0.89	0.85	0.57
CSIn	0.65	−0.42	0.89	1.00	0.73	0.47
DI	0.83	−0.35	0.85	0.73	1.00	0.87
DIIMF	0.87	−0.16	0.57	0.47	0.87	1.00

two indices. The final two columns, respectively, display the values of the IMF proxy and the corresponding country ranking as reported in Balino et al. 1999.

The Spearman rank correlation coefficient between DI (column 2) and DIIMF (column 4) is 0.91. Major differences in the magnitude of the dollarization indices appear in those countries that have a large share of observed dollar FCC net inflows, notably Russia, Latvia, Yemen, Argentina, Saudi Arabia, Mozambique, and Nicaragua. The foregoing dollarization indices understate the true amount of foreign currency in circulation in these countries to the extent that some countries also employ other foreign currencies as cocirculating currency.

7.3.2 *Indirect Methods of Estimating Foreign Currency in Circulation*

Indirect estimates (Seitz 1995; Doyle 2000) suggest that 84–193 billion DMs are in circulation abroad. Although these studies are incapable of determining the location of these large estimated overseas holdings, anecdotal evidence suggests that many of the transition countries of central and eastern Europe employ the DM as a cocirculating currency. In Russia and the Baltic nations, dollars play the leading role of cocirculating currency, but in Bulgaria, the Czech Republic, Hungary, Slovakia, Slovenia, Croatia, and Bosnia and Herzegovina,[10] the DM is believed to be the dominant foreign currency in circulation. In Poland, and perhaps in some other transition countries, the situation is particularly complicated, since dollars and DMs are cocirculating and there is no direct means to measure DM FCC holding directly for these countries.[11] We therefore require the development of indirect measures of DM FCC holdings.

Table 7.2
Comparison of different dollarization measures

Country	DI (in %) (1)	RANK for (1) (2)	DIIMF (in %) (3)	RANK for (3) (4)	Difference (in percentage points) (5=1−3)	IMF Study[a] (in %) (6)	RANK for (6) (7)
Angola	6.3	26	1.3	25	5.0	n.a.	
Argentina	68.5	4	48.9	4	19.6	43.9	5
Armenia	36.1	12	33.6	8	2.5	20.4	15
Bolivia	83.5	1	78.8	1	4.7	82.3	1
Bulgaria	49.8	9	42.2	6	7.6	28.4	9
Costa Rica	40.8	11	35.5	7	5.4	31.0	8
Estonia	18.6	21	16.0	21	2.5	11.4	18
Hungary	26.7	15	26.6	13	0.1	26.6	11
Indonesia	20.9	18	20.7	16	0.2	n.a.	
Israel	18.0	23	17.9	19	0.2	n.a.	
Jordan	19.3	20	16.4	20	2.9	15.2	17
Kuwait	16.9	22	15.3	22	1.7	n.a.	
Kyrgyzstan	18.1	24	15.4	23	2.7	n.a.	
Latvia	56.8	5	31.1	9	25.7	31.1	7
Mozambique	45.5	10	29.1	11	16.4	32.6	6
Nicaragua	77.3	2	62.1	2	15.2	54.5	3
Peru	54.0	6	53.9	3	0.1	64.0	2
Poland	19.5	19	15.2	24	4.3	20.4	16
Romania	28.9	14	28.5	12	0.4	21.7	12
Russia	77.2	3	30.4	10	46.9	20.6	14
Saudi Arabia	36.0	13	17.9	18	18.1	n.a.	
Tanzania	50.0	17	46.4	17	3.6	n.a.	
Turkey	23.3	8	18.0	5	5.3	46.1	4
Ukraine	26.3	16	21.1	15	5.3	26.9	10
Venezuela	9.2	25	0.2	26	9.0	n.a.	
Yemen	50.7	7	25.8	14	24.9	20.9	13

Note: n.a. = not available.
[a] Balino et al. 1999 data from their table 1 are reported in column (6). Column (3) represents the same measure (DIIMF) based on the data set independently gathered for the present study.

The first indirect method of measurement we propose is the *denomination displacement method*. The hypothesis underlying this method is based on anecdotal evidence that suggests that cocirculating currency is typically used for larger transactions, such as the purchase of automobiles, consumer durables, and real estate. In dollarized countries where people use U.S. currency as means of exchange, it is well known that most transactions are accomplished with the largest-denomination bills available, that is, with US$100 bills. Similarly, for those countries that use nondollar cocirculating currencies, many transactions are carried out with larger-denomination notes (such as DM 500 and DM 1,000 bills). Our hypothesis is that countries that are heavily (unofficially) dollarized with large-denomination foreign bills will have domestic currency (LCC) denomination structures that are unusually skewed away from higher-denomination domestic bills. Denomination displacement occurs as higher-denomination FCC bills substitute for the high-denomination LCC bills.[12] As such, knowledge about the denomination structure can be used as an indicator of the extent of FCC.

The second method we propose for estimating DM FCC is to investigate the demand for money in highly dollarized countries for which we have data on the actual amount of U.S.-dollar FCC. Our aim is to estimate an empirical demand function for dollar FCC that depends upon independent variables that can be readily measured in those countries for which the DM FCC is unknown. If we can find known dollarized countries that have behavioral and structural similarities to countries with unknown DM FCC, we can use the parameters obtained from estimated dollar FCC demand functions to simulate the unobserved demand for DM FCC in transition countries.

7.3.3 Preliminary Findings Employing the Denomination Displacement Method: The Case of Croatia

Before we compare denomination structures of selected countries,[13] it is useful to describe the denomination structure of Croatian currency. The Croatian currency consists of kuna (HRK) notes, issued in denominations of 5-, 10-, 20-, 50-, 100-, 200-, 500-, and 1,000-HRK bills, which have the same face value denominations as DM bills. Table 7.3 displays the nominal denominations of both kuna and DM notes as well as the approximate kuna value equivalent of DM notes.

Table 7.3
Value structure of kuna and DM notes

Kuna (HRK)	5	10	20	50	100	200	500	1,000
DM	5	10	20	50	100	200	500	1,000
Approximate kuna value equivalent of DM bills	20	40	80	200	400	800	2,000	4,000

The circulation of the higher-denomination DM notes (200, 500, and 1,000) tends primarily to displace the 1,000- and 500-kuna notes.

The kuna denomination structure is displayed in figure 7.2 for the period 1994:6–1999:9. In September 1999, 32.4 percent of the value of all HRK notes in circulation with the public was in the form of 100-HRK notes; 24.4 percent was in 200-HRK notes, 19.3 percent in 500-HRK notes, and 11.8 percent in 1,000-HRK notes, with the remaining 12 percent in the smallest-denomination notes.

Figure 7.2 reveals that there were no dramatic changes in the kuna denomination structure during the observed period. Observations of denomination structures in other countries suggest that rising price levels that increase the average transaction size will induce an upward shift in the denomination structure. This tendency is predicted by models that assume transactors will attempt to economize on the number of bills used in any given transaction. As transaction size increases, economic actors will choose to hold a larger proportion of large-denomination bills. A gradual shifting away from lower-denomination notes toward higher-denomination notes is evident in the Croatia data.

Figure 7.3 displays in greater detail the temporal development of the largest-denomination kuna notes. The proportion of 200-HRK notes rises sharply as these notes appear to replace the 100-HRK note. The 500-HRK notes are roughly stable until the end of 1997 and thereafter reveal a gradual upward trend. The largest (1,000-HRK) notes, however, reach a peak of roughly 20 percent of circulation at the end of 1997 and then decline to roughly 12 percent by September 1999. Therefore the dynamic denomination structure evidence suggests that whatever level of currency substitution had been achieved in Croatia by mid-1994 was not significantly altered until the end of 1997. Although there is evidence of denomination displacement in the highest-denomination notes since the end of 1997, there is little evidence from these initial denomination structure data to support

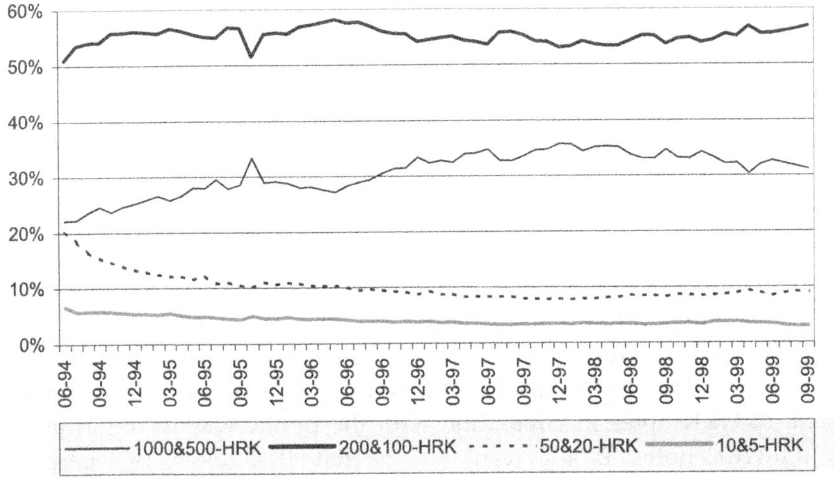

Figure 7.2
Denomination structure of kuna notes in circulation with the public (in value terms)

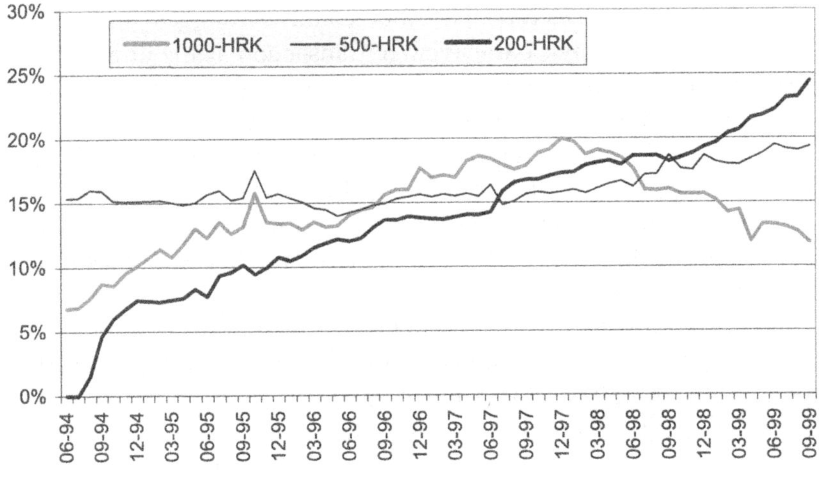

Figure 7.3
Percentage of large-denomination notes in circulation

Table 7.4
Denomination structures for selected countries: Exchange rate conversion

		Percentage of notes in value class		
Country	Year	\$0–\$10	>\$10–\$50	>\$50
Russia	median 96–97	38.0%	54.3%	7.6%
Slovak Republic	median 94–98	8.5%	65.3%	26.2%
Romania	median 93–98	100.0%	0.0%	0.0%
Hungary	median 93–98	17.8%	82.2%	0.0%
Bulgaria	median 97–98	44.8%	55.2%	0.0%
Latvia	median 95–98	19.3%	57.5%	22.1%
Estonia	median 95–98	31.5%	68.5%	0.0%
Czech Republic	median 93–98	8.2%	63.3%	28.5%
Armenia	median 96–98	64.0%	36.0%	0.0%
Israel	median 95–98	7.6%	69.2%	23.2%
Venezuela	median 95–98	87.6%	12.4%	0.0%
Saudi Arabia	median 95–98	2.6%	26.4%	71.1%
Croatia	median 94–98	12.5%	54.2%	33.3%

the notion that the extent of currency cocirculation changed dramatically between mid-1994 and the end of 1997.

We now turn to the denomination structure evidence concerning the extent of currency substitution in Croatia. Our aim here is to compare the denomination structure of kuna notes with those of other countries. In particular, we are interested in examining the Croatian note denomination structure as compared to those from other transition countries for which we have independent evidence of the extent of dollarization.

To make denomination structures comparable, we have defined three denomination categories in terms of U.S. dollar values: small-denomination notes, having a value of \$10 or less; mid-sized-denomination notes, having a value greater than \$10 and less than \$50; and large-denomination notes, having a value in excess of \$50. The exchange rate is used to convert from local currencies to dollars. The percentage of notes in each size category is presented in table 7.4, which reveals sizable differences among countries. The Slovak and Czech Republics appear to have high percentages of large-denomination notes compared to other countries (Saudi Arabia being the exception) and a denomination structure not unlike that observed for Croatia. Hungary appears to have an unusually high

Table 7.5
Denomination structures of selected countries: Purchasing power parity conversion

	Percentage of notes in value class purchasing power parity adjusted			Currency substitution indicators	
Country	\$0–\$10	>\$10–\$50	>\$50	\$FCC/POP[a]	CSIn[a]
Russia	9.4%	83.0%	7.6%	\$374	63.0%
Slovak Republic	6.9%	12.0%	81.3%	—	—
Romania	25.8%	68.3%	0.0%	\$2	1.8%
Hungary	3.3%	13.7%	82.2%	\$2	0.3%
Bulgaria	24.3%	20.6%	55.2%	\$58	38.7%
Latvia	0.0%	49.7%	50.3%	\$354	50.7%
Estonia	6.6%	24.9%	68.5%	\$29	4.6%
Czech Republic	4.3%	13.0%	83.0%	n.a.	n.a.
Armenia	29.0%	35.0%	36.0%	\$1	5.3%
Israel	4.0%	66.0%	30.0%	\$24	2.3%
Venezuela	57.2%	42.8%	0.0%	\$74	15.8%
Saudi Arabia	3.1%	26.0%	70.9%	\$1,096	36.5%
Croatia	6.0%	58.8%	35.7%	—	—
Germany	2.1%	12.0%	85.9%	—	—
Netherlands	2.1%	9.4%	88.4%	—	—

Note: n.a. = not available.
[a] Average values for 1996–1998.

percentage of medium-denomination notes, whereas Romania appears to have only small-denomination notes.

Since denomination structures will depend upon the size distributions of transactions, table 7.5 displays the denomination structures employing the more appropriate purchasing power parity index for converting local currencies into dollar values. The last column of table 7.5 depicts two currency substitution indicators: per capita foreign currency holdings and the fraction of the effective M1 money supply made up of foreign currency in circulation.[14] Table 7.5 also includes the denomination structure estimates for Germany and the Netherlands.[15] Based on the PPP conversion, it appears that Hungary, the Czech Republic, and the Slovak Republic have denomination structures very similar to those of Germany and the Netherlands, whereas the structures for Bulgaria, Croatia, and Russia appear quite different.

Figure 7.4 displays the simple observed relationship between CSIn and the percentage of high-denomination notes for eight of the ten

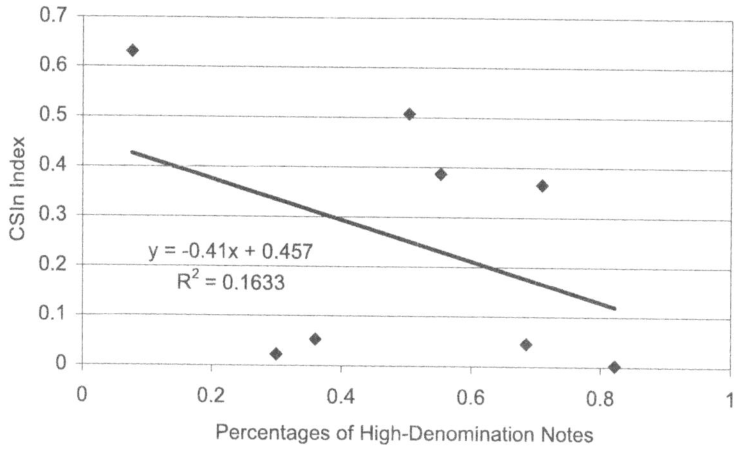

Figure 7.4
Currency substitution and denomination displacement

countries in table 7.4.[16] Consistent with the denomination displacement hypothesis, we note that Russia has the smallest percentage of high-denomination bills (15.3 percent) and is also the most highly dollarized of the selected transition countries. Bulgaria is also quite highly dollarized, but to a smaller extent than Russia, and shows a higher proportion of notes in the large-denomination range (59.6 percent). Hungary, which has the lowest currency substitution indicator, also has the highest percentage of domestic notes in the large-denomination category (87.4). Croatia's denomination structure appears to lie somewhere between those of the two most dollarized countries. If Croatia were assumed to lie on the simple regression line, we would expect its CSIn to be approximately 30 percent. Given the CSIn and the observed level of LCC and LCD, one could infer the unknown amount of FCC. It is impossible, however, to draw any firm conclusion from these preliminary results because (1) some other explanatory variables are missing from the regression in figure 7.4, and (2) CSIn for some countries in the sample is incompletely measured, because in countries like Bulgaria and Hungary, the DM also plays the role of a competing foreign currency.

To enable us to obtain a better estimate of the parameter linking the dollarization measure to the share of high-denomination domestic notes, table 7.6 presents the results of a regression model that employs the logarithmic transformation of the narrow currency sub-

Table 7.6
Regression results

Ind. variable	Equation (7.1)
CONST	1.7694
	(1.9)
DENOM	−4.0447
	(−3.6)
ROM	−3.9804
	(−4.3)
PRIVATCON	−0.0004
	(−3.7)
R^2	0.47
Standard error of regression	1.59

Note: *t*-tests in parentheses; dependent variable LCSIn.

stitution index (LCSIn) as the dependent variable and DENOM (the value share of domestic currency in the highest denomination class); PRIVATCON (per capita household consumption expressed in U.S. dollars corrected for PPP) and ROM (a dummy variable for the Romania outlier) as independent variables. Given the regression presented in table 7.6, it is possible to obtain an estimate of the unknown amount of foreign currency in circulation in Croatia by substituting the known values of the independent variables for Croatia and solving the equation for the unknown quantity FCC.

Our estimate indicates that for 1994–1998, the average dollar value of the DMs in circulation in Croatia was US$402 million or a total of approximately 0.8 million DMs. This represents 0.4–1.0 percent of the estimated total of DMs believed to be circulating abroad.

We regard this preliminary estimate as an illustration of the denomination displacement method. A more reliable estimate would require a larger number of countries in our sample, refinement of the sample countries to exclude those believed to hold DMs in addition to dollar FCC, and perhaps a more refined measure of the skewness of the denomination structure itself.

7.3.4 *Demand for Money Approach: Estimating Foreign Cash in Circulation from Currency Substitution Ratio Simulation Models*

In this section we attempt to estimate the unknown temporal path of FCC in Croatia by estimating a currency substitution ratio model for

Argentina. Once we have found a satisfactory model for Argentina, we use the parameters of the model to simulate the time path of the unknown amount of FCC held in Croatia. Argentina was chosen for this initial simulation effort because its history of hyperinflation followed by periods of stabilization is similar to that of Croatia. It is also a country for which we have obtained reliable estimates of the actual extent of dollarization based on the CMIR data. Unlike those for transition countries, data for Argentina span a period of two decades. Moreover, both Croatia and Argentina also hold a surprisingly large fraction of BM deposits in the form of FCD. At the end of 1998, the FCD/BM ratio was .697 for Argentina and .692 for Croatia.

Our first effort to model the currency substitution phenomenon employs a simple partial-adjustment model[17] applied to the logarithmically transformed dollarization index (LUDI), so that the fitted dependent variables fall within the interval between zero and one.[18]

$$\text{LUDI} = -\ln\left[\frac{(1-\text{UDI})}{\text{UDI}}\right]. \tag{7.12}$$

The explanatory variables of the dollarization process are those typically employed to explain the demand for money in situations in which foreign currency and foreign currency deposits are available substitutes for domestic money. In particular, we employ as regressors the lagged value of the dependent variable, the expected depreciation of the exchange rate (DLEX), a banking crisis variable (CRISIS)[19] and a ratchet variable (RATCHET) to capture the persistence effects that have been observed in dollarized countries (Kamin and Ericsson 1993) when network externalities produce incentives for the continued use of a foreign currency even after inflation or exchange depreciation effects have moderated. Specifically, the equation estimated for Argentina and subsequently used to simulate the quantity of FCC in circulation in Croatia is

$$\begin{aligned}\text{LUDI} = {} & c(1) + c(2) * \text{LUDI}(-1) + c(3) * \text{DLEX}(+1) \\ & + c(4) * \text{RATCHET} + c(5) * \text{CRISIS}.\end{aligned} \tag{7.13}$$

While $c(1)$ is a constant, $c(2), c(3), c(4)$, and $c(5)$ are parameters related to a specific variable (see table 7.7). RATCHET takes the form of the highest previously attained rate of depreciation of the exchange rate.[20]

Table 7.7
Regression results, Argentina, 1979–1998

	LUDI
constant	−0.5839
	(−4.1018)
LUDI(−1)	0.81197
	(19.0302)
DLEX(+1)	0.13781
	(2.23524)
RATCHET	0.25687
	(4.0945)
CRISIS	1.67477
	(4.56825)
R^2	0.97744
Adjusted R^2	0.97624
Durbin-Watson statistic	2.51075

Note: t-statistics are reported in parentheses.

Table 7.8
Estimated long-run coefficients

Dependent variable	LUDI
DLEX(+1)	0.73
RATCHET	1.37
CRISIS	8.91

The results of the ordinary least squares estimate obtained for Argentina are reported in table 7.7. All of the coefficients have the expected signs, and all are significant at the five-percent level. Table 7.8 presents the corresponding long-run estimate of the key coefficients of the model presented above.

Figure 7.5 displays the actual and simulated values of UDI for Argentina for 1978–1999 based on the estimated equation presented in table 7.7. The figures reveals that dollarization in Argentina began in the early 1980s and then accelerated dramatically during 1989–1990 as a result of a severe hyperinflation. Despite subsequent successful stabilization efforts, the unofficial dollarization index remained stubbornly around 70 percent.

Figure 7.6 presents the estimated values of the unofficial dollarization index simulated for Croatia ($\widehat{UDI}$) on the basis of the equations for these variables estimated for Argentina. The overall pattern

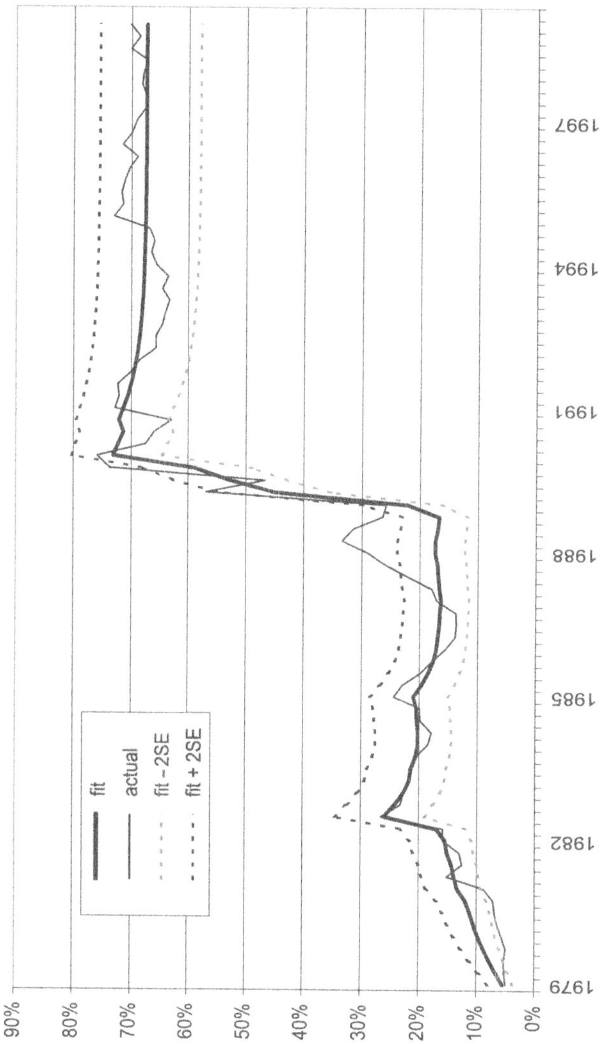

Figure 7.5
Actual and simulated UDI for Argentina

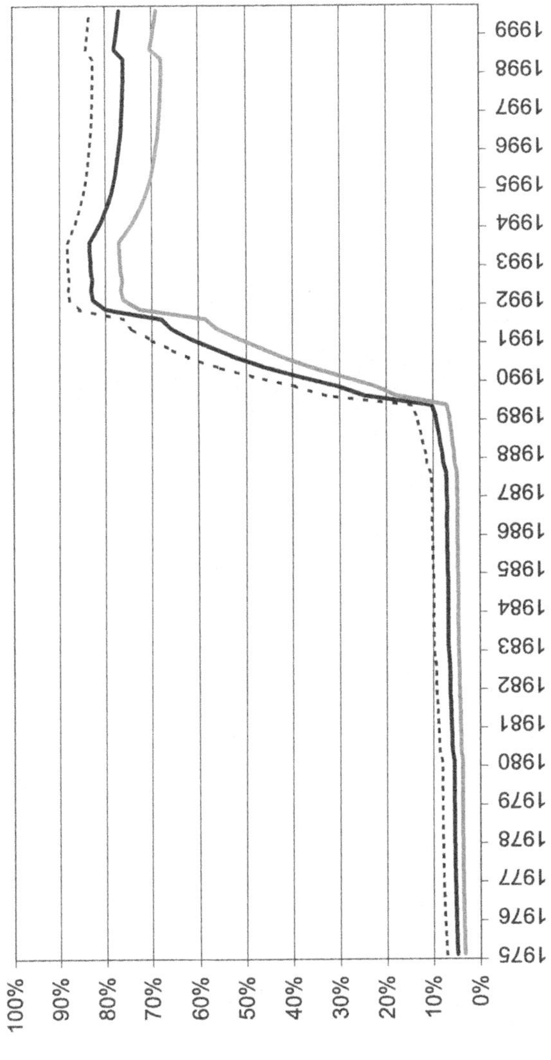

Figure 7.6
Simulated unofficial dollarization ratios for Croatia

of the dollarization process simulated for Croatia appears to be very similar to that of Argentina. Both countries experienced hyperinflation episodes in late 1980s during and after which their economies became increasingly dollarized. The estimates suggest that the extent of dollarization was so extensive as to make the process virtually irreversible. The Croatian simulation suggests that most of the dollarization of the economy took place before the period of Croatia's attainment of monetary sovereignty. This seems consistent with the denomination displacement method findings for Croatia (presented in figure 7.7 with two standard errors):

Our basic aim is to employ the estimates of $\widehat{UDI}$ to obtain an estimate of the unknown amount of FCC in Croatia, which is believed to be held in the form of DM. Given an estimate of the dollarization ratio, we can derive the corresponding estimate of $\widehat{FCC}_{UDI}$ as a function of the actual amounts of M2 and FCD observed in Croatia:

$$\widehat{FCC}_{UDI} = [(\widehat{UDI} * M2) - FCD]/(1 - \widehat{UDI}). \tag{7.14}$$

Figure 7.8 displays the estimated per capita dollar values of FCC holdings for 1992–1999 obtained by the UDI simulation approach as well as the estimate obtained by the denomination displacement method. As revealed by the figure, the UDI simulation estimates a significantly higher level of FCC than the denomination displacement approach.

Table 7.9 presents the estimates of the dollar value of FCC in Croatia for 1991:4–1999:2 and shows the percentage of the total currency supply estimated to be held in the form of foreign currency. The table reveals that the estimated per capita holdings and the percentage of the currency supply held in the form of FCC seem to be unusually high. The estimated fraction of currency held in the form of FCC in Croatia is roughly 10–15 percent higher than the corresponding ratio for Argentina. In the immediate aftermath of the worst hyperinflation in Argentina, the FCC/total currency ratio reached a maximum of 89 percent and subsequently declined to a range of 76–80 percent. Most transactions in Argentina are now quoted in U.S. dollars, and dollars themselves openly circulate for even common purchases. This is not the case in Croatia, where common purchases are quoted and conducted in kuna and only large transactions are actually effected in DMs. We therefore suspect either that the FCC estimate is overstated, or else that the large estimated

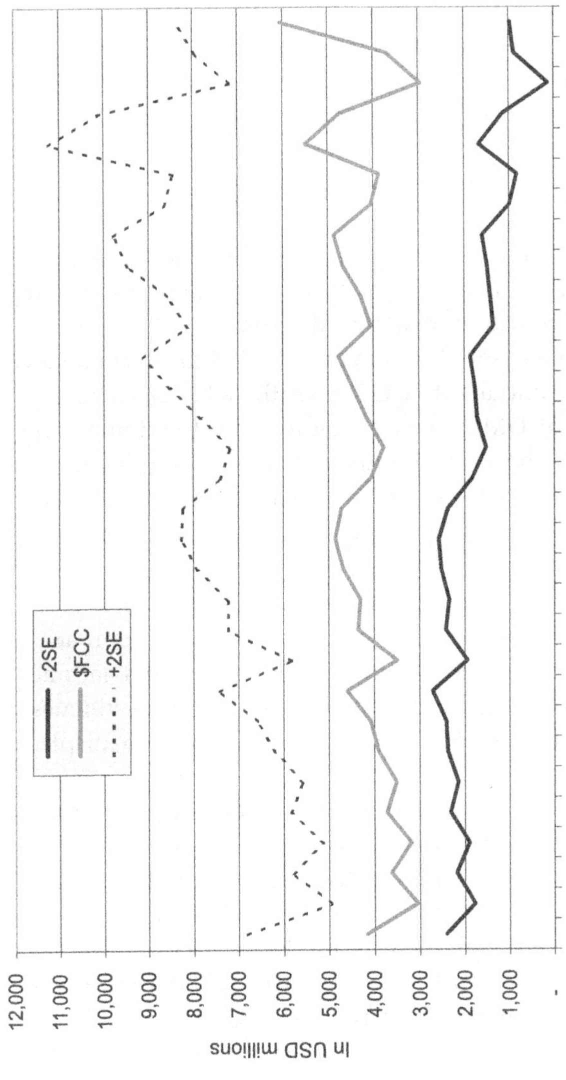

Figure 7.7
Simulated dollar value for FCC in Croatia

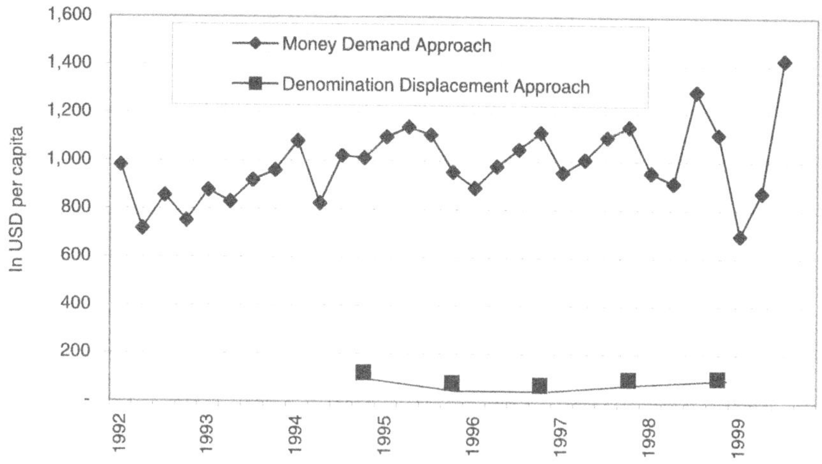

Figure 7.8
Estimated FCC per capita in Croatia

FCC holdings serve largely as a store of value rather than a medium of exchange.

Dollarization developments in Croatia and Argentina do not necessarily represent a universal pattern; it is likely, however, that when currency substitution occurs on a large scale, network externalities in the use of currency (Dowd and Greenaway 1993) take hold and it becomes ever more costly to switch back to local currency even if expected inflation and exchange rate depreciation are brought under control. Proper measurement of FCC is crucial for understanding the true nature of unofficial dollarization, as well as for a proper assessment of the likelihood of flight back to local currency usage after stabilization. These predictions are crucial for policymakers' choice of the exchange rate regime: if unofficial dollarization becomes entrenched and irreversible after stabilization, it is ever more difficult to derive the often-cited benefits from flexible exchange rates.

7.4 Concluding Remarks

In an effort to overcome the "unobservability" problem that has plagued the currency substitution literature, this chapter presents direct estimates of the amounts of U.S. dollar foreign currency in circulation in many countries. Traditional measures of dollarization employed in earlier literature have largely relied on foreign currency

Table 7.9
Estimated values of FCC and CSI in Croatia, 1991–1999

Date		Per capita FCC (Dollars)	CSI (Percentage)
Year	Quarter		
1991	Q4	993	95.1
1992	Q1	727	95.2
1992	Q2	865	95.4
1992	Q3	760	95.2
1992	Q4	888	97.5
1993	Q1	839	97.4
1993	Q2	930	97.6
1993	Q3	973	95.3
1993	Q4	1,096	95.0
1994	Q1	833	92.7
1994	Q2	1,036	92.2
1994	Q3	1,024	90.3
1994	Q4	1,114	90.4
1995	Q1	1,156	89.4
1995	Q2	1,123	88.8
1995	Q3	966	86.8
1995	Q4	900	86.6
1996	Q1	990	86.7
1996	Q2	1,063	86.4
1996	Q3	1,136	86.1
1996	Q4	965	84.5
1997	Q1	1,020	84.6
1997	Q2	1,114	85.1
1997	Q3	1,159	85.5
1997	Q4	965	84.4
1998	Q1	922	83.3
1998	Q2	1,308	86.2
1998	Q3	1,128	84.1
1998	Q4	703	81.0
1999	Q1	884	83.3
1999	Q2	1,442	89.0

deposits as an indicator of currency substitution, because actual measures of foreign currency in circulation were unavailable. Employing aggregated data derived from CMIRs on dollars inflows to and outflows and from the United States, we estimate the amounts of U.S. dollars in circulation in a sample of twenty-six countries. These new estimates of the location of U.S. currency held overseas permit a refinement of definitions and indicators of currency and asset substitution as well as broader indices of the extent of unofficial dollarization. We find that traditional measures of dollarization are highly correlated with asset substitution but perform poorly as measures of currency substitution and unofficial dollarization in countries that use U.S. dollars extensively as a cocirculating means of exchange.

A remaining obstacle for the understanding and measurement of currency substitution and unofficial dollarization is the absence of any direct estimates of nondollar foreign currencies in circulation in many of the transition countries of central and eastern Europe. Many of the transition countries employ DMs as a cocirculating medium of exchange, and aggregate estimates suggest that between 30 and 69 percent of DMs circulate outside the borders of Germany. Hence, DM cash in circulation in these countries must be estimated by indirect methods. We propose a denomination displacement method and a demand for money method to determine the unknown amounts of DMs in circulation in transition countries. We illustrate both approaches by undertaking preliminary estimates of the amount of DMs in circulation in Croatia.

Preliminary analysis suggests that this is a promising line of research, the predictions of which could be tested during the upcoming experiment in the year 2002, when the euro is set to replace the national currencies of EU countries. What is required is the establishment of a centralized information tracking system that systematically records the magnitude of euros exchanged for EU national currencies in transition countries. Since the introduction of the euro currency within the EU is the responsibility of each EU country's central bank, the obvious candidate for the supervision of the information tracking system for non-EU countries is the European Central Bank, which bears ultimate responsibility for the formulation of monetary policy in the EU. If monetary policy is to be conducted effectively, a necessary condition is knowledge concerning the effective money supply in circulation within the EU, which in turn requires knowledge of the level and changes in the usage of euros outside the EU boundaries. Similarly, monetary and fiscal policies as well as indicators of economic activity in transition countries require knowledge of the extent of unofficial euroization in these countries.

The methods for determining the amounts of nondollar cocirculating currencies developed in this chapter can be used to obtain estimates of the amounts of euros that may be required when DM-ization becomes euroization. Such estimates should help to facilitate a timely and smooth transition. If the transition is successfully monitored and accurate information is systematically collected, researchers, policymakers, and national accountants all stand to gain from this unique experiment.

Notes

This chapter is largely an outcome of the first author's stay with the Croatian National Bank in the position of independent consultant from October to December 1999. This paper was prepared and presented prior to the introduction of the euro currency on January 1, 2002. On November 5 and 6, 2001, The Croatian National Bank in cooperation with the International Monetary Fund sponsored a conference in Zagreb of Central and Eastern European Central Banks. The aim of the conference was to establish uniform procedures among participating central banks to monitor the euro's introduction and to establish an ongoing data collection system designed to obtain direct estimates of the stocks and flows of foreign currencies in circulation in CEE countries. This data collection effort is presently under way.

1. For an elaboration of the irreversibility problem, see Guidotti and Rodriguez 1992 and Balino et al. 1999.

2. We ignore those rare institutional circumstances in which transfers between foreign currency deposits are employed for transaction purposes.

3. Balino et al. (1999) choose to define highly dollarized countries as those whose FCD/BM ratio exceeds 30 percent. The major shortcoming of this definition is that it takes no account of FCC. Further study is required to determine whether there exists a unique value of the dollarization index that represents a threshold effect at which point dollarization is likely to become irreversible because of network externalities. Mongardini and Meuller (1999) define the degree of currency substitution as measured by the ratio of FCD to total deposits.

4. Officially dollarized independent countries include the Marshall Islands, Micronesia, Palau, and Panama.

5. In some countries foreign banknotes may simply be hoarded and treated purely as a store of value. When this part of FCC can be estimated, it should be treated in the capacity of money as the store of value and included in the asset substitution index.

6. Again, readers should keep in mind that the definition of ASI also depends upon the particular institutions of a nation. Its quality is high when the amount of FCD and

LTD used for transaction purposes is low in comparison to the amount of those deposits used as income-earning assets.

7. In June, 2000 some $520 billion was in circulation, suggesting that $208–312 billion may in circulation overseas. The official U.S. government estimate based on a modified version of the proxy measure proposed by Feige 1994 was $247 billion.

8. Estimates of travelers' expenditures and net remittances are obtained from the Bureau of Economic Analysis, Survey of Current Business, Balance of Payments Accounts.

9. The street value of a kilogram of cocaine is approximately $20,000. If the proceeds from the sale of cocaine were equally divided between $10 and $20 bills, the weight of the cash to be exported would exceed the weight of the imported cocaine. Four hundred fifty U.S. bills weigh approximately one pound.

10. Bosnia and Herzegovina have introduced a currency board system that issues "convertible mark" as a local currency.

11. A carefully designed information system that tracks the exchange of DMs into euros during the year 2002 conversion would enable central banks to obtain direct estimates of the amount of FCC.

12. Rostowski and Shapiro (1992) analyze Russia's unique experiment of introducing, during the period of hyperinflation, a stable secondary currency that effectively replaced the primary currency. The primary currency that was devalued by the inflation was used only for small transactions, and citizens demanded only small denominations of primary currency notes. On the other hand, the secondary currency, which was not affected by inflation, was used for large transactions and as a store of value, resulting in a demand for high-denomination units of secondary currency notes.

13. Denomination structures and values of local cash supply per denominations are usually not publicized, so we relied on direct data requests to the central banks of various nations. We obtained data for ten countries from our sample: Armenia, Bulgaria, Estonia, Hungary, Israel, Latvia, Romania, Russia, Saudi Arabia, and Venezuela.

14. Our estimate of foreign currency in circulation is based on the direct measurements obtained from CMIRs, described above.

15. The denomination structures for Germany and the Netherlands are based on median estimates for 1992–1996.

16. Romania and Venezuela are outliers. We suspect that U.S. dollarization is largely not relevant for Romania, where DMs are believed to be the dominant competing foreign currency. In the case of Venezuela, we suspect that the direct measures of dollar holdings may be biased as a result of money laundering associated with a common border with Colombia.

17. At a later stage in the research we may attempt to employ an error correction model with cointergration procedures, but the partial-adjustment model was chosen as a first approximation because of its simplicity and the ease of interpreting its results.

18. A similar transformation is employed by Mongardini and Mueller (1999).

19. Andy Berg of the IMF generously provided the bank crisis variable.

20. A number of ratchet variables were tested, including the past peak inflation rate, depreciation rate, and currency substitution index. All were highly significant, and the past peak depreciation rate was chosen to simplify the simulation.

References

Baliño, Tomás J. T., Adam Bennett, and Eduardo Borensztein. (1999). Monetary Policy in Dollarized Economies. Occasional paper no. 171, International Monetary Fund, Washington, D.C.

Calvo, Guillermo A. (1999). Fixed vs. Flexible Exchange Rates: Preliminary of a Turn-of-Millenium Rematch. ⟨http://www.bos.umd.edu/econ/ciecalvo.htm⟩.

Calvo, Guillermo A., and Carlos A. Végh. (1992). Currency Substitution in Developing Countries—An Introduction. Working paper no. WP/92/40, International Monetary Fund, Washington, D.C.

Dowd, Kevin, and David Greenaway. (1993). Currency Competition, Network Externalities and Switching Costs: Towards an Alternative View of Optimum Currency Areas. *Economic Journal* 103 (September): 1180–1189.

Doyle, Brian M. (2000). "Here, Dollars, Dollars ..." Estimating Currency Demand and Worldwide Currency Substitution. International finance discussion paper no. 657, Board of Governors of the Federal Reserve System, Washington, D.C.

Eichengreen, Barry, and Ricardo Hausmann. (1999). Exchange Rates and Financial Fragility. Working paper no. 7418, National Bureau of Economic Research, Washington, D.C.

Feige, Edgar L. (1990). Defining and Estimating Underground and Informal Economies: The New Institutional Economics Approach. *World Development* 18, no. 7 (July): 989–1002.

Feige, Edgar L. (1994). *The Underground Economy and the Currency Enigma, Public Finance and Irregular Activities.* In *Proceedings of the 49th Congress of the International Institute of Public Finance,* 119–136. Berlin. Reprinted in Fiorentini, G., and S. Zamagni (ed.), *The Economics of Corruption and Illegal Markets.* International Library of Critical Writings in Economics. City: Edward Elgar, 1999.

Feige, Edgar L. (1996). Overseas Holdings of U.S. Currency and the Underground Economy. In S. Pozo (ed.), *Exploring the Underground Economy,* 5–62. Kalamazoo, MI: W. E. Upjohn Institute for Employment Research.

Feige, Edgar L. (1997). Revised Estimates of the Size of the U.S. Underground Economy: The Implications of U.S. Currency Held Abroad. In Owen Lippert and Michael Walker (eds.), *The Underground Economy: Global Evidence of its Size and Impact,* 15–208. Vancouver: Fraser Institute.

Fry, Maxwell J. (1997). *Emancipating the Banking System and Developing Markets for Government Debt.* London and New York: Routledge.

Guidotti, Pablo E., and Carlos A. Rodriguez. (1992). Dollarization in Latin America: Gresham's Law in Reverse? *International Monetary Fund Staff Papers* 39, no. 3 (September): 518–544.

Hausmann, Ricardo, Michael Gavin, Carmen Pages-Serra, and Ernesto Stein. (1999). Financial Turmoil and the Choice of the Exchange Rate Regime. Working paper, Interamerican Development Bank, Washington, D.C. Available online at ⟨http://www.iadb.org/oce/pdf/financial_turmorl.pdf⟩.

Ize, Alain, and Eduardo Levi-Yeyati. (1998). Dollarization of Financial Intermediation: Causes and Policy Implications. Working paper no. WP/98/28, International Monetary Fund, Washington, D.C.

Kamin, Steven B., and Neil R. Ericsson. (1993). Dollarization in Argentina. International finance discussion paper no. 460, Board of Governors of the Federal Reserve System, Washington, D.C.

Mongardini, Joannes, and Johannes Mueller. (1999). Ratchet Effects in Currency Substitution: An Application to the Kyrgyz Republic. Working paper no. WP/99/102, International Monetary Fund, Washington, D.C.

Porter Richard, and Ruth Judson. (1996). The Location of US Currency: How Much Is Abroad? *Federal Reserve Bulletin* 82 (October): 883–903.

Rostowski, Jacek, and Judith Shapiro. (1992). Secondary Currency in the Russian Hyperinflation and Stabilization of 1921–24. Discussion paper no. 59, Centre for Economic Performance, London School of Economics, London.

Sahay, Ratna, and Carlos A. Végh. (1995). Dollarization in Transition Economies: Evidence and Policy Implications. Working paper no. WP/95/96, International Monetary Fund, Washington, D.C.

Seitz, Franz. (1995). The Circulation of Deutsche Mark Abroad. Discussion paper no. 1/95, Economic Research Group of the Deutsche Bundesbank, Frankfurt am Main.

Index

Aancans, Helmut, 201–202
ABILITY indicators, 34–38
Acquis communautaire, 193
Adequacy. *See* Reserves
Africa, 49, 96
floating and, 116
imports and, 106–108
reserves and, 131
short-term external debt of, 143
Annual Report on Exchange Arrangements and Exchange Restrictions (IMF), 69, 77–78
Appreciation bubble, 179, 182
Argentina, 2, 103
BSLF and, 181
regression analysis on, 238
reserves and, 136
short-term external debt of, 148
Arteta, Carlos, 47–94
Asia, 2–3, 95
banking crises of, 2–3, 6, 48
external factors and, 63
international financial crises and, 96 (*see also* International financial crises)
private net flows and, 4
reserves and, 102–103
short-term external debt and, 111
Asset substitution index (ASI), 222

Bank credibility index (BCI), 222–223
Banking crises, 85–94. *See also* International financial crises
Asia and, 2–3, 6, 48
bailouts and, 96
causes of, 48–49
cost of, 5–6
data sources for, 75–79
dating of, 55–59, 79–82
deposit insurance and, 4, 49, 54, 69–72, 84
exchange rates and, 62–66, 83
external factors of, 62–66
floating and, 61 (*see also* Floating)
GDP and, 65–66
implications for, 74–75
inflation and, 49
instability and, 48
institutional quality and, 72–74, 84
Latin America and, 48
liberalization and, 48–51, 67–69
literature on, 49–55
macroeconomic analysis of, 49–50, 54, 59–61, 74
nonperforming asset measurement and, 56–57
regression analysis and, 59–62, 83
reserves and, 61–62
reverse causality and, 65
Volcker disinflation and, 62
Banking sector liquidity fund (BSLF), 180–181
Bank of International Settlements (BIS), 34
Bank Secrecy Act, 224
Barro-Gordon equation, 31
Blejer, Mario I., 1–15
Bond yields, 100
Borrowing
passthrough and, 33–38
SIN measure and, 33, 35, 38–42
Brazil, 2, 95
floating and, 116
reserves and, 106, 127
short-term external debt of, 139

Bretton Woods system, 100
Broad money, 138
 capital flight and, 149–154
 effective, 220–221
 equations for, 220
 LUDI and, 237
Budgets, 61–62
Bundesbank, 181

Camdessus, Michel, 95
Capital. *See also* Reserves
 broad money and, 149–154
 control of, 104–105
 developing countries and, 100–101
 errors/omissions of debt and, 151–152
 EU and, 165 (*see also* European Union (EU))
 euroization and, 180–186
 flight, 105, 149–154, 159n35
 mobility and, 101
 Mundell-Flemming model and, 171–176
 short-term debt and, 102–103, 109–113, 115
 social return on, 99
 special drawing rights and, 120–124
Capitalism, 170
Caprio-Klingebiel study, 56–59, 70, 76, 89n50
Central and Eastern European (CEE) countries, 178
 dollarization and, 219–220
 euroization and, 180–186
Central bank model, 28–33
 ABILITY indicators and, 34–38
 estimations and, 38–42
 exchange rates and, 114
 GDP and, 39–41
 passthrough and, 33–42
Chamfort, Sebastien Roch Nicolas dit, 13
Chile, 115
 reserves and, 132
 short-term external debt of, 144
China, 2, 106
 reserves of, 133, 157n17
 short-term external debt of, 145
Colombia, 133, 145
Common Agricultural Policy (CAP), 207
Communism, 170
Contingent credit line (CCL), 122, 125
Crises. *See* Banking crises; International financial crises
Croatia, 219
 currency substitution models and, 236–243
 denomination displacement method and, 230–236
 FCC data for, 242–244
 LUDI and, 237–238
Currency, 2–3. *See also* Exchange rates
 banking crises and, 55–59 (*see also* Banking crises)
 capital flight and, 149–154
 central bank model and, 28–33
 CMIRs and, 224–226, 245
 crashes, 65
 Croatian, 230–244
 cross-border flow of, 224–226
 Czech Republic, 223
 denomination displacement method and, 230–236
 dollarization and, 10–12, 19 (*see also* Dollarization)
 euroization and, 10, 180–186 (*see also* Euroization)
 FCC measurement and, 223–243, 245
 foreign, 167, 217, 220–243, 245
 German mark, 11–12, 194–196, 219–220, 228, 230–231, 241, 245
 international financial crises and, 95 (*see also* International financial crises)
 laundering and, 225–226
 Maastricht criteria and, 176–180
 Mundell-Flemming model and, 171–176
 passthrough and, 33–43
 SIN measure and, 33, 35, 38–42
 substitution, 217–222, 234–243
 super-fixed exchange rate and, 19
Currency and Foreign Transactions Reporting Act, 224
Currency and Monetary Instrument Reports (CMIRs), 224–226, 245
Currency substitution index (CSI), 222
Current accounts
 appreciation bubble and, 179
 equations for, 168, 170
 EU applicants and, 166–169
 euroization and, 201
 fiscal policy effects on, 169–171
 Maastricht criteria and, 176–180
 Mundell-Flemming model and, 171–176

Czech Republic, 2, 223
Maastricht criteria and, 179
reserves and, 127
short-term external debt of, 139

Debt
errors/omissions of, 150–153
euroization and, 202
European Union and, 166–169
FDI and, 155
fiscal policy effects on, 169–171
foreign currency and, 167
Mundell-Flemming model and, 171–176
reserves and, 102–103, 117–120 (*see also* Reserves)
short-term external, 109–113, 115
special drawing rights and, 120–124
Demirgüç-Kunt study
banking crises and, 49–50, 54, 56–57, 76, 85n13, 88n47, 89n50
deposit insurance and, 69–70
liberalization and, 67, 69
Denomination displacement method, 230–236
Deposit insurance
banking crises and, 4, 49, 54, 56, 78, 84, 69–72
GNP and, 72
institutional quality and, 73
OECD members and, 89n54
Deregulation, 12–13
Detragiache study
banking crises and, 49–50, 54, 56–57, 76, 85n13, 88n47, 89n50
deposit insurance and, 69–70
liberalization and, 67, 69
Deutsche mark, 11–12
distribution of, 228, 230–231
dollarization and, 219–220, 245
euroization and, 194–196
UDI and, 241
Devaluation, 28
banking and, 47 (*see also* Banking crises)
central bank model and, 29–33
vicious cycles of, 28
DIIMF index, 221, 227–228
Dollarization, 195, 247–249
Croatia and, 230–243
definitions for, 220–223
demand for money approach and, 236–243
DIIMF index and, 221, 227–228
FCC measurement and, 223–243, 245–246
IMF and, 219
Latin America and, 219
liability and, 169
Lithuania and, 195–196
models for, 20
super-fixed exchange rates and, 19
unobservability and, 243, 245
unofficial, 217–223
"Double-mismatch" approach, 64
Duisemberg, Wim, 194

Early warning systems (EWSs), 108–109, 112
Economist Intelligence Unit, 115
Edison, Thomas Alva, 13
Effective broad money, 220–221
Effective narrow money supply, 220–221
Eichengreen, Barry, 47–94
Eichengreen-Rose study, 50, 54–55, 63, 86n20
Emerging markets, 14–15, 156–162
access to, 101
assessing framework for, 96
banking crises in, 47–94 (*see also* Banking crises)
broad money and, 138, 149–154
capital flight and, 149–153
deregulation and, 12–13
exchange rate and, 8–12 (*see also* Exchange rate)
external debt and, 139–148
FDI and, 155
floating and, 21–28 (*see also* Floating)
foreign direct investment and, 4–5
IMF classification and, 1–2
imports and, 96–97
international financial crises and, 96 (*see also* International financial crises)
Mundell-Flemming model and, 171–176
OECD members and, 2
private net flows to, 4
reserve adequacy and, 7–8, 103–120, 127–148 (*see also* Reserves)
short-term external debt and, 109–113, 115
vulnerability and, 1–15
Enhanced Structural Adjustment Facility (ESAF), 95

Equations
asset substitution index (ASI), 222
bank credibility index (BCI), 222
Barro-Gordon quadratic loss function, 31
broad money, 220
central bank model, 29, 31
currency substitution index (CSI), 222
current account, 167–168, 170
DIIMF index, 221
domestic price fall, 178
effective broad money supply (EBM), 220
effective narrow money supply, 221
FLEX, 33
income, 29
inflation/devaluation, 29–30
interest parity condition, 29–30, 178
interest rate intervention, 26
logarithmically transformed dollarization index (LUDI), 237
Mundell-Flemming model, 171–172, 174, 176
narrow currency substitution, 222
narrow money supply, 221
quasi money, 220
reserve intervention, 24
unofficial dollarization index (UDI), 222
utility function, 167
Euroization, 10, 213–216, 245–246
advantages of, 196–198
capital effects and, 183
CEE countries and, 180–186
convergence issues in, 205–207
cost/benefit analysis of, 180–186, 204
currency board for, 183, 186, 194–195, 197–200
currency exchange issues in, 186–188
current progress of, 195–196, 208–211
debt and, 202
deutsche mark and, 194–196
disadvantages of, 198–204
EBRD and, 205–207
improved trade and, 207, 212
inflation and, 182
interest rate effects and, 181
liability, 169
Maastricht criteria and, 205–207
pegs to, 195, 201–204
real convergence and, 182–183
reserves and, 187–188, 199
seigniorage and, 199
shocks and, 182
special drawing rights and, 196, 202
European Association Agreements, 207
European Bank for Reconstruction and Development (EBRD), 205–207
European Central Bank (ECB), 181–182, 186–188, 212
enlargement issues of, 194
euroization and, 199–200, 204
monetary policies of, 203
European Economic and Monetary Union (EMU), 9–10, 165
appreciation bubble and, 179
conditions of, 193–194
currency board for, 194–195
derogations and, 193
euroization and, 180–186, 193–213 (*see also* Euroization)
Maastricht criteria and, 176–180
European System of Central Banks (ESCB), 180
European Union (EU), 9, 193–194, 245–246
applicant-country trends and, 166–169
current accounts and, 166–169
FDI flows and, 168
fiscal policy effects on, 169–171
growth rate of, 165
Harrod-Balassa-Samuelson effect and, 165–167
improved trade access and, 207, 212
indirect FCC measurement and, 228–230
liberalization and, 74–75
Maastricht criteria and, 176–180
Mundell-Flemming model and, 171–176
supply factors and, 168–169
Exchange Rate Mechanism, 169, 193
Exchange rates, 8–12
banking crises and, 55–59, 62–66, 83 (*see also* Banking crises)
capital flight and, 105
central bank model and, 29–33
data sources for, 77–78
double mismatch and, 64
equilibrium and, 189n16
euroization and, 186 (*see also* Euroization)
external factors and, 62–66
FLEX index and, 28, 33, 39, 41–42
floating and, 19–28 (*see also* Floating)
interest rate volatility and, 26–28

model for, 19–20
Mundell-Flemming model and, 171–176
optimal, 104
passthrough and, 33–42
reserves and, 24–25, 28, 100, 103, 150–153
shocks and, 55
super-fixed, 19
Exports, 176–180
euroization and, 207, 212
Mundell-Flemming model and, 171–176

Faulend, Michael, 217–249
Federal Reserve, 103, 196, 200, 225
Feige, Edgar L., 217–249
Financial policy
banking crises and, 47–94
Croatia and, 230–236
dollarization and, 223–249
euroization and, 10, 169, 180–188, 193–216
European Union and, 165–191
exchange rate and, 8–12, 19 (*see also* Exchange rates)
floating and, 19–28
foreign direct investment and, 4–5
independent, 19–20
inflation and, 13
international financial crises and, 95–162
Maastricht criteria and, 176–180
models for, 20–21, 28–42
Mundell-Flemming model and, 171–176
passthrough and, 33–44
reserve holding and, 7–8 (*see also* Reserves)
vulnerability and, 1–15
FLEX index, 28, 33, 39, 41–42
Floating, 43, 125
banking crises and, 61, 64
Brazil and, 116
data sources for, 78
estimations and, 38–42
exchange rates and, 19–20 (*see also* Exchange rates)
FLEX index and, 28, 33, 39, 41–42
IMF classification and, 21, 64–65
model for, 28–33
passthrough and, 33–38
reality of, 21–28
reserves and, 24–28, 112, 114, 150–153 (*see also* Reserves)
risks of, 19
Russia and, 116
RVEI index and, 26–28
RVER index and, 24–25, 28
South Africa and, 116
Fluctuation bands, 179
Foreign currency deposits (FCD), 220–221
Foreign currency in circulation (FCC), 217, 220–221
Croatia study and, 230–236
denomination displacement method and, 230–236
direct measurement of, 223–228
indirect estimation of, 228–230
substitution models and, 236–243
UDI and, 241
unobservability of, 243, 245
Foreign direct investment (FDI), 4–5
Frankel-Rose study, 65

Germany, 11–12, 219
Bundesbank, 181
currency of, 11–12, 194–196, 219–220, 228, 230–231, 241, 245
euroization and, 187
Globalization, 120–124
Goldstein, Morris, 122–123
Government
bond yields, 100
BSLF and, 180–181
foreign debt and, 167
Great Depression, 47, 98
Greenspan, Alan, 7, 103
Gross domestic product (GDP), 39–41, 48
banking crises and, 61, 65–66
Harrod-Balassa-Samuelson effect and, 166–167
liberalization and, 69, 78
macroeconomic analysis and, 77
reserves and, 99
Gross national product (GNP)
banking crises and, 61
deposit insurance and, 72
macroeconomic analysis and, 77
Guidotti, Pablo, 7, 102–103

Harrod-Balassa-Samuelson effect, 9, 165–167
euroization and, 182
Maastricht criteria and, 176–180
Hausmann, Ricardo, 19–46

Heller, Robert, 98–99
Hong Kong, 2, 104
reserves and, 116–117, 137
short-term external debt and, 109, 149
Hungary, 2
reserves and, 134
short-term external debt of, 146

Imports, 96–97
euroization and, 207, 212
GDP and, 99 (*see also* Gross domestic product (GDP))
Maastricht criteria and, 176–180
Mundell-Flemming model and, 171–176
reserves and, 99–101, 106–107
Ricardian equivalence and, 170
India, 116
reserves and, 128
short-term external debt of, 140
Indonesia, 2
reserves and, 128
short-term external debt of, 140
Inflation, 13
banking crises and, 49, 51
Brazil and, 2
central bank model and, 29–33
euroization and, 182
Maastricht criteria and, 176–180
Mundell-Flemming model and, 172
vicious cycles of, 28
Volcker disinflation and, 62
Interest rates
banking crises and, 54, 63
bond yields and, 100
central bank model and, 29–33
current accounts and, 170
euroization and, 181
exchange rate volatility and, 26–28
external factors and, 63
IMF and, 95
liberalization and, 49
M2 ratio and, 108, 116, 150
Mundell-Flemming model and, 171–176
parity condition for, 178
short-term debt and, 102–103
war chest and, 104
International financial crises
bank bailouts and, 96
changing nature of, 95–96
country-level analysis of, 95, 125–126
developing economies and, 95–96
global architectures and, 124–125
official involvement and, 96
post-Asia crises and, 102–103
reserve measures for, 102–120, 126–148
SDRs and, 120–124, 126
trade-related adequacy and, 97–101
International Monetary Fund (IMF), 11
bailout and, 96
banking crises and, 48, 96
borrowing costs and, 119
classifications of, 1–2, 64–65
devaluation and, 28
dollarization and, 219
exchange rates and, 21
external vulnerability and, 98
inflation and, 28
international financial crises and, 95
liberalization and, 69
Poverty Reduction and Growth Facility, 95
reserves and, 96–97, 101, 119
short-term external debt and, 109, 111
special drawing rights and, 120–124
Turkey and, 115–116
U.S. and, 122–124
International Monetary Stability Act (2000), 199–201, 203
Interventions
RVEI index and, 26–28
RVER index and, 24–25, 28

Kapteyn, Arend, 95–162
Keynes, John Maynard, 98–99, 170
Korea, 106, 116
reserves and, 129
short-term external debt and, 111, 141

Latin America, 2
banking crises and, 48
dollarization and, 219
international financial crises and, 96 (*see also* International financial crises)
reserve-holding cost and, 117
Laundering, 225–226
Least-developed countries (LDCs), 22, 27
Liability dollarization, 169
Liability euroization, 169
Liberalization, 12, 48, 74, 88n41, 90n61
banking crises and, 50–51, 67–69
data sources for, 78
EU and, 168

FDI flows and, 168
GDP and, 69
institutional quality and, 73
interest rates and, 49
Lindgren-Garcia-Saal study, 56–58
Lipton, David, 121–123
Liquidity, 158n21
BSLF and, 180–181
Mundell-Flemming model and, 172
special drawing rights and, 120–124
Liquidity-at-risk standard, 7, 103
Lithuanian Currency Board, 195–196
Local checkable deposits (LCD), 220–221
Local currency in circulation (LCC), 220–221
Local currency time and savings deposits (LTD), 220
Logarithmically transformed dollarization index (LUDI), 237–238M

Maastricht Treaty, 9, 165, 175, 193
conformity implications for, 176–180
convergence issues and, 205–207
H-B-S effect and, 176–180
pegged rate and, 178–179
special drawing rights and, 196
Mack, Connie, 199
Macroeconomic analysis
banking crises and, 59–61, 74
data sources for, 77
EU and, 165 (*see also* European Union)
Malaysia, 2
reserves and, 134
short-term external debt and, 111, 146
Markets. *See* Emerging markets
Mathematics
exchange rates and, 19–20
FLEX index and, 28, 33, 39, 41–42
least squares method, 238
RVEI index, 26–28
RVER index, 24–25, 28
standard deviation, 24–26
Mexico, 2–3, 95
external factors and, 62
imports and, 106–108
rescue of, 123
reserves and, 117, 129
short-term external debt of, 141
Models
ABILITY indicators and, 34–38
central bank, 28–41, 114
currency substitution, 236–243
current account, 166–169
dollarization and, 20
estimations and, 38–42
exchange rates and, 19–20
FLEX index and, 28, 33, 39, 41–42
GDP and, 39–41
Heller, 98–99
Keynesian, 99, 170
liberalization and, 67–69
Mundell-Flemming, 165, 171–176
partial-adjustment, 237
passthrough and, 33–42
reserve benchmark, 103–120
RVEI index and, 26–28
RVER index and, 24–25, 28
Mundell-Flemming model, 165, 171–176

Narrow currency substitution index, 222, 234–236
Narrow money supply, 220–221
National central bank (NCB), 180, 187–188
New Arrangements to Borrow, 122
Nuti, D. Mario, 193–216

OECD members, 2
banking crises and, 61–63, 84
deposit insurance and, 72, 89n54
floating and, 20
institutional quality and, 73–74
Mundell-Flemming model and, 176
Opportunity cost, 99–100
Original-sin measure, 33, 35
passthrough and, 38–42

Panizza, Ugo, 19–46
Partial-adjustment model, 237
Passthrough, 43–44
measurement of, 33–37
original sin and, 38–42
Pegs. *See also* Reserves
debt and, 202
euroization and, 195, 201–204
floating and, 112, 114 (*see also* Floating)
Maastricht criteria and, 178–179
Peru, 130, 142
Philippines, 2
reserves and, 130
short-term external debt of, 142

Poland, 2
BSLF and, 180–181
euroization and, 183, 186–187, 190n23, 199
Maastricht criteria and, 179
reserves and, 135
short-term external debt of, 147
Political stability, 115
Poverty Reduction and Growth Facility, 95
Prices, 177–178
Private capital flow, 4–5

Quasi money, 220

Regression analysis
Argentina, 238
banking crises and, 59–62, 83
data sources for, 76–79
Relative price change, 177–178
Report of International Transportation of Currency or Monetary Instruments, 224
Reserves, 7–8, 87n24, 125–126
banking crises and, 61–62
broad money and, 138, 149–154
cost of holding, 99, 117–120
developing countries and, 100–101
early warning systems and, 108–109, 112
economies of scale and, 99–100
errors/omissions and, 150–153
euroization and, 187–188, 199
exchange rates and, 24–25, 28, 100, 103
external liabilities and, 103
floating and, 20–28, 112, 114
growth in, 106
IMF and, 96–97, 101, 119
imports and, 101, 106–107
international financial crises and, 96
liquidity and, 103, 158n21
M2 ratio and, 108, 114–116, 150
minimum benchmark for, 103–120
new adequacy measures for, 102–103
official financial support and, 105
opportunity cost and, 99–100
post-Asia crises and, 102–103
private support and, 105–106
SDRs and, 120–124
shocks and, 102, 119–120
short-term external debt and, 109–113, 115
trade-related adequacy and, 97–101
Ricardian equivalence, 167, 170
Romania, 234
Rostowski, Jacek, 165–191
Russia, 2–3, 95, 115, 126
floating and, 116
imports and, 106–108
private net flows and, 4
reserves and, 106, 117, 131
short-term external debt and, 111–112, 143
RVEI index, 26–28
RVER index, 24–25, 28

Seigniorage, 199
Shocks
data sources for, 78
euroization and, 182
exchange rates and, 55
insurance premium and, 119
reserves and, 102, 119–120
Short-term external debt (STED), 109–113, 115
account deficit and, 158n23
data by country, 139–149
SIN measurement, 33, 35
passthrough and, 38–42
Skreb, Marko, 1–15
Smuggling, 225–226
Social capital, 14
Sonje, Velimir, 217–249
Sosic, Vedran, 217–249
South Africa
floating and, 116
imports and, 106–108
reserves and, 131
short-term external debt of, 143
South Korea, 2
Special drawing rights (SDRs), 120
euroization and, 196, 202
systemic threats and, 121–124, 126
Stein, Ernesto, 19–46
Stock prices, 47
Summers, Larry, 199
Supply factors, 168–169
Sweden, 193

Taiwan, 2
Thailand, 2
reserves and, 132
short-term external debt of, 144
Trade-related reserves, 97–101
Transition Reports (EBRD), 205

Turkey, 2–3
 reserves and, 115–117, 135
 short-term external debt and, 109, 147

United Nations, 98
United States
 currency distribution of, 2–3, 223–225
  (*see also* Dollarization)
 currency stability and, 199
 IMF funding and, 122–124
Unofficial dollarization index (UDI), 222.
  See also Dollarization
 Argentina, 238–239
 Croatia, 240
 FCC, 241
U.S. Council on Foreign Relations, 122
U.S. Customs Service, 224
U.S. International Monetary Stability
  Act, 199–201, 203
Utility function, 167

Value-at-risk standard, 7
Venezuela, 136, 148
"Visegrad Three," 168
Volatility
 exchange rate/interest rate, 26–28
 exchange rate/reserve, 24–25, 28
Volcker disinflation, 62
Vulnerability, 1, 13–15. *See also* Floating
 banking and, 3
 deposit insurance and, 4
 euroization and, 197, 199–200
 exchange rate and, 8–12
 external, 98
 foreign direct investment and, 4–5
 measurement of, 6–7
 1990s and, 2, 4
 reserves and, 7–8 (*see also* Reserves)
 Russian crises and, 2–3

Wijnholds, J. Onno de Beaufort, 95–162
World Bank, 48
World War II, 47, 97

Made in the USA
Monee, IL
04 July 2024

61214228R00148